# PRAISE FOR *LARGER THAN YOURSELF*

"I have been blessed to be part of several incredible movements, including the Birmingham Children's March, led by Dr. King in 1963. I marched and went to jail because I believed in something larger than myself. Thibault Manekin's gripping real-life stories, and the principles he's observed about how movements come to be, are valuable lessons about how we can bring ideas and dreams to life. His book inspires us with the confidence to take on the seemingly impossible."

— **Freeman A. Hrabowski III**, president,
University of Maryland, Baltimore County

"Thibault Manekin's journey shows what's possible when we tap into the power of collective leadership and when we lead with love."

— **Wendy Kopp**, CEO and cofounder of Teach For All
and founder of Teach For America

"*Larger Than Yourself* is a book I didn't know I needed. Thibault Manekin uses the complex elements of his personal story to convey the transformative power of human connection, despite the many differences between us all. Manekin is a true leader on and off the page and understands the energy needed to get through these challenging times. This book should be required reading for all who dare to live with purpose. Highly recommended."

— **D. Watkins**, *New York Times* bestselling author of
*The Cook Up* and *The Beast Side*

"Thibault Manekin has used his life experiences — from building bridges through sport in areas of conflict to developing communities (both literally and spiritually) — to create inspiring movements. If you want to build a better organization, project, neighborhood, or world, and turn ideas into movements, *Larger Than Yourself* is an illuminating and inspiring guide to getting there."

— **Ronald M. Shapiro**, attorney, sports agent,
and *New York Times* bestselling author of *The Power of Nice*

"While I'm a huge believer in our personal master plans, Thibault Manekin's journey reminds us that nothing great can be accomplished by one individual alone. At a time of unparalleled upheaval and worldwide uncertainty, when old industries need reinvention and new ways of working must emerge, *Larger Than Yourself* provides both the inspiration and the road map for that change — and shows us that we are stronger united than divided."

— **Chris Wilson**, artist and bestselling author of *The Master Plan*

# LARGER
## THAN
# YOURSELF

# LARGER
## THAN
# YOURSELF

**REIMAGINE** INDUSTRIES,
**LEAD** WITH PURPOSE
& **GROW IDEAS** INTO MOVEMENTS

## THIBAULT MANEKIN
Foreword by **Wes Moore**

New World Library
Novato, California

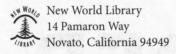

New World Library
14 Pamaron Way
Novato, California 94949

Text design by Tona Pearce Myers

Library of Congress Cataloging-in-Publication Data

Names: Manekin, Thibault, author.
Title: Larger than yourself : reimagine industries, lead with purpose & grow ideas
    into movements / Thibault Manekin ; foreword by Wes Moore.
Description: Novato, California : New World Library, [2021] | Summary: "A guide
    for contemporary entrepreneurs who are seeking to create businesses that are
    profitable, innovative, and socially responsible"-- Provided by publisher.
Identifiers: LCCN 2021025216 (print) | LCCN 2021025217 (ebook) | ISBN
    9781608687596 (paperback) | ISBN 9781608687602 (epub)
Subjects: LCSH: Manekin, Thibault. | Businesspeople--United States--Biography. |
    Social entrepreneurship. | Social responsibility of business. | Social movements.
Classification: LCC HC102.5.M25 A3 2021 (print) | LCC HC102.5.M25 (ebook) |
    DDC 338/.04092 [B]--dc23
LC record available at https://lccn.loc.gov/2021025216
LC ebook record available at https://lccn.loc.gov/2021025217

First printing, November 2021
ISBN 978-1-60868-759-6
Ebook ISBN 978-1-60868-760-2
Printed in Canada on 100% postconsumer-waste recycled paper

 New World Library is proud to be a Gold Certified Environmentally Responsible Publisher. Publisher certification awarded by Green Press Initiative.

10   9   8   7   6   5   4   3   2   1

To Charlie, for helping me open my eyes and my heart.

And to my two incredible sons, Finley and Durban.
Always remember: there is no mountain so tall
we won't climb it and no wave so big we won't ride it.

# Contents

## PART III: GROW    181

## PART IV: EVOLVE    241

# Foreword

I'll never forget the first time I heard a Thibault Manekin speech. It was the spring of 2016, over five years ago now, and I had just walked off-stage following my talk at the tail end of Baltimore's Light City event. Inspired by festivals like South by Southwest in Austin, Texas, Light City is a celebration of the creative spirit of my hometown of Baltimore, and it was an honor to participate as a speaker for the inaugural edition. Over the prior few days, the city's famous waterfront had transformed into a spectacle of light exhibitions, music performances, parades, local cuisine, and panels on innovation and thought leadership. I had moved back to Baltimore after a few years living in New York City and, as with many other native Marylanders, the festival had reinvigorated my excitement about the future of the city. There was a tinge of exhaustion in the air, and about half of the crowd had either filed out or were on their way out after I wrapped up my speech. By that point the sense was that folks had been given enough to think over and were ready to go home. Then Thibault appeared as Light City's final speaker.

If we hadn't met leading up to the event and spoken earlier that day, I might have thought he'd stumbled out there by mistake. Thibault sauntered up to the podium wearing a simple pair of jeans and moccasin loafers. The event wasn't exactly a black-tie affair, but most presenters wore dresses or slacks and sports coats — these were business leaders, after all. In true form, Thibault set down his speaking notes, rolled up the sleeves of his casual plaid button-up, and addressed the audience with an enthusiasm so sincere it caught me off guard.

"Last one, right?" Thibault announced, eliciting a few hoots and hollers from the crowd. "Cool — we are almost there."

I'll admit it: I was ready to call it a day myself. Had a few folks not approached me for photos or to sign copies of my first book — *The Other Wes Moore* — I might have headed for the exit. What I couldn't have imagined, as Thibault began stitching together the narrative of his journey, was that by the time he was done speaking I'd be feeling bad for the half of the crowd that left early. They missed out on something massive.

In many ways Thibault's book *Larger Than Yourself* is an extended and expanded, full-fledged version of his speech that day. He tells of how an impromptu soccer game he played with Zulu children in a rural village in South Africa lit a flame of belief in him that sports could bridge divides with PeacePlayers, the nonprofit he helped start. Through his words, he brings us to visit the old tin can factory that inspired him to reimagine the real estate industry as a way to use the built environment to empower underserved communities with his development company, Seawall. He writes as he speaks: with the emboldened passion of someone who truly understands how privilege can and should be leveraged for good. Onstage and on the page, Thibault is imbued with a unique brand of wildness, optimism, and candor about his own experience. But what still strikes me most — just as it did five years ago — is his ability to distill the lessons of his truth into actionable principles.

Thibault's set of principles — *get out of your comfort zone, put purpose first, never claim ownership of an idea, build inside out, banish* can't/no *from your vocabulary, grow with love,* and *great movements need leaders* — are not just instructive to those who do nonprofit work but equally practical in the private sector. They are useful not just in bringing our entrepreneurial dreams to life and enhancing our careers but in bringing forth the best version of ourselves so that we can help shape the best version of our world. It's one thing to tell your story; it's quite another to give others the chance to sculpt their own. To be at once inspirational and instructive is a tough task for even seasoned writers, and I applaud Thibault for managing to strike this balance in his first book.

When he was wrapping up his speech that day, as our shared hometown of Baltimore was primed to do the hard work of continuing to unite our divided city, Thibault told us that if we followed these principles, our bravest ideas could grow into movements. In that moment, I thought about all the things I'd been a part of that had grown and flourished. I considered all those that had crashed and burned. Thibault was onto something. There is a fine line between an idea becoming a movement and it getting stuck, never to reach its potential.

I was mesmerized. This man was genius and so human at the same time. Invigorated by Thibault's speech, I asked myself a question when he stepped offstage: *What if growing brave ideas into principle-driven movements is exactly what Baltimore desperately needs to do to evolve?* Now, reinvigorated by Thibault's book, I find myself asking new questions: *What if principle-driven movements — in this time of a fiercely divided populace, racial violence, and a shockingly inequitable society — are what the United States needs to reckon with and redefine itself? What if, on a planet in the throes of environmental catastrophe and besieged by a deathly pandemic, principle-driven movements are among the world's most valuable weapons in the fight for our right to exist and thrive? How different might the future look if dozens, hundreds, even thousands of principle-driven movements took root?*

These possibilities make the hair stand on the back of my neck, the same way it seems to every time I get to hear my friend Thibault speak now, whether onstage or in our conversations together. Sometimes I wonder about what might have happened had the other half of the crowd stayed put at the Light City event back in 2016. What might have percolated in the heads and hearts of the audience? What ideas would already have turned into movements?

What I do know is that from his inspiring life journey and as delivered in his moving speech, the Larger Than Yourself movement has sprouted. This book is the next step in its growth. It will not be the last.

Wes Moore, *New York Times* bestselling author of
*The Other Wes Moore*
Baltimore, Maryland
May 2021

# Introduction

I was ten years old the first time I saw how deeply divides cut. I was at home with my parents, watching the climax of the Oscar-nominated movie *Mississippi Burning*. In the movie, a group of white men dressed in Ku Klux Klan suits gathered outside a church, gripping makeshift weapons in their hands. Crickets chimed in the warm evening air. The glow of truck headlamps illuminated the dirt road as a group of Black men, women, and children filed peacefully out of their place of worship. When they saw the mob — their heads covered with white hoods — they ran.

These men chased the people down. They tackled them. They beat them. The screams cut into the night air, and in the end, a small boy — who appeared to be my age — knelt praying in front of the church. Before the last hooded man kicked the praying boy, I ran away myself.

I burst into my room and buried my face in my pillow. I cried so loud I didn't even hear the footsteps of my parents coming in. I tried to stop sobbing, but I couldn't. My parents didn't try to stop my tears; they simply sat down and comforted me. *Mississippi Burning*, a crime thriller based on the murders of civil rights workers who were registering African American voters in the South in the 1960s, changed my life forever.

The winding road that took me from that childhood moment

across the world to some of the most divided countries on the planet —
and, unexpectedly, back to my hometown of Baltimore — eventually
inspired me to tell a story of my own. I had seen, heard, and learned
too much along the way to remain silent. As an adult, looking back on
my experience as a young boy watching *Mississippi Burning*, I can now
recognize that my pain and anguish pale in comparison to the pain and
anguish of folks who endured this and countless other acts of hatred
firsthand. Reflection allows us all to see things that weren't apparent to
us right away.

This book in your hands is not a memoir, although it might feel
like it at times. I do retrace my growth from a son to a father, from a
dreamer to a leader, but I've deliberately not spent too much time on
myself. What follows is intentionally light on personal details.

This is a book about how small ideas can grow into movements.
I've been lucky enough in my short professional career to participate
in several that changed me and, at least in my eyes, in some small way
changed the way the world turns. I've observed a process and set of
principles that are key to bringing movements to life. To highlight
those principles, I've divided the book into four parts. The first three
parts document three separate movements, each unique. The fourth
and shortest part captures the spirit of a movement I feel bubbling up
for the future. The chapters in each section tell the story of how I remember the movements unfolding. While it's possible that the other
people who were involved may remember specific events differently
or in another chronological order, I've chosen to tell the story in a way
that focuses on the lessons that I learned. The patterns that emerge between these movements offer a subtle but instructive best-practices list
for how this phenomenon happens — how the wave builds and how
to ride it. For readers who are looking to dive deeper into the principles themselves, I've included an expanded discussion section with
questions for each chapter; these appear at the end of the book as an
appendix. I advise first reading the book in full before turning to the
discussion section so the lessons from the stories can be best applied to
readers' own lives and current projects.

While I recognize the part I've played in helping nurture good ideas — pouring the water that allowed them to blossom into full-blown movements — the last thing I would want readers to come away with is a sense that this story is mine alone. It's not. Movements, by definition, require an entire army of people, many of whom don't even realize the role they are playing beyond that special sensation of being part of something very important.

There are far too many of these people and stories for me to include all of them in this one book. Still, I chose to provide a glimpse into some of their lives in a specific way. Four separate vignettes kick off each of the book's four parts. My hope is that readers will continually be reminded that movements are about real people who take real actions to be part of something meaningful. The story would be incomplete if it didn't portray the raw spirit of these individuals, and the vignettes are my best attempt at telling that tale. I should reiterate that the moments in the book that focus on others — whether in PeacePlayers or Seawall, South Africa or Baltimore — are simply my interpretations of their stories. I welcome other perspectives and hope that the book opens the doors to even more conversations. In the end, I offer this book as one story, not *the* story.

I've elected to change some names throughout the book to protect the privacy of certain people involved. I've also chosen to use some racial terminology when writing about my experience in South Africa — including words some readers in the United States and elsewhere might find offensive — in order to remain authentic about the way South Africans themselves talk about their own racial makeup. I did not take this decision lightly and recognize the impact of racial terminology over time. I appreciate the inherent power I wield in even making such a choice — when so many others have no say in how they're described or by whom — and have chosen to use this power with care in order to more fully illustrate the racial dynamics at play in South Africa as I experienced them. Finally, I'm aware that some of my heavily used words, like *movement* itself, might already carry their own definition for readers. I ask that we all keep our minds open to new ideas. After all, flexibility is what building movements and reinventing industries is all about. It's how we bridge divides.

Back when I was a young boy, even before I saw that violent movie scene, I had wondered why there was a division between Black people and white people. Growing up in Baltimore, a city that is over 60 percent Black, with massive racial disparities, you'd think I would have come across scenes of racial tension in my own life, but I really hadn't. I grew up in a privileged, predominately white bubble. After I saw the divide, however, I couldn't unsee it. That movie forced me to dive deeper to understand our country's complicated past. Back then, it was hard to wrap my head around how slavery could have existed and trace how the legacy it left reached into the present. As a young boy, I didn't understand it any more than I understood why my friends who were Black went home from school to houses considerably smaller than mine. I'd always had a nagging sense that the circumstances were all so unfair, but watching the scenes in *Mississippi Burning* crystallized something that I never forgot. From that moment on, even if I wasn't fully aware of it yet, I began to step out of my bubble, out of my comfort zone, to explore the divide. Looking back as an adult, I understand that choosing to see the divide or not is a privilege on its own. People of color don't have that choice.

I'd had another formative experience only a couple of years earlier. I remember being in the family station wagon when my dad pulled over on the side of the highway. He had explained that we were going to join some people for what he described as a special moment. Peering curiously out of my window as my dad put the car in park, I saw a huge line of people, all linked together. We got out and walked over to take our place in a chain that would include more than six million Americans holding hands. It was May 25, 1986, and that event on a beautiful Sunday became etched in history as Hands Across America, when Americans were encouraged to link hands across the country to raise money to fight poverty. I stood there with my family for fifteen minutes, holding hands with complete strangers and connected with people from every background imaginable. During that quarter hour, I thought about kids my age, all the way on the other side of the country in California, doing the exact same thing. My mind raced.

What was this force that was so powerful that it could bring millions of people together, at one point in time, for one specific purpose? How did everyone get focused on one thing? How was this even possible?

I was incapable of comprehending the reality of all these people connected across the entire United States, but I felt, for the first time, the massive energy that being part of a movement stirs in all of us. I felt proud to be there.

History has shown that Hands Across America turned out to be more symbolic — or even superficial — than useful in changing the way people experiencing poverty were treated or acknowledged, yet it did bring awareness to at least one young person, me. That experience started me thinking about what brings us together.

More than thirty years later, a part of me has still never left that line. I remember the feeling of the springtime air that day. The neon-colored clothes so many people were rocking. My heart pounding so hard I could feel it in the palms of my hands, as I served as a link in this chain of something that was clearly massive. In the same way, another part of me has never forgotten that scene in *Mississippi Burning*. I remember our family's living room. The stiffness of our couch. The big, boxy 1980s-style TV. That crash of sadness, the hysterical crying about the cruelty over something so trivial as skin color, my parents talking me through it. I remember trying to wrap my little head and heart around our country's bloodstained history. My mom's hands on my back.

Over the years, the events depicted in the film — which took place in 1964, only a couple of decades before my first viewing — got closer and closer in my mind. It wasn't all that long ago. I'd see flashes of that past in the present. I watched buildings burn on TV as members of the National Guard surged through the streets of Los Angeles during the 1992 uprising following the acquittal of the police officers who beat Rodney King. On field trips to museums in Washington, DC, I saw collections of photos with signs designating areas "Whites Only," taken only a few decades before I was born. Most recently I've followed the unfair deaths of too many people of color at the hands of our country's police forces. *Mississippi Burning* felt more current, not less, the older I grew and the more aware I became of the privilege that came with the color of my skin.

On my journey to adulthood, I also felt those pounding sensations of movements deepening like the sound of a stampede drawing near. When my work or hobbies brought me closer to people, I felt the energy that true connection brings. I felt a certain nearness and oneness that come in those rare moments when we are swept up in the collective energy toward a common goal.

Watching that film was the first time I remember deeply hurting without understanding the logic behind the suffering depicted on the screen. Standing hand in hand with those millions of people was the first time I remember feeling part of something larger than myself. Ultimately, these two experiences spurred a curiosity in me. I'm now in my early forties with young sons of my own, and I don't feel any closer to knowing what keeps us divided, but I am no less obsessed with seeking a solution. I've discovered that's where movements come in. They link us together and help us step into those divides. United in a movement, we're empowered to do what we could never do alone.

# Part I

# DREAM

I'm sitting across the table from my friend Charlie. His beautiful dark-brown face is framed by a patchy beard and a thin helmet of hair, both a fuzzy blend of silver, pewter, and cotton white. The delicate web of lines angling from his eyes reminds me of the trails seawater leaves behind on the sand when the tide washes out.

To my twenty-four-year-old self, there's no more welcoming face in the world. Maybe that's why I'm still sitting here in my family's dining room, elbows resting on the tablecloth as we stare into each other's eyes. The creaking of the wood chair beneath me is the only sound against the faint clatter of the rest of the family cleaning up in the kitchen. Traces of another lovingly prepared dinner still waft in the air. I wish I could capture this moment, put it in a jar, and take it with me. Soon I won't be so spoiled by delicious home-cooked food and the joy of Charlie's company.

"So, where you're goin', how you gonna get there?" he asks in his Baltimore drawl.

"I'm taking an airplane, Charlie," I say. "It's a long way from here to the place I'm going."

The ancient fellow — some say he's more than a hundred years old — pauses for a moment. "You know the problem with airplanes, don't ya?"

"Nope," I admit. "What's that, Charlie?"

"If it runs out of gas, you ain't got nowhere to go."

With that, Charlie smiles his priceless, toothless smile and wheezes out his trademark chuckle. I can't help it. I begin laughing too.

■ ■ ■ ■ ■

Back in early 1990, I was on the verge of becoming a teenager. My three sisters — Lauren, Sophie, and Celine — were ten, seven, and four. During much of my childhood we'd lived in a modest house in the city of Baltimore, but after the birth of my youngest sister, my parents decided the family had grown too big to fit there comfortably. Thanks to the success of the family real estate company where my dad worked, we'd bought a larger house north of the city in the rolling green countryside off the Falls Road Corridor in Baltimore County. To the outside observer we were a model family. We had a successful dad, a stay-at-home mom, four healthy kids, and a big new house. What very few people knew was that this was actually our toughest moment.

My parents' relationship was in question. Even though I blocked most of it out, from what I remember, they were trying to figure out whether they still loved each other. The move to the new house and the uncertainty about the marriage proved too much for my mom. Suddenly, she fell into a deep depression and had to be taken away from us. She was admitted to the kind of hospital that at twelve years old I could only understand as a place where they kept crazy people.

One day, I was forced by my dad to visit her. I remember driving past the ominous 140-year-old stone gatehouse of Sheppard and Enoch Pratt Hospital. We slowly wound our way through the sprawling, dark, and depressing campus of one of the oldest mental health institutions in the country. Eventually my dad parked next to an even more frightening building, its cupola seeming to disappear in the thick gray clouds that hung low in the sky. Standing outside its century-old brick exterior, I felt like I was in a bad horror movie. We checked in and went upstairs. Finally, we were led to a room for visitors and told to wait.

My dad and I sat in complete silence at a table with an empty chair across from us. The heavy air in the room suffocated any small talk. There was a palpable tension. I was scared. Part of me wanted to just get up and run out of there, but as I heard footsteps down the hall and watched the door swing open, I changed my mind. I wanted to grab my mom and flee together.

I hardly recognized the woman who entered the room. She sat down. She had the same facial features and hair as my mom, but she was somehow different. She wore an expression I'd never seen before. It was as if someone had pressed the pause button on her usual lively, warm demeanor and left her flat and vacant.

I sat across from this woman who looked like my mom, unable to speak. My dad did the best he could to start a conversation between us, asking me to tell my mom about my recent basketball game, but all I could do was sit there stunned, staring at my mom and searching for the spark she'd had in her eyes my whole life. What I found was something unrecognizable. She simply stared back as though she was looking right through me, like I wasn't even there.

*Where is my mom? Who took her away? How did this happen?*

Until that moment, I had only known her as the most incredible mother in the world. Her love and thoughtfulness were like a warm blanket. It was large and thick enough to cover not just her family but everyone she touched. I had always assumed that she was invincible, that we were invincible.

The visit was short. The conversation was shallow. Before I knew it, my mom was led by a nurse back out of the room. My father told me it was time to go, and the two of us went out the way we came. My mom, he said, would not be coming with us today.

On the car ride home, I thought about her. While I knew that my mom's journey toward motherhood had its own challenges, I was too young to grasp the full extent of them. At eighteen, against the wishes of her parents, she had taken a giant leap of faith and emigrated from the tiny village in France where she had grown up to the United States. When she left her parents and five older brothers behind, she'd pinned her hopes on the budding relationship between her and my father working out. From that very first choice, the culture shock had always been too much for her. While my dad's family welcomed her, the closed-minded country club lifestyle they lived was such a departure from the way my mom saw the world. In 1946, right after the Second World War, my dad's father, Harold, had founded a real estate brokerage company with his brother, and they grew it to the point that the name *Manekin* was synonymous with real estate in the greater Baltimore area. My free-spirited mother didn't want to fit into the mold they expected of her any more than she wanted to fit into the world she left behind in France. The harder she tried, the more lost and purposeless she felt. Even I noticed, as a young boy, that she wasn't totally acclimated to life in Baltimore. I loved that she was foreign, though, and different from all the other moms. I was proud of her, just the way she was.

As my mom worked with the professionals in the hospital to get better, I tried to make sense of it all. The experience of that one visit crushed me, and I vowed to never go back. I couldn't. My mom was my number one. Now she appeared to be gone, an unrecognizable shell of her former self. I couldn't handle it, so I turned away from it all. As I prepared to turn thirteen, I simply hid from the reality of my family's problems. I was in denial. To me, we were still the perfect family, and I couldn't admit to myself or to anyone else that we were struggling. The truth was that none of us really knew whether we'd make it out in one piece or not.

After a couple of months in the hospital, followed by almost a year of ongoing care and hard personal work, my mom started coming out of the fog. During her recovery, while I pretended that none of it was happening, my parents did the opposite. They confronted it head-on and never gave up on each other, slowly but surely beginning to re-ignite that flame that keeps two people together.

By the winter of 1991, my mom was almost back to her amazing self. With her own mom, my French grandmother, in town to help her get back on her feet, she and my dad decided to go out on a much-needed date night to a restaurant tucked away in a local shopping center just down the road from our new house. The two of them enjoyed a quiet meal where they were able to connect without the commotion of a house full of kids. They both arrived at a new appreciation for the love they shared, a love that had inspired my mom to cross an entire ocean fifteen years earlier. A love that had them fight for each other at their most challenging time.

Baltimore winters can be brutal, and that evening a particularly biting cold spell hit town. As they walked back to the car after dinner, my mom held on to my dad tightly to stay warm. Nearing the parking lot, she noticed a thin man curled up on a bench. She was drawn to him. That deep curiosity about life and compassion for every human being — which she had brought with her to this country, then lost — had finally been reclaimed.

"Good evening, sir," she said in her charming French accent from the safety of the sidewalk.

There was no response.

She left my father's side and approached the bench.

"Excuse me." She gently cleared her throat in a way that caused the man to stir. "I'm sorry to bother you. My name is Brigitte." She pointed to her husband. "This is Donald. What is your name?"

The man woke from his doze and shifted his body.

"I'm Charlie Barber." He lifted his head slightly from the bag he was using as a pillow.

"Mr. Barber, it's a pleasure to meet you," she said. "Do you have a home?"

"Sure do." He pointed at the bench. "Right here."

For a moment, my mom considered Charlie's age. He looked elderly enough to be her grandfather. "Mr. Barber, if you don't mind my asking, how old are you?"

"Don't know. Lost track of the time, I suppose," he said with an endearing giggle.

My mom smiled, charmed by his directness and his ability to be so lighthearted despite his circumstances. My parents said their goodbyes and continued on toward the car. As they walked, a freezing wind blasted them, a reminder of the growing severity of the winter.

My parents' entire conversation on the car ride home revolved around Charlie.

"Donald," my mom said, "there is something powerful about that man we just met."

They discussed the best options for Charlie. There were shelters. There were social services. There was the prospect of offering financial help, but the more they talked about it, the more complex that solution became. The reality was that they didn't know anything about Charlie's story. They didn't know how much of his present lifestyle was circumstance and how much of it was choice. They only had a name and a single brief encounter. Eventually, they pulled into our driveway with only more questions about whether it was their place to do anything at all.

Later that night, the temperature plunged far below freezing. Even bundled up in her warm and cozy bed, my mom still felt cold. She couldn't sleep, and she couldn't stop thinking about the man on the icy bench less than two miles away.

So at 2:00 a.m. she got up, grabbed a pillow and several warm blankets, and drove back down to Green Spring Station. She found Charlie still on the bench, dozing in the fetal position to conserve warmth. She gently tapped his shoulder a few times to wake him up.

"Hello, I'm so sorry to bother you again. I met you earlier," she said once she had his attention. "I thought that maybe you could use a pillow and another blanket. Please take these and go back to sleep. I'll come again tomorrow."

Shivering in the freezing nighttime air, she stayed for just a few minutes to make sure he was well wrapped up, then drove back to finally get some rest.

True to her word, the next day she returned. The first thing she did was visit some of the nearby shops and ask the storekeepers about the gentleman sleeping on the bench. My mom discovered that Charlie had been living in the Green Spring Valley area since he was a young boy, when he'd been a sharecropper on nearby farms. She also learned that he was homeless and had been residing on the benches of Green Spring Station for years, making a little bit of money running errands for shop owners and receiving donations from passersby. He used to sleep in an abandoned shack in the woods behind the center until a developer acquired the land and bulldozed the shelter.

The first few people my mom spoke with liked Charlie. While nobody knew him intimately, they said he was harmless, and they indicated that people genuinely enjoyed seeing him every day. One owner, however, responded much differently.

"Oh, don't worry about him. He smells, and he doesn't belong here.

But the shopping center has new management coming in, and hopefully they'll be getting the police to make him leave. Now, how can I help you?"

"You already have, thank you." My mom turned and left the store.

She began walking around the shopping center, looking for Charlie. She checked the benches, but he wasn't there. Then she saw a heap of boulders to the side of one of the walking paths. She could see a man sitting on one of the stones, dangling a leg over the edge.

"Hello again," she said as she walked up to Charlie. "Mr. Barber, I understand that you have a home here, but if you are ever in need of help, please find a way to give me a call."

She handed him a piece of paper with her phone number on it, and the two of them chatted for a few more minutes. Feeling that she had accomplished what she could for the time being, my mom headed home.

A week later, at 7:00 a.m., she got a call from a woman who said, "I have someone here named Charlie who asked me to contact you."

"Oh yes, I know Charlie," said my mom, excited at the mention of a man she had spent less than ten minutes with. "Please put him on."

Charlie got on the line and skipped the small talk. "Can I come over to your house?"

Without hesitation, my mom jumped into her car to pick him up and bring him home.

■ ■ ■ ■ ■

Ten years later, as Charlie and I sat laughing together at the dinner table before my next big adventure, he had become a member of our family. He'd moved in with us from the day my mom first brought him home. After he moved in, my mom spent years trying to piece together Charlie's story. He couldn't remember his birthday or how old he was. He didn't have a social security card or any other kind of identification.

The only family Charlie mentioned having was a sister who'd become a maid for a wealthy family in Roland Park decades earlier.

She made raising the family's five kids her life's work and didn't venture outside of that environment. They hadn't spoken in many years, and Charlie showed no interest in reconnecting with her or any part of his past. All he saw was the present moment, and nothing about it seemed to bother him, not even having to sleep on the shopping center's benches.

Most interesting of all was how indifferent he was about piecing together his past. He never talked about having fallen in love or whether he had any kids — or whether he had wanted either at any time in his life. We knew he'd lost the place he called home and no longer had contact with his sister, but on the rare occasion he spoke about those sorts of losses, he did so with a trademark emotionlessness that left us unsure of whether there was something deeper or whether he'd simply come to terms with where he found himself and didn't need the kind of wraparound narrative completeness that our family wanted for him.

Many people questioned my parents' decision to bring a homeless man into the house, saying it was unsafe for the children. That conversation never fazed any of us. My mom was spectacular, and she did extraordinary things on a regular basis. Nothing she did surprised us, even as she was still acclimating back to regular life, and adding our new housemate was no exception.

Charlie had his own room, and he ate both breakfast and dinner with us every day, plus lunch on the weekends. On weekdays, we dropped him off at Green Spring Station, where he claimed he worked, on our way to school. On our way back, we picked him up.

For all of us, Charlie became more than just another member of the family. He had joined us when we were at our breaking point. After his arrival, my mom's recovery accelerated. She wasn't just returning to her old self; she had somehow arrived at an even better place, in large part because she rediscovered her ability to help others. My parents emerged stronger as a couple.

I was so caught up in my own head as I grew into my teenage years that Charlie's presence took a bit longer to have an effect on me, but it was equally profound when it did. Not knowing how to cope with all the family confusion and the task of growing up, I had turned to my peers for comfort and support. As time churned on, I made a lot of the trademark bad decisions of high school. It was only after several years with Charlie that I began to recalibrate my priorities and the direction of my life.

My moods and behavior often changed on a whim, but his presence and love remained steady. He was a constant reminder that there wasn't any room to complain about anything. I had no right to be a jerk to my sisters or my parents. In Charlie's presence, I began to realize that I could never take anything for granted because he had seen a million more hardships in his lifetime than I would ever see in mine.

Charlie, sitting for hours at the head of the kitchen table and simply observing in silence, had a powerful effect on us. We all cleaned up a little more. We were on our best behavior. We tried a little harder. We cared more. We loved more deeply. It's not like Charlie was ever judging us; he just kept us honest and always striving to be our highest selves. He was a guiding light, a unifying force, in ways none of us could have ever imagined — a new part of the family who reminded us why family itself was so important, which was something I had almost given up on.

Although many people had initially voiced concerns about our decision to allow Charlie to live with us, many others complimented our family for doing so much for him as the years wore on. The reality was that he did as much for us as we did for him. He was there when we needed him the most. Charlie's presence in our house shaped the human beings my parents, my sisters, and I became. He taught us the value of getting out of our comfort zone. He showed us how to walk in other people's shoes before passing judgment. He helped us better understand our privilege and why we should do everything in our power to use it for good. He brought back my mom to me.

■ ■ ■ ■ ■

That's why this night after dinner, a month after I have just turned twenty-four, Charlie and I are simply sitting across from each other. It feels right. It also feels much more lighthearted compared to the discussions I've been having with the rest of my family and friends about my big decision. I'm about to leave this warm, happy, safe life behind. I'm leaving my family. I'm leaving Charlie.

"You know what you're gonna do when you get over there? Know what it's gonna be like?" Charlie asks.

"No idea." I laugh. "Only one way to find out."

Then Charlie flashes a knowing smile. Here is a man who lives life one day at a time. He is a guy who can't afford to be paralyzed by fear of the unknown.

"So, do you wanna come to South Africa with me, Charlie?"

I know his answer before I even ask the question. Charlie can't be bothered to go anywhere. Plus, I know he'd never leave my mom's side. All the same, I still want to invite him.

"You kidding?" he says, still smiling warmly. "Already told you, I'm not going on no plane."

I know I'll miss Charlie's smile every day I'm gone. It's one of those special comforts I don't need distance to appreciate. He's become one of the most significant people ever to come into my life, and I love him deeply. Somewhere during our talk, I find the last bit of courage I need to set off on the journey. I don't know it yet, of course, but there at the dinner table with Charlie I find the strength to embark on the quest that started when I was eight years old, excited by the power of holding hands with strangers, and took shape when I was ten, shocked by the rawness of a film. As my journey continues, I remain obsessed with figuring out what keeps us apart and how to bring us together.

# 1

# Comfort Zone

*"The comfort zone is the great enemy to creativity;*
*moving beyond it necessitates intuition, which in turn configures*
*new perspectives and conquers fears."*

— DAN STEVENS

The tires skidded to a halt, and a cloud of amber dust curled around our sky-blue 1980 Volkswagen Golf. For the last hour I'd grown used to watching the metal hood vibrate above the bumpy dirt road like a ship bouncing across a choppy crimson sea of African dirt. Now we were parked, our rickety vehicle idling with a little tin wiggle on the side of the road. Over the hum, my heart pounded against my ribs.

"This is exactly what they told us not to do," I said.

We were deep in rural South Africa. The Drakensberg mountain range punctuated the horizon. In the foreground, a plain dotted with dung huts and patches of trees stretched toward infinity. Immediately below us was a slope and below that a field. Dozens of Zulu kids — maybe a hundred — fanned out across it, some tiny toddlers, others nearing their teenage years. Since we were perched high up on the road, we had no way to figure out whether they were doing anything organized. It looked like the kids were merely playing. Some chased their friends; others lounged in the large patches of African grass that jutted skyward.

I glanced over at my buddy Sean, the only other passenger in the vehicle. He was gazing down at the field, his face drenched in sweat. Vusi, which is what we called our two-decades-old German transport, lacked a lot of modern conveniences, but on those hot days, air-conditioning was what we missed most.

We still had more than one hundred miles to go before we were back at our apartment in Durban, and though the continent itself was all still so new to me, the one message that had been pummeled into my head was that I should be afraid. Tales of tourists disappearing, rapes, and kidnappings were among the first things I heard from white South Africans I knew back in the States when I'd told them where I was headed.

"South Africa is great to visit," one said. "As long as you stay in the well-policed game parks, beachfront resorts, and upscale restaurants."

"The country is dangerous enough for a white guy," another explained. "But if you go for a drive, don't pull over, don't stop at red lights. Don't get out."

"Whatever you do," a third told me, "don't go into any rural areas or townships."

The white South Africans I had met in my first week in Durban confirmed that pit stops on dirt roads in the middle of rural areas were definitely a bad idea.

Now, only a week after arriving in the country, Sean and I turned to face each other in the sweltering car. There was risk, sure, but when we locked eyes and exchanged a nod, I knew what that meant. I flipped off the ignition, creaked open my door, and jumped out. We popped the trunk, grabbed the lumpy donated basketball that we always carried with us, and walked over to the edge of the steep hill that led from the road to the field below. Without the rumble of Vusi's engine, all I could hear floating through the breeze was the bubbly sound of children at play.

Sean and I slowly and carefully made our way down the hill with our beat-up basketball, heading toward the throng of children. The kids immediately noticed us. The two-hundred-foot hill was staggeringly steep, and as slowly as we tried to move, we inevitably picked up speed. My heart and lungs slammed against my chest from a mixture of fear and adrenaline, and we kicked up a dust storm as we scrambled down, struggling to stay upright. To the kids it must have looked like we were charging toward them, two six-foot-plus white guys mounting an attack.

As Sean and I neared the bottom of the hill, skidding our sneakers to a stop as the ground leveled out, fear and panic had spread among the kids, and they began to prepare for the worst. The youngest ones started crying and sprinted as fast as their tiny legs would carry them toward the woods on the opposite side of the field. The older kids walked uneasily to the base of the hill, fists clenched, ready to fight for their turf if need be.

■ ■ ■ ■ ■

One week before Sean and I charged down that hill toward those Zulu children in the vast South African field, I'd kissed my mother goodbye at the bustling drop-off lane outside Dulles Airport in Washington, DC.

"I'm proud of you, Thibault," she said, tears running down her cheeks.

We had been through some tough times, my mom especially, but she had never given up. She had taught me so much about the world outside of our slice of Baltimore, the different kinds of people out there, and how we should treat one another. I pulled her in close for one last hug. I knew her tears stemmed from pride that I was chasing my dream of making the world a better and more united place, a mission she had inspired in me since I was young. I needed to get out to see the world, and she knew that. The upper-middle-class bubble I grew up in never felt right to my mom, and she did all she could to make sure that my three younger sisters and I understood that the world was a vast and powerful place, full of amazing people, ideas, and different ways of being.

It was early 2002, and I had recently graduated from Lehigh

University. While most of my friends headed off to Wall Street, law school, or big-five accounting firms, I knew that wasn't me. I wanted to live in other countries, explore different cultures, and feel like I was doing something that mattered. As unconventional as my choice was, my mom supported it wholeheartedly, because that's how she and my dad had raised us. Mixed with her pride, though, was a touch of fear. We'd both heard stories that would make any mother nervous for her son's safety. I squeezed her a little bit tighter to let her know that I'd be just fine.

With my backpack strapped on and my suitcase in hand, I walked over to my dad. We exchanged a powerful hug, but he showed no emotion. He gave nothing away. I could tell from the strong grip of his arms wrapped around me that he too approved of my choice, that he was proud as well. As I embarked on my own journey to become a man, the one I looked to as a stable, reliable role model remained the soft-spoken dad I'd always known.

"I love you guys," I said.

With that, I turned and walked into the massive terminal, open to whatever experience came my way. As I waited to check in for my sixteen-hour flight on South African Airways, the anxiety and uncertainty I had been feeling moments before slowly began to fade.

As I stood in line, my mind flashed back to three months earlier, when I had unexpectedly reconnected with Sean Tuohey, a friend from college. Our meeting had completely altered the trajectory of my life.

Sean had also chosen a different path for himself. After college, he had gone overseas to play professional basketball in Northern Ireland. While there, he took a side job coaching kids in a program that worked to help Catholic and Protestant children find common ground through sports. These two religious groups had been locked in a low-level war known as the Troubles for nearly four decades. Even though a truce had been called in 1998, the younger generation had inherited the hatred for the opposing side that dated back centuries.

The more Sean worked with the program, the more he started to see the positive impact it was having in Northern Ireland. Sean's professional hoops career never took off, but he fell in love with the idea that sports could unite deeply divided countries. Through a connection with a local police chief, Sean was introduced to another divided country, South Africa, and he was ready to try out the concept on his own.

Sean came back to his hometown of Washington, DC, and with the help of his older brother, Brendan, formed a nonprofit organization called PeacePlayers. The plan was to go into war-torn and deeply divided countries and use sports to get children from both sides of the divide to meet each other, find common ground, and — hopefully, over time — become friends.

After college, I did not immediately cross paths with Sean again, but then a mutual friend told me that Sean was over in Africa coaching hoops. Because I had grown up playing sports, and because I had been deeply curious about Africa from as far back as I could remember, this kind of work fascinated me, and I wanted to learn more. Without even knowing whether Sean had an internet connection, I shot him a message. He replied within hours, saying that he was on the way home for a visit following his first spell in South Africa.

"Let's get lunch," his email said in closing.

A week later, over a long meal in Baltimore, Sean started off by telling me about the low-level Northern Ireland league he had played in, where his teammates smoked cigarettes and drank pints of Guinness at halftime, and about the kids' program there. Sean had seen the power of sports to unite Protestant and Catholic children, but he felt that a program like that could be run differently, perhaps even better and at a larger scale. He then began telling me stories of showing up in South Africa for the first time and moving into the YMCA in Albert Park, one of the most volatile neighborhoods in Durban. He mentioned some coaches he had recruited to help, who had endured the horrors of apartheid, the authoritarian system based on institutional racism that was a white supremacist way to govern South Africa. It treated non-white people as less than human. He talked about the lawlessness of the country. He described the challenge of learning to surf in shark-infested waters and visiting *sangomas* (traditional healers) when he got sick. He told me about townships, which were planned, segregated communities outside the main urban areas. These deliberately underdeveloped informal settlements housed racial groups from Indians to Black people to "Coloureds" — the name given to the mixed-race group in South Africa, which was a legally defined racial classification during apartheid and is a designation still used today, showing how the racial power dynamic continues to operate — each in geographic and ethnic isolation. Like favelas in Brazil or shantytowns the world over, these unregulated neighborhoods were often deprived of even basic civic services. Sean explained that the prospect of danger was always present in those areas and that the rawness of human life was on full blast.

I hung on his every word.

Sean also explained the program to me. PeacePlayers was still in its infancy, but the more he talked, the more I fell in love with his straightforward proposition: sports have an amazing ability to break down barriers and unite people. Sitting there at lunch, I realized how simple an idea it was. I thought back to most of my best friends, guys I had played sports with since I was a kid. I thought about the times we had laughed together and cried together, about the high school basketball championships we had lost, and about how closely we had worked as a team to get there. I thought about great sports movies where a group of men or women who society said didn't belong together bonded with one another through the love of a game. PeacePlayers was expanding upon that idea, with intentionality.

*What would happen if we went to war-torn countries and helped bring kids from both sides of a conflict to play sports together? Was it too far-fetched to think the kids could find common ground and eventually become friends? Could that gradually start to change the course of the future in a country or region, one kid at a time?*

If the plan was to build social bridges in severely divided countries, it required a tool. Though there were a lot of sports to choose from to achieve this goal, Sean focused on basketball, and not simply because it was the game closest to his heart. In South Africa, sports also divided the country. The white people played rugby and the Black people played soccer. Basketball was neutral. It was a relatively new sport. It hadn't gotten much traction and didn't come preloaded with generations of stigma. Kids from all sides of the conflict — white kids, Black kids, and everyone in between — could be equally interested. Sean believed that if he could get them at a young enough age — around ten to twelve years old — they might not have formed irreversibly negative opinions about one another yet, the way so much of the older generations already had.

Toward the end of the lunch, Sean explained that he was the only employee of the organization and that his older brother, Brendan, was raising money for it during any spare moment he could find outside his day job.

That three-hour lunch with Sean wasn't enough for me. Over the next few weeks I had several more meetings with him and Brendan, sitting in the basement of their parents' house, and I hit it off with both of them. Those meetings were exhilarating, and I asked tons of questions: What funding did we have? Were our coaches in South Africa volunteers or were we paying them? Where were we getting our hoops? Were white kids and Black kids playing together? Was the program working?

None of us really knew what we were doing at the time, but we were driven by what felt like an enormous force. I hadn't been to South Africa yet, but I could close my eyes and picture it all — the kids, the coaches, the games, the possibility. I wanted to take on something that I could grow with, something that could grow with me. The potential in the idea that sports could unite was utterly compelling. I wanted in.

In February 2002, with not much more than a couple of high fives — no contracts or legal documents — I joined the ambitious organization that promised me a shot at helping to unite the world. We had only $8,000 in our bank account, raised mostly from friends and family, but at the time, that backing felt huge.

Thinking back on all this while waiting to board my flight to South Africa, the uncertainty came in waves. I didn't have any idea what I was getting myself into, how my life there would unfold, but there was something else in the mystery. There was an excitement. It had begun with the decision to join the program, but it certainly hadn't ended there.

I was eager to see what I was made of. On the one hand, my privileged upbringing inspired a curiosity about how the world worked outside of the bubble I grew up in, with family trips in the summer to Maine and visits to see my mom's family in France from the time I was born. On the other, that same privilege haunted me. My last name came with expectations. The color of my skin came with assumptions. My address was in a safe neighborhood. At home, I didn't always feel like I had the space to make my own way, to define myself. Still, the favorable circumstances of my life came with the question of what I was going to do with them. Abroad, I felt like I would be empowered to test out answers in a way that I couldn't in my own backyard. This opportunity to dive in headfirst with PeacePlayers gave me a shot at finding out, underneath it all, what I was really about.

■ ■ ■ ■ ■

Back at the base of the hill in rural South Africa, Sean and I stood in front of the semicircle of kids that had formed around us. They no longer looked like the carefree group of school-age children we had seen milling about from our car. The older boys, most of them shoeless, were on the front line, their nostrils flaring in and out, their chests pumped up. We stared at the faces that surrounded us, the tension as thick as the mixture of anthill clay and cow dung on the round Zulu huts that edged the field. Our eyes locked with theirs. We knew immediately that we weren't thinking the same thing.

*Who are we to them anyway? Just a representation of the ever-present racial tensions between Black people and white people that still run through South Africa? Why would they welcome us? Why wouldn't they fight us?*

Those kids had every right not to trust us. It had only been eight years since apartheid had ended. It was still fresh in people's minds, especially those in the rural tribal areas like the one we found ourselves in that day. We fit a profile they'd been taught to treat with caution, if not hostility. To complicate matters, we also didn't speak their language. There was no verbal way to calm the escalating situation. We couldn't explain we were American. The fact that we were white by itself meant that building trust was going to be a tall order. All we had was a ball, and not one they appeared accustomed to seeing.

I was worried about whether the younger kids had run back to the village to get their fathers and what kind of trouble that might bring. Realizing that we needed a way to make friends, and fast, I took three cautious steps forward and extended my right hand, palm up, toward the nearest boy in the circle. Our eyes met. I softened my shoulders and put a big smile on my face. The muscles in his cheek hardened, his jaw clenched even tighter. I took another step forward, and everyone apart from this one boy took a step back, their stares unwavering and their fists curled closed.

Understanding that I needed help in demonstrating my peaceful intentions, I turned back to Sean and reached my outstretched hand to his. We demonstrated a quick high five. The kids didn't blink. A sharp silence had crept across the field. Sean extended his own hand and I returned the high five, both of us smiling. We repeated the exercise several more times, exaggerating the motions and hoping that our goofiness might make these kids-turned-warriors laugh and understand that we had come to have fun, not to hurt anyone.

Eventually, I turned back toward the first boy. His expression had softened. His eyes relaxed slightly. A few of his friends were cracking curious smiles and whispering to one another in Zulu. I could hear the light clicking of their tongues, but at that point, I had no idea what they were saying. As our eyes met again and my hand extended toward him for the second time, the smiles and giggles stopped. Taking a deep breath, he slowly walked toward me until we were only a few feet apart.

He raised his hand in the air, pausing for a moment to look back at his friends. Seeing no objections, he burst into a huge smile as he swung his hand with all his might to smack mine. I grabbed my hand in exaggerated pain, hopping around and blowing on my fingers as if to cool the burn. His buddies erupted into laughter and started jumping up and down. He then extended his own palm. The kids grew silent again, and I returned the high five, just not quite as hard — my hand still stung.

From that moment on, Sean and I didn't have enough hands. Kids climbed over one another in pursuit of high fives. Hearing all the laughter and commotion, the little kids who had run into the woods crying had sprinted back and were crawling under the legs of their older friends trying to get in on the action. For half an hour it was a high-five fest. Over and over, the dark, hardened skin of rural mountain life clapped against our soft white hands.

When the high-five craze wore off, we naturally picked up the ball. Sean took one half of the kids, I took the other. Without a hoop, basket, or even pavement, the sport was chosen for us: soccer. Two boys ran in opposite directions to mark off goals on either end of the expansive field.

The impromptu game began, and the smiling faces hardened once again; each kid had something to prove. I hadn't played soccer since I was in high school, and the hazardous terrain — patches of dirt, rocks, and the odd tree stump — was so different from the smooth grass fields and AstroTurf I had grown up playing on. About ten minutes in, with the score tied at zero and after a timely steal, a young boy on my team passed me the ball. Soccer wasn't my strongest sport, but I wanted to attempt something that would excite the kids. I planted my left foot into a patch of that soft red dirt and swung my right foot through the ball as hard as I could.

As if in slow motion, our cheap plastic basketball left my shoe and sailed above the other players. Time stood still. I watched. Sean watched. All the kids watched. The ball floated through the air, turning ever so slightly at the end and sailing between the two trees that marked our makeshift goal, past a diving ten-year-old goalie.

Immediately, I felt like ducking in shame. I hadn't really meant to score on this kid. He was less than half my age and appeared to be half my height.

*What am I supposed to do?*

Panicking, my mind defaulted to a soccer game I'd seen on TV a few days before. I took off my shirt, stretched my arms out wide, and began running toward midfield. I think they call that celebration "the Airplane."

"Gooooooaaaaaal!" I yelled out, adrenaline pumping through my veins, my feet feeling like they might lift off the ground.

As I ran, I heard a rising noise behind me. Glancing over my shoulder, I expected to find Sean chasing me down to tell me to get ahold of myself. Instead, I saw quite a different sight.

They were chasing after me — not just the fifty or so kids from my team, but the entirety of Sean's as well. Some had their shirts off and their arms stretched out, and all had massive smiles plastered on their faces. "Oooooooohhhhhh!" they hollered, trying to mimic the sound of my scream.

The tears came right away, flooding down my cheeks. It was as if I could feel every step of the nearly ten-thousand-mile distance between me and my hometown in the States. The shell that had surrounded me — the one that protects us all from the perceived danger of the outside world — had cracked. With each stride, more of the shards fell away. Here we were, Sean and I, two white guys running around with a hundred Zulu kids in total jubilation because a round object had traveled from one place to another. We didn't share a language. We couldn't have grown up more differently. It was crazy, but it also, somehow, made perfect sense. It confirmed what we'd expected about the potential of sports to unite. We were onto something.

Soon we'd be back in Durban, totally pumped about digging into the idea we had crossed an ocean to test out. But for now, the goodbyes could wait. The drive too. For a bit longer we kept going, the giant mass of us, doing "the Airplane" across the field below the booming African sky, the glowing pinks and oranges of the sun finally beginning to dip behind the mountains on the horizon.

# 2

# Purpose First

*"Sport has the power to change the world. It has the power to inspire.
It has the power to unite people in a way that little else does."*

— NELSON MANDELA

"The NBA?"

I couldn't tell who shouted it, but those three letters cut through the thick afternoon air as Sean nodded affirmatively.

"The NBA," he added coolly, facing a half circle of young men and women, mostly college age, who'd gathered on the set of concrete steps. A few days had passed since the spontaneous soccer game in the mountains, and I was meeting this group for the first time.

Sean continued. "That's right. PeacePlayers is officially on the map."

"*Hayibo*," another voice said, using the Zulu word for *disbelief.* "They are supporting the program?"

"Of course," said Sean, grinning. "How could they say no? We are the feeder program they have always hoped for. We are going to help put these guys on the international map."

Gasps and murmurs of excitement rolled through the small crowd. Sean's comment was true, but it did not reveal the entire picture. The NBA was supporting us with a measly $5,000. A month earlier, when

Sean, Brendan, and I had met with league representatives in a Manhattan high-rise, they had given us a big fat *no* to our initial suggestion of a $100,000 donation. I'd never asked anyone for so much money. When I'd worked briefly in fundraising for the United Way right after college and before PeacePlayers, asking anyone for $1,000 was a big deal. Saying "one hundred thousand dollars" at twenty-four years old with a straight face to a bunch of NBA suits was another thing entirely. Even with the absurdity of the number, we had gone into the meeting with great confidence. Not only were we going to develop the game of basketball abroad, but we would use it as a tool to unite countries. It was perfect, something the NBA would want to get behind in a major way. We were so convinced they'd say yes to our big ask, their comparatively small contribution caught us all off guard. We were missing something from our presentation but weren't sure what. Sean had a way of taking it all in stride, though. He had that rare blend of goofiness and passion that made him charismatic.

Now he continued addressing the group in South Africa. "I missed you guys while I was in the States the last two months," he told them. "We made great progress raising money and telling your stories to our board of directors back home, and now it's time to talk about the next phase of PeacePlayers."

We'd arrived at the outdoor amphitheater at the Durban Institute of Technology (DIT) a few minutes earlier. The university, which was one of two main institutions of higher education in Durban, was a half-hour stroll from Durban's downtown, harbor, and beaches. The small amphitheater was part of a larger campus courtyard, and the sounds of college life hummed merrily around us like a breeze.

"And what I'm really excited about, even more than the NBA, is to introduce you to my boy," Sean said, turning to me. "This is Thibault. He left an incredible career with the United Way — a great job at a large and stable organization — to help us blow this program up. He took a massive leap of faith to roll out here with us. He came here to make us legit."

With that, the floor was mine. Fresh off our soccer game in the mountains a couple of days before, I was pumped up and ready. In front of me were faces to match the names Sean had been telling me about. These were the dozen coaches he had recruited when he established the program on his first trip to Durban.

"*Sanibonani*," I said, my broken attempt at a formal greeting in Zulu, which I accompanied with a wide smile. No reaction.

Sean had made them laugh. I searched for some way to connect. I tried again in a less formal way, the same smile glued to my face.

"*Atah mujitas*," I said, the equivalent of "What's up, dogs?" in English. This brought some chuckles, and a few eyes darted curiously toward me, but the rest of the group just stared at their feet.

Uncertainty swept through my body. The group stayed quiet. I had to trust that it would happen; it would just take time.

"Sean has told me so much about every one of you, and I can't wait to get to know you. I want to meet your friends and your families," I continued. "I want to come watch you practice. To be honest, I'm not the greatest ballplayer in the world, so I know there's a lot I can learn from you too."

Beginning to fear that I would never break through, I swallowed hard and felt the sweat beading on my forehead.

"This is your program; it's not ours. Your job is to make it into whatever you dream it can be. This is your chance to change the future. This is your fight. This is your country. My job, and Sean's job, is to be behind the scenes helping you all bring the idea to life."

I had never really led before. I felt I had never been a good enough big brother to my three younger sisters. While I had been captain of many teams in high school, I had always let fear, uncertainty, and self-consciousness drive the way I related to my teammates.

But now, I felt an amazing sense of calm. No one knew who I was there. No one knew who my family was. I wasn't Donald Manekin's son. I was a blank slate in South Africa, totally open to what was to come. The only thing I knew for sure at that moment was that it was my job to help everyone around me shine.

I pulled out a paper I had folded in my back pocket. Asking the coaches to digest all the information about the program and comprehend the size of the opportunity in front of us felt like asking them to drink from a fire hydrant. Now I needed to channel it all into a single message. What better way to do that than with someone who understood South Africa's great challenges and complexity better than we Americans ever could?

"I want to read you an email I received two weeks ago before I came to this country. It was from Bongani Nkosi, my first South African friend, who picked me up at the airport when I got here," I said, glancing over at Bongani and remembering the massive hug we had exchanged at the airport when he had first picked me up a little over a week before. He was the guy who had given me the Zulu name of *Thokozani*, which means *happiness*.

At five foot ten, Bongani is solidly built, with strong shoulders and powerful legs. His dreadlocks fall neatly against his South African national team basketball jersey. His gaze is soft and steady, his eyes a deep, vast brown.

Bongani grew up in the 1980s, when the apartheid system was brutally cracking down on anyone who opposed its power. His childhood in the township of KwaMashu wasn't simply one of extreme poverty; it was also one of terrifying violence. It's not something he likes to talk about. It's not something he advertises or offers up freely to prove a point, but it's also not something that he'll ever forget.

I looked down at the page in my hand and began reading Bongani's email:

Thibs, can I call you that? Well this is only for the time being until we hook you up with a nice African name. Man, thank you so much for all that you are doing for this team. I know that you are what we need to get to where we can go. Thanks for giving up your work for this. I think when you see those kids, you'll understand and you won't have regrets. I'm 21, doing my third year of psychology at the University of Natal. I have always dreamt of making a difference and influencing someone positively. I've been playing for 7 years and coaching for 6. I have no clue about the business structure and all the other admin stuff but I know that this is a good thing we got going and I know that it changes lives. I know that it's what my city and country need. I believe in this.

I paused and looked up, seeing my audience beginning to pay care-ful attention, then kept reading.

> Where do I see us going? I see this program flying so high. I see it being the most talked about thing around here since Nelson Mandela being released. I see it restoring a hope and passion for life that our generation is losing.

I scanned the crowd again. They were totally captivated; the name *Mandela* was a lightning rod. I had read this email more than a hun-dred times since receiving it two weeks earlier. Every time I read it my heart beat faster.

> I don't think this game will be won in the first ten minutes of play. We gotta go all the way. We will expand to other provinces until this becomes a national thing.

I let those words sink in for just a moment before wrapping up.

> I do understand that this requires a plan. That is why I'm glad I'm not Sean or Thibs because I know nothing about plans.

Laughter bubbled among the audience and heads bobbed in agree-ment as many of them glanced back over at Bongani — who was sitting in the back row quietly listening — as I folded the paper and put it back in my pocket.

Bongani and I had deeply connected from the minute I received that first email. He has this amazing energy — a spectacular laugh where he jumps up and down — and an unwavering commitment to doing the right thing, no matter how hard the road will be to get there. When you are in Bongani's presence, he makes you feel as if you are the most important person in the world, that you can do anything. His piercing eyes lock onto yours as if he is staring into your soul. He looks for answers that you might not even know exist. He peers past the words that come out of your mouth. He has that rare talent of knowing what makes you tick.

I scrolled my gaze back from Bongani to the audience and continued.

"Now, I don't know if Sean and I know everything about plans either, but I do know that what Bongani wrote touched my heart," I said. "His words helped put me at ease and made the decision to join you here in South Africa a simple one."

Very few coaches looked at me. A week into my time in South Africa, I had already learned that Black people tended to avoid eye contact with white people — not just because it had been culturally taboo during apartheid but because it could lead to real trouble.

"If Bongani's right — and I believe he is — and this is going to be as big as Mandela being released, then we're going to need coaches like you and as many of them as we can get," I said. "But we need you to be more than coaches; we need you to understand that you are the heartbeat of the program."

By the end, I had given what I figured might have been the best speech of my life, but I couldn't tell how it had been received. I didn't care. I knew we were at the beginning of something magical, and I knew that trust, deep relationships, and love would take time to build.

Sean thanked me and called everyone up to the front of the space. He brought us all into a huddle. We were close enough to feel one another's breath, the smell of the day's sweat on our backs. Our hands lay on top of one another's, some of them clammy and warm, others cold and firm. Sean pumped us up and we started jumping around, shoulder to shoulder, the fabric of our shirts moist from the heat.

"On three, PeacePlayers!" he shouted, like we were about to tip off for a championship game. "One ... two ... three!"

"PeacePlayers!" we screamed, our voices echoing off the amphitheater and into Durban's evening air, the passing college kids staring at us like we were maniacs.

As the huddle dispersed, I felt a massive hand on my shoulder. I turned around and it was Thabang, all seven foot one of him. I shook his hand and my eyes followed his arm all the way up to his wide grin. The average height for most Zulus is around five foot six, and this guy towered over everyone else. We'd met the week before. He was a gentle giant who was a superhero with kids.

"T-Bose, Sean's right. You are here to make us legit," he said warmly, looking right into my eyes. "We are lucky to have you."

*Really?*

The doubt came as soon as Thabang let go of my hand.

*Am I capable, at twenty-four years old, with my limited knowledge of this new place, of helping? If so, what is that going to look like?*

I thought I was in South Africa to motivate and uplift guys like Thabang, but here he was flipping the script. His words felt as good as that soccer game in the mountains a couple of days before. I just wasn't sure whether I believed them.

■ ■ ■ ■ ■

Months before Sean introduced me to the informal assembly at the amphitheater, PeacePlayers had begun to grow organically. He'd planted the first seeds on his initial visit. First, schools were recruited to participate. The pitch was simple: the program would build a basketball court at each school and supply two coaches to work with both male and female fifth graders (ten- to twelve-year-olds) twice a week to prepare for a citywide basketball tournament for kids from all over Durban.

The schools in the city — and in South Africa as a whole — were almost completely segregated by race. There were Black schools, Coloured schools, white schools, and Indian schools. We knew we were going to have to first get kids and schools to fall in love with the game of basketball and then build trust for the program in each of these racially divided schools. Only then could we realize our ultimate goal of bringing kids of different backgrounds together to play.

The purpose of the program was to bridge divides through basketball, but without amazing coaches, achieving it would be impossible. Though the kids who participated were our focus, the coaches were the immediate concern. If this was going to work, they needed to embrace and own the program's purpose more than anyone else.

Thabang was the perfect example of what we needed. Even though he was over seven feet tall, he wasn't a very good basketball player. This wasn't surprising; no one had ever worked with him on his game. In fact, years before, Thabang had been burned by the sport. Because of his impressive height, a college scout had found him one day and promised him a plane ticket to America and a spot on a team. Thabang had showed up at the airport, carrying a suitcase holding everything he owned in the world, but the scout never arrived. The experience shattered Thabang's confidence in his own skills, but it quadrupled his desire to see basketball succeed in South Africa. What he lacked in skills he made up for in passion, love, and commitment. He never wanted another kid to experience what he had gone through.

Like Bongani, Thabang had grown up in a township during apartheid, and he wanted desperately to be part of reversing centuries of oppression. He cared less about teaching kids to dribble a basketball than he did about showing them how to live healthy and united lives, something he didn't get to experience growing up. He was the poster child of a coach for our program.

In the initial clinics, Thabang was always exceptional, despite his lack of game skills. For most of the kids, the fact that he could hit the rim with a shot was impressive, let alone that every now and again the ball would actually go in. At Clifton School, one of the most affluent schools we worked in, a room full of white kids would listen intently not because Thabang had a ball but because he was charismatic and full of energy. One simple warm-up he enjoyed was telling kids at the beginning of a session, "When I blow my whistle, start running." Then, as the kids would prepare to take off, he would shout, "One, two, three, GO!"

Every single kid would start sprinting.

"What are you doing?" he'd ask, a fake sternness etched on his face as he tried to hold back his laughter. "I didn't blow my whistle."

Not only did this make everyone laugh, it also taught the kids to be present and pay attention to what happened in the moment.

The kids hung on his every word. They didn't know that Thabang wasn't a great basketball player. They loved him because he cared, and he approached each coaching opportunity with raw passion, whether he was working in a white school in the suburbs or a Black school in a township or rural area.

Basketball itself almost didn't matter. It could have been baseball, or volleyball, or cricket. PeacePlayers began to grow because we led with our purpose to bridge divides through sports, not because we thought we could sell the sport of basketball. To a certain extent, we were actually reimagining the game altogether, taking something the world understood to work one way and completely changing it. The dedication of coaches like Thabang, and their desire to empower these kids who were trapped in the divide they had inherited — now that was why PeacePlayers was really starting to take off.

■ ■ ■ ■ ■

The days came fast. We had massive failures almost every day, but we followed them up with even greater successes. It was a whirlwind. Seeking some stability, we locked down a headquarters. The same woman who had been the link for Sean from Northern Ireland to South Africa let us use a few of the empty desks in her fancy high-rise office downtown.

Walking into the office to work every day made it feel that much more real. We had working phones, internet, access to a printer, and even a conference room we could use. At first it was just Sean and me, but that changed quickly as the program began to grow. When we started to have dozens of Black coaches visiting us each day, the older white office workers whose space we were sharing stared in disbelief, and the security guards — who let Sean and me pass without question — interrogated every one of them. On the one hand, the sweaty basketball clothes probably didn't help. On the other, it was another lesson learned in the realities of segregation. While it was easy for me as a white American to press on regardless, I developed deep respect for the way our coaches — who grew up under the enormous weight of racism, judgment, and the physical and psychological violence of the apartheid regime — also kept charging forward.

Bigger obstacles were popping up all the time. We soon discovered that most of our coaches and their families had never had bank accounts. We figured out the banking system and worked to get them set up legitimately so we could organize our payroll, which until then had consisted of Sean handing any coaches he happened to bump into whatever he had in his wallet.

There was no handbook on how to do any of this. Decisions had to be made on the fly. We knew we had to establish ourselves as a professional program in order to take things to the next level, but despite all the progress, there were no guarantees we'd get there. We had a direction and momentum, but a growing tension in leadership had reached a breaking point.

■ ■ ■ ■

On an overcast July day, a full three months after I'd arrived in South Africa to help get PeacePlayers off the ground, Sean and I found ourselves back in Vusi. This time, instead of driving down windy roads in the stunning South African countryside or hustling to a coaching clinic, we were scooting along in traffic toward a rental car lot. We weren't alone. Sean's friend Christine was in the car with us. July is the coldest month in South Africa, but temperatures in Durban never dipped too low, and it rarely ever rained that time of year, so the dark and ominous clouds in the sky were unusual. The same went for the vibe in the car.

*What am I going to say to him?*

No one spoke a word. The only noises I could hear were the tires against the road and the VW's throttling gears when they shifted. The transmission in my head was also thrashing around violently.

*How is this going to work?*

With things at PeacePlayers running smoothly on the surface, Sean felt it was a good time to join his friend from the States — who'd come down to check out our program in Durban — on an out-of-town adventure. As most people did when they visited, Christine had spent a week with us in the city. Then she planned to head off to explore the rest of South Africa's beauty. She and Sean were driving north to

Kruger National Park, a popular safari destination and one of Africa's largest game reserves, which runs along the border between Mozambique, South Africa, and the tip of Zimbabwe. After their trip, Sean was heading back permanently to Washington, DC, to join Brendan, who had left his day job to focus all his energy on the program. From there, both of them would continue helping to run PeacePlayers full-time.

In the few months since that first coaches' meeting at the Durban Institute of Technology, the program had accelerated. People were coming out of the woodwork to join. The vast majority of our coaches were Black, with a very small handful of white, Coloured, and Indian coaches. It seemed like everyone was telling his or her friends about this awesome job where you could not only get paid to coach basketball, but also be a part of a groundswell that was working to change the way South Africa looked at itself. Most of us don't ever get the opportunity to be a part of something as powerful as that, something that can help to reverse hundreds of years of oppression, death, and war.

*Do I tell him before he leaves?*

I had a million things I wanted to say, but I kept my mouth shut.

*I don't want it to come out the wrong way. I don't want to fight.*

The thing that was weighing on me was that I couldn't wait for Sean to leave. What had started as an epic adventure among the peaks of the Drakensberg mountains had begun to sour. The more time Sean and I spent together, the more we realized how incompatible we were. Our ideas of leading and inspiring were polar opposites. Sean had no filter, and he was quick to criticize and humiliate our coaches in public. A growing number of them had been approaching me, complaining about Sean. He asked a lot of them, and they felt he was too harsh. He yelled. He was intense.

*I get what they're saying. I see it too, but is it even my place to call him out?*

I gripped the steering wheel.

*I wouldn't even be here if it weren't for Sean. He's my hero.*

As I grew into my leadership role in the organization, I had my own doubts about how Sean wanted to run things. I was genuinely interested in the coaches' lives. I'd sit with each of them for hours just listening to their life stories. Connecting with the coaches mattered deeply to me, but Sean felt that getting too close was a bad idea. He thought I was soft. He felt that the coaches came to me with concerns and requests because I was a pushover.

For several of these young men and women, it was their first time touching a basketball. Sean was in their face about technical mistakes, where I focused on the human side. He criticized ball-handling skills and even shooting styles. Even when he was trying to be lighthearted, which he often was when there were kids around, I could sense when the coaches felt deflated. It was clear to me that the spirit and excitement that got them involved to begin with was starting to ebb. I noticed how some coaches started to avoid Sean when he came around.

*But is he right? Am I too soft? Can leading my way work any better?*

While I couldn't wait for him to leave so I'd be free to explore my own kind of leadership, and even though the honeymoon phase of our partnership had passed and our styles were clashing, I still just wasn't completely sure of myself.

*With him gone, what's going to happen?*

I stared straight ahead, flicking on the windshield wipers as a light rain began to fall.

The awkwardness in the car was palpable. This was the first time Sean would be leaving the program entirely in my care. While we were civil, the tension had grown heavy between us, and it was weighing on me more and more with every passing moment.

"At last," Sean announced as I pulled into the rental car lot.

"Yep," I confirmed.

Christine opened the door as soon as the car was parked and hopped out as fast as she could. I had grown close with her too, but I could tell she just needed to escape the awkward situation she had found herself in. I got out and gave her a hug, then turned my attention to Sean.

"Man," I said, my voice shaky with uncertainty, "I love you."

It was the truth. I had never considered him a regular friend. Even though our styles were different, I still looked up to him. He gave tough love, sure, but it was love all the same.

"I'm so in awe of what you created," I said. "I'm so thankful for having had the opportunity to begin to bring an idea to life with you. Along with my dad, you are one of the most inspiring guys I've ever met."

We slapped hands and brought it in for an embrace. It felt good to share my feelings, to send him off with a compliment and a sincere thank-you. There was more I wanted to say, but this wasn't the time.

Initially, he did not reply to the words I had spoken. Instead, he turned and began walking toward Christine, who'd made her way ahead. Then he stopped and spun around.

"You know what, man?" Sean said. "Maybe you're just the number-two guy."

With that, he left.

*What the hell is that supposed to mean?*

Blood pumped into my face. The skin on my neck and all the way down to my arms started itching. I flushed red.

I was pissed off. Outraged. Beyond furious, so angry I could have smashed the side-view mirror as I turned back toward the car, but underneath it all I was embarrassed. As good as the trajectory of the program seemed, I hadn't come that far personally. He hit me right where I still doubted myself the most.

*Here I am thinking I've made progress, thinking maybe I have a shot at being a decent leader, and this guy, who I just told I respected like my dad, throws it back at me.*

The pain was sharp and deep. Sean's dismissal burned on through my chest all the way down to my heart.

I climbed into the VW, threw the car into gear, and headed back toward the city, feeling more self-conscious than I ever had before and lost about what to do next.

# 3

## Shared Ownership

> *"Bringing people together is what I call 'ubuntu,' which means 'I am because we are.' Far too often people think of themselves as just individuals, separated from one another, whereas you are connected and what you do affects the whole world. When you do well, it spreads out; it is for the whole of humanity."*
>
> — DESMOND TUTU

Not long after Sean left South Africa, I began to regain my composure and confidence. One day I stood gripping a faded orange rubber basketball in both hands and glanced up. Beautiful clumps of scattered clouds, which had hung in the sky all afternoon, were starting to glow red and orange as the sun was finally ready to dip. I leaned forward onto my toes, hovering just behind the makeshift basketball court's freshly painted three-point line, the handmade metal basketball hoop's rim sparkling in the magic-hour light just a couple of dozen feet in front of me.

I was deep in Umlazi, the fourth-largest township in the country. Despite the warnings of white South Africans, we felt like superheroes out there. Kids dropped everything they were doing whenever they saw us walking the streets. They'd chase us, screaming, *"Umlungu!"* – the

Zulu word for *white person* — laughing and grabbing our hands, asking us to pass them the balls we always had with us.

Now, as I stood on the court that late afternoon with the ball in my hand, trying to decide what move to make, a voiced squeaked, "Tea Pot."

Gift, a charming ten-year-old who was smaller than a lot of his peers, stood panting in his favorite place on the court, hands open, eagerly awaiting a pass. He was a few feet away from the hoop, just within layup distance. Some kids called me Thibault, others T-Bone, but Gift's chosen nickname was Tea Pot, which he always said with a huge smile on his face.

There was something special surrounding the program by this time. There was a contagious energy around everything we did, a feeling of invincibility, of being a part of something important, of almost not being able to keep up with the intense grassroots growth. PeacePlayers was booming, completely driven by the coaches and their dedication to the program, by the enthusiasm of the communities where we were working, and by the speed at which the kids were falling in love with the sport. That initial group of twelve young men and women I had met at DIT had quintupled, and we were now at sixty coaches. We were in more than forty schools — Black, Coloured, Indian, and white — across the greater Durban area. The township of Umlazi, where it all started, remained the most active location.

Gift had been among those most likely to hang around long after the regular practices were over for the day, hoping for the chance to take a few extra shots with the coaches. We knew it didn't matter if we let the kids stay late; most were free to make their way home on their own schedule.

Stepping up to guard me was Menzi Zungu — a coach we affectionately called Appetite, for the massive figure he cut and for his love of all things delicious. At six foot four and 250 pounds, he was a South African version of Shaquille O'Neal, with an endearing smile, a dash of joviality, and a genuine quickness on his feet. His massive sneakers dwarfed mine on the slab of concrete that had become Umlazi's most popular place to play hoops.

Walking through the township with Menzi felt like rolling with a celebrity. He was an ultra-recognizable figure in town: the people's mayor. He grew up in Umlazi without a dad, but as the eldest of his mother's many children, he had learned leadership skills out of necessity, without ever being taught.

Menzi scooted over to block my path, a massive smile on his face, as if to acknowledge that he knew that I knew there was no way I'd ever get by him. For an instant, I faked like I was going to try to shoot over his head — also a recipe for failure — before flinging my thumbs at an angle down against the ball, sending a bounce pass skipping against the concrete into Gift's shaky arms.

Even though he'd fumbled passes all afternoon, this time the youngster received the ball cleanly, hopped up, bumped his layup off the backboard, and watched it dink around before falling through the hoop.

Gift's hands shot skyward as his shoeless feet landed back on the ground, his bare toes splayed out on the cracked cement like every other kid on the court that day and most of the days we played in Umlazi. His eyes lit up. He let out a scream of excitement and sprinted toward me.

"*Yebo!*" Menzi shouted the Zulu word for *yes*, smacking his hands together to applaud the move.

By the time Gift reached me, Menzi and I were jumping in the air in celebration, bumping shoulders. Gift and Menzi had spent months together trying to iron out the basics of basketball control. Gift's progress was staggering, a true testament to his coach.

As the splashes of light continued thinning on the court, we thanked Gift and the others who'd stayed behind to play. I trotted over to my bag and began getting myself ready to drive home to my comfy apartment overlooking the ocean on Durban's beachfront. While I squirted some water into my mouth and wiped down my face, Menzi approached.

"My mama," Menzi started, slinging his sweaty arm over my shoulder, "said you are coming for dinner."

"Sure, Menzi," I said without a second thought, thinking I'd come back on a future afternoon for an early supper with his family. "What day?"

"Tonight, of course." He grinned.

I felt the smile slide off my face but tried not to wear the worry that stirred inside me. While I'd learned the value of expanding my horizons since coming to South Africa, there was one rule Sean and I had tried to adhere to when it came to the townships in the early days: get out before dark. I usually took the warnings that frightened white South Africans gave about the townships with a grain of salt, but if there was one constant in all the horror stories, it was that the bulk of the danger seemed to lurk in the nighttime hours.

"Man, you are crazy. Don't you know *umlungus* don't stick around the township after dark?" I said, laughing and packing my things.

"I got you, *umlungu.*" The Zulu rolled smoothly off Menzi's tongue as he pulled me closer toward him in a loving bear hug. "You are safe with me."

Menzi knew that white South Africans rarely went into the townships, let alone stayed past dark. In fact, had this been a few months earlier, it's unlikely he would have even suggested the idea. He would have been the one ushering me out of Umlazi well before it got dark to ensure I felt comfortable and safe. Now, though, with the extended summer daylight hours, the spirit of our recent work, and a general good feeling, he had decided today was the day. What was most clear about Menzi's invitation was that he wouldn't make it unless he felt I'd be okay.

"It's time you had a proper township *braai,*" Menzi added, referring to the traditional South Africa–style barbecue to heighten the offer's appeal.

Maybe it was the reassuring gleam in his eyes, the softness with which he spoke, or merely the fact that I was salivating at the thought of grilled meat after a long day's coaching, but I settled on an answer. "Let's do it."

Much of Umlazi was built on hills, and finding stretches of flat pavement for our basketball games had been a challenge. Menzi had been instrumental in showing us the location for the court we were on that evening. Some government-funded agency had built tennis courts there years ago, and although they'd long since fallen into disrepair, the pavement was still in place. We brought in portable hoops, painted some lines, and turned it into a basketball court. Our coaches called this court "the Island" on account of the river that separated it from the rest of the township.

I followed Menzi across the sewage pipe, about 150 feet long and only 2 feet around, that served as the improbable bridge connecting the Island to the rest of Umlazi. Although legend has it that King Shaka Zulu gave Umlazi its name — which means something close to *sour* — after drinking from a stream in the area, Menzi had told me that a decade ago, the township rivers here were filled with beautiful, clean, flowing water, which he and his siblings actually spent hours splashing around in. Looking down at the enormous ditch beneath us, however, it was clear that those bathing days were long gone, as there was almost as much sewage and trash as there was water. Crossing was an act of acrobatics. One wrong step meant a fifteen-foot tumble into the contaminated river.

"T-Bose, don't fall," Menzi said, laughing hysterically as I struggled to keep my balance. "The hospitals around here aren't that good."

There was something about the way Menzi cruised across the sewage pipe. There was something about the Island itself. The whole setting exuded a palpable allure. Coaching hoops in the townships was already tricky enough; add to that crossing a massive river of sewage each day. There was something so unique about everything we did out in the township. It made me appreciate how determined our coaches were to succeed.

That sense only grew as we wound our way through the town's network of dirt paths. We passed the uneven slabs of slanted metal roofs on the boxy residences, which had imperfectly laid brick walls, and made our way toward an unassuming cinder-block house. Squawking chickens fled out of our way as we reached the home, and the singe of Durban's pungent peppers wove its way into my nostrils. Menzi waved me toward the *braai*, the sounds and smells putting me even more at ease.

■ ■ ■ ■ ■

As I prepared to meet Menzi's family, I thought about how far we all had come. The township work was really taking off, in large part because of the incredibly warm reception we received there. We couldn't grow fast enough to keep up with the number of schools that wanted to get into the program. Soon the word about PeacePlayers had spread throughout the Durban area, and a group of key leaders had stepped up to help.

The eldest in our group was Craig Gilchrist, a really cool, six-foot-seven white guy who was one of the best big men in South Africa during his prime. Craig took on the role of basketball manager. Our marketing manager was Ryan Douwie, a Coloured kid with an infectious personality who had a marketing degree and claimed to have dropped ten three-pointers during a single game. Bongani, who was more interested in the community work we were doing than in the actual game of basketball, served as the program's community manager.

During those early days before Sean returned to America, we spent countless hours locked in rooms with these three guys, whiteboarding out their visions. At best we were facilitators, taking notes and pushing them to dive deeper. We helped them think not about what the program was but about what the program ought to be.

*What if we stop listening to all the people who tell us on a daily basis that what we set out to do can't be done? What if it isn't about putting a ball in a hoop at all? What if the game itself is secondary to our purpose? What if we help reinvent what the sport of basketball can be?*

In addition to helping with the simple logistics of running the program, enabling these coaches had created a sense of shared ownership and authorship. From this place of partnership, Douwie suggested that PeacePlayers build a system of area managers who would each oversee the group of coaches and schools within their district. For example, Umlazi would have its own manager; Lamontville — another nearby township — would have its own manager; and the same for Durban North, Durban South, and so on. This was a great idea, and it allowed us to promote some key coaches to management positions as the program continued to explode. We had expanded into eight different geographic areas throughout Durban as schools continued to pile into the program. Each school had two coaches, but we clearly needed more of an organizational infrastructure if things were going to run smoothly as we grew. This is why it made sense to promote the young men and women who were shining stars.

Menzi joined our coaching staff early. When we started appointing area managers, who would be paid 1,600 rand per month (about $160 per month at the time), which was a little over double what we paid coaches, there was no question that he was the perfect fit for the Umlazi post. Menzi, like many of his peers in the townships, had never finished high school, so his English wasn't the best and his reading and writing were still a work in progress. But what he lacked in formal education, he made up for in pure heart and passion.

For Menzi, PeacePlayers was everything. It was his universe. It was his chance to change his country. While he may never have been able to completely articulate that, you could see it in the amount of love he put into each and every one of the kids, teachers, parents, and coaches he worked with on a daily basis. When Menzi found out he was being promoted to area manager, he jumped up and down and hugged everyone around him, his reaction itself confirmation that his peers chose wisely. I have never met anyone as committed as Menzi in my life.

■ ■ ■ ■ ■

Menzi's family, all ten of them, were outside their house getting things going for the *braai* when we arrived. They had heard so much about PeacePlayers, and they couldn't wait to meet one of the *umlungus* who was stirring things up. They also seemed determined to make sure that my first township *braai* was a memorable one.

Menzi's little cousins scrambled after two of the chickens that had been scurrying around the house and brought them to Menzi's mom. She instantly decapitated them, plucked their feathers, cut them up, and threw them over the fire to grill.

With no father in the picture, Menzi's mom was clearly the head of the family. This was her kingdom, and everything ran directly through her. Mama Zungu was almost as big as Menzi, and she gave me a huge hug. She saw to it that I felt right at home.

Within minutes of our arrival, a full-on party erupted. Our hosts had each chipped in several rand until there was enough to run to the local shebeen and buy a case of Black Label forty-ounce beers. Neighbors wandered over to see if it was true that a white guy had come for dinner, after dark. Soon music started playing, and African beats flowed through the hot summer night. Time stood still under a big half-moon as we all forgot what we had been taught to believe about where we should hang out and who we should spend our time with.

At some point, as the party appeared to be on cruise control and Mama Zungu could relax, she came up to me and put her huge arm around me. In heavily accented English, she began talking.

"*Ey*, T-Bose," she started. "We love you guys and what you are doing for our country."

"Thank you, mama," I responded. "Please know that it's not what we are doing for your country — we are just along for the ride. It's Menzi and all his friends who are doing this work for South Africa."

Her tone changed and her smile disappeared as she turned to face me more directly. She put two huge hands on my shoulders.

"T-Bose, I have one request. Please?"

"Of course, mama, anything."

"Take these damn basketball poles out of my house," she said sternly, her greasy apron hanging from her neck.

I had no idea what she was talking about.

She went on to explain that every evening Menzi walked half a mile to the Island, and he carried, one at a time, the four portable hoops we had purchased across the sewage pipe back to the house so he could store them in the family's living room for the night. This was a living room in a 400-square-foot house where ten people slept. Then Menzi woke up early the next morning and brought all four 150-pound hoops back to the court so they would be there when the kids showed up to play.

Never has my heart glowed with as much pride while being lectured. As Mama Zungu begged me to get the hoops out of her living room, I gave her an enormous hug. I thanked her for her son and promised we'd invest in some permanent equipment.

Off the top of my head, I couldn't think of a single person who would do something like that for his job. Menzi carried those hoops because he didn't want anyone stealing or damaging them at night. Growing up, he didn't have hoops to play on, a dad to play with, or coaches to empower him. He wasn't about to let the next generation grow up without those things too.

I could tell you countless similar stories of countless other young men and women who took similar ownership of their work. In doing so, they added to the momentum and changed the trajectory of their country. Menzi owned PeacePlayers. His heart ran it. This was his program. There was nothing he wouldn't do for it. And he wasn't alone.

# 4

# Outside Listening In

*"There is no power for change greater than a community discovering what it cares about."*

— MARGARET J. WHEATLEY

The casket was open. Mourners filed forward to pay their respects, myself among them. I got to the last step but wasn't sure I could take it. My feet felt cemented to the floor. Rain pelted the razor-thin scrap-metal roof. Above the din of the weather and the sobs of mourners, the boxy township church in Lamontville was a symphony of Zulu hymnals.

"*Hamba nathi,*" the voices bellowed. "Walk with us."

They'd been singing for hours, long before I'd arrived. I'd come to give my love and support for Nathi Kheswa, one of our PeacePlayers coaches, who served as the area manager for the township of Lamontville. Nathi had been with us from the beginning, and he had just lost his partner. He greeted me beside the casket with a one-armed hug.

"*Ngiyabonga,* brother," Nathi said quietly, tears running down his cheeks, his eyes red. "Thank you."

With his spare arm, he clutched his three-month-old daughter, Anelisa. While I was expressing my condolences, the baby's eyes darted between me, her father, and the scene unfolding around us. She was too young to understand the rawness of the moment or the fact that she'd never feel the warmth of her mother again. The space was packed, standing room only. Generations of Zulu women stood together at the front of the church, while the men packed the rear. The rain had kept no one away, and those Zulu songs filled the cold moment with abundant warmth.

"*Hamba nathi, mkhululi wethu*," they sang. "Stay with us, our redeemer." "*Mkhululi wethu, mkhululi wethu, mkhululi wethu.*"

Nathi's wife, Lwazi, occupied the casket at the front of the church. When I'd heard the news of her passing, it had crushed me. Nathi was different from so many of the boisterous, outgoing, and energetic coaches who worked with us. He was calm, soft-spoken, and humble, but he had a smile that could electrify a room. Like so many of our coaches, he was also someone I'd connected with on a personal level. He was a superstar for the program, but on top of that, he'd become one of my closest friends. I'd watched him beam with pride at his newborn child. I knew he'd envisioned a bright future with his wife.

A week before the funeral, when Nathi had first told me that she had passed, he had given me an unusual explanation for her death.

"Fits, seizures," Nathi had told me. "Seizures are what killed her."

Not wanting to cause him any additional grief, I'd left it at that. I'd taken Nathi's word for it, even if I didn't completely understand what he meant. Now as I stood in front of him, the casket beside us, the rhythm of the hymns helped spur a courage in me to have a look inside.

I took the last step toward the modest wood box, gazed down at her, and immediately realized I'd been missing something. The once beautiful young woman I'd known — the woman whom Nathi had loved and who had given birth to their precious Anelisa — was little more than skin and bones. Her hair was wiry, her eyes sunk back into the sockets, her skin thin and dull. Her face was almost unrecognizable as that of the lively soul we'd all come to adore. There was nothing left. I imagined that the corpse probably weighed sixty pounds.

I understood what I'd been missing. This was no seizure. This was

HIV/AIDS. She had died of AIDS, and no one would admit it. I turned away from the casket as the voices began a new hymn.

"*Senzeni,*" they sang. "What have we done?"

Death had hung around us since I first got to South Africa. When you watched young children play in the poorer areas, you rarely saw their parents with them. The grandparents took over. In the townships and rural communities, where the epidemic was much more severe, roughly a third of the population was HIV positive. An entire generation — that of Nathi and his wife — was vanishing.

"*Senzeni,*" the funeral singers wailed. "*Sono sethu ubumnyama, sono sethu yinyaniso, sibulawayo, mayibuye i Africa.*" "What have we done? Our sin is that we are Black, our sin is the truth, they are killing us, let Africa return."

I couldn't hold back the tears as I turned to hug Nathi and Anelisa once more. I cried for him. I cried for his daughter and their family. I cried for his wife, gone too soon. I cried because in South Africa, when someone died from AIDS, families invented a story about it. They couldn't bear the thought of facing the fierce stigma associated with the disease. But most of all, I cried because I was scared that we would lose our own coaches or kids all because none of us were able to talk about it openly.

■ ■ ■ ■ ■

HIV/AIDS had ripped apart the fabric of families, villages, townships, and communities throughout South Africa. To make matters worse, Jacob Zuma, the deputy president of the country at the time, on trial for raping an HIV-positive woman, told the entire world that he could not get the disease because he had showered after having unprotected sex with her. This was the kind of message leaders were sending out to the young people in the country.

As an outsider, I was petrified. Before I had arrived in South Africa, the closest I had come to HIV/AIDS was when Magic Johnson announced he had the disease when I was in seventh grade. Beyond that, the problem was so distant it wasn't something I ever thought about.

Which is why, the second I got off the plane in Durban, I was afraid. I didn't share drinks with people. I was scared about dating. I didn't care whether someone came from one background or another, I was on high alert; I approached the whole situation with total fear. Many people said that the disease was constantly mutating, maybe even airborne. While I knew better than to believe everything I heard, in those early days it was 100 percent on my mind, and I chose to play it as safe as I could.

Regardless of how I felt about it, the reality was that huge swaths of young adults were dead or dying, and if nothing was done, their children would suffer the same fate. Few people knew how to talk about HIV/AIDS, much less grasped how it actually attacked the body or how to prevent it. Many didn't even believe the virus existed.

Fortunately, some of the people who did believe it was real had come into contact with the PeacePlayers program, and we were open to their suggestions. Our whole team understood that the ideas we worked on didn't belong to us and that we could only be successful if we listened to new information and adjusted the program accordingly. Because of this approach, opportunities to improve upon the PeacePlayers model abounded, and school administrators and parents took advantage of our open communications to make suggestions for the benefit of the program. That included the issue of HIV/AIDS education, which crystallized when a group of parents and teachers approached us one day. They told us we had captured their kids' attention in a way they had never been able to do before. They explained that their kids hung on our every word and that we needed to harness that connection to talk about HIV/AIDS.

"Please find a way to talk to them, to keep them safe. To keep them alive," one concerned mother told us that day.

With that simple yet powerful request, the PeacePlayers life skills program was created. Though it was a huge undertaking, we accepted the challenge and put a significant portion of our resources toward developing a curriculum primarily focused on HIV/AIDS. Knowing what we didn't know, we partnered with Harvard University's School of Public Health, the University of KwaZulu-Natal, and several other nonprofits to develop a world-class interactive life skills curriculum focused on empowering our coaches, the generation that was the most impacted. They would, in turn, teach the girls and boys they worked with. Those moms were right. Our coaches had captured the attention of these kids in a way that none of us saw coming, and we could use that to help them stay safe.

There was a new schedule. Practice was an hour long, two days per week. The last twenty minutes were spent sitting in a shaded area, where the coach delivered the life skills messages. The curriculum was set up as an interactive conversation in an age-appropriate way that, for the first time ever, made it acceptable for these kids to open up in a safe and nonjudgmental environment. Our coaches weren't parents or teachers lecturing them not to have sex. They were inspiring role models and heroes whom our kids really looked up to.

One day, several months after Nathi's wife passed away, I watched him deliver the messages from the curriculum to a group of kids in Zulu. Standing under the shade of a beautiful African tree in Lamontville, he looked every kid in the eye. He was able to talk seriously when he needed to, but he also got them to smile and laugh at some points. I was so proud to see how far he'd come since he'd tried to cover up his wife's death with the seizures story.

Afterward, I asked him what he'd said to the kids.

"I told them, 'I know you don't want to think about this because I didn't want to think about it either.'"

I thanked him for being brave and helping to get the word out.

"You don't need to thank me, Thokozani," he said. "I'm just grateful I get the chance to talk to them about it. I wish someone would have done the same for my generation."

Because of the coaches' deep commitment to these kids, and because they were bringing the kids to this new and exciting sport, the children listened to their every word. It happened just as the mothers had predicted it would.

We doubled down on the program by making the sessions mandatory. If you missed life skills, you didn't get to practice or play in the game. If you didn't practice or play in the game, you weren't on the team. And if you weren't on the team, then you weren't a part of Peace-Players. No one was going to risk that.

Because the parents felt like they owned the idea and the program, they had a deep sense of pride of authorship in what was being created. The community had stepped up and expanded the roles and responsibilities of the coaches, empowering them to carry an important torch forward. The community gave guys like Nathi, who needed it more than most, a chance to become heroes to the younger generation.

■ ■ ■ ■ ■

After some time teaching the life skills curriculum, Nathi himself started to feel weak. He was familiar with the symptoms and knew what they meant. Still, in South Africa, it took such courage to go get tested. The reward for his bravery was a diagnosis: Nathi also had HIV/AIDS.

After years of working with the kids, helping them both on the court through basketball and off the court through the life skills curriculum, he had changed. Even as he was physically getting weaker, his character was the strongest it had ever been. He came forward and told his colleagues at PeacePlayers the truth.

When Nathi broke the news, I was home in the States hosting a fundraiser. I'll never forget getting that phone call from my good friend, Andrew Gordon, one of the other Americans who had come on board early to help shape the trajectory of the program.

I couldn't sleep that night thinking of Nathi. I lay in my comfortable bed in Baltimore and reflected on how lucky I was even to have the seemingly simple gift of being educated about the dangers and transmission of HIV/AIDS. Coming from so little, Nathi had managed to become such a force for good. His commitment and impact were massive despite his lack of basic education. He didn't have Bongani's hoops skills and charisma, Thabang's height, or Menzi's size, but he found his own way to make a powerful difference.

After hearing the news, I wanted to hop on the next flight back to South Africa and see Nathi right away. I'd been planning to be back in a week, but that wasn't soon enough. One of my best friends had just received a death sentence. I hadn't heard of anyone in South Africa surviving the disease. There was medicine floating around the country at the time, but at best it seemed to slightly delay the inevitable. With my mind reeling, I got up in the middle of the night to write him a letter. The message was simple: *tell your story; you never know who it could help.*

Had we been just a basketball program and had we not created this platform for the community to feel both empowered and capable, Nathi would have likely died alone, without the hope of saving hundreds, if not thousands, of young people. Without the life skills program, Nathi wouldn't have a legacy to leave behind for his daughter, Anelisa. Instead, because the community planted that seed — and because we listened to them, not superficially, but deeply — not only did Nathi leave his mark, but he also helped break the taboos around HIV/AIDS in South Africa.

While we did everything we could to get Nathi the medication and care he needed, the disease eventually won the fight and Nathi passed away. Despite growing up without either of their parents, his children would grow up HIV/AIDS free and go on to thrive in South Africa. Because of Nathi and his work, and the work of so many others who wanted to carry his torch forward, lives continue to be saved every single day.

# 5

## *Can't/No* as the Motivator

*"Be realistic: demand the impossible."*

— CHE GUEVARA

"**Y**ou boys are doing amazing work," said Brian Mitchell, the head-master of Clifton, the predominantly white school where Thabang and Bongani coached.

Bongani had accompanied me to Clifton to help with a big ask, and Brian invited us to have a seat on the couch in his office. It was a large, imposing space. Leather-bound books filled the massive shelves, with potted plants below them. Brian took a seat behind his commanding wooden desk.

"I never thought I'd say this," he began, "but our boys are really keen on this basketball thing. Pulling those okes off the rugby field isn't easy, but you boys seem to have really gotten to them."

"Thanks, Brian." I grinned at his use of the common South African slang *oke*, which meant something like *dude*. "It's been a blast working with your kids, and we're happy they're having fun."

"For over a year now," I continued, "we've been coaching your kids twice a week, scheduling matches against other schools around here, and even hosting several citywide tournaments where all of the kids in the program get to come together for a giant day of basketball."

He nodded. "I was at that last tournament you guys held. It looked like there were thousands of kids there. I have no idea how you all pulled that off."

Bongani and I laughed nervously, and I knew we were both remembering how hard that day was to put together and how proud we were to make it happen.

I said, "Those tournaments are fun because they allow us to really focus on our mission of using sports to bridge divides, because there are schools from all over Durban that attend. And that's exactly why we're here today."

Brian smiled and gestured for us to continue.

"We're ready to take PeacePlayers to the next level," I added.

I paused as the headmaster leaned forward. Then I said, "Last week we got a call from Linda Mgobozi, one of the producers at the South African Broadcasting Corporation. She heard about what we are doing, and she wants to run a national TV news story about the program."

"Brilliant," said Brian. "That will be great exposure for you guys."

I paused again, this time for effect. I gathered myself for what I was about to say.

"Brian, Linda and SABC want the story to be about a white school traveling to a school in a Black township to play a game against each other."

I glanced over at Bongani, who nodded his approval.

"They want the township school to be Saphinda in Umlazi and the white school to be Clifton."

Brian never flinched. He remained cool and composed as I invited him to do something that would have caused most white South Africans at the time to fall out of their chairs.

We spent a few more minutes talking through logistics. I knew Brian's heart was in the right place. Just the fact that he had allowed Clifton to participate in PeacePlayers at all was more than most of his affluent-white-school counterparts had done, but I saw his body language change as he understood the offer. When we were finished, Brian explained that he'd give the opportunity some thought.

Clifton had become a huge supporter of the program. Their kids had excelled. PeacePlayers had become a part of the school's fabric. But getting them to go into the townships was a big ask. Nothing like what we were suggesting to Brian had ever been done. I thought that the chance to be a part of the national TV segment would tilt things in our favor. I was wrong.

The call came a few days later.

"No," Brian told me over the phone.

I calculated the exact wording I wanted to use.

"This is an unprecedented opportunity," I argued. "Clifton and Saphinda would be paving the way for the youth of this country going forward."

"The answer is no," the headmaster continued. "It simply doesn't fit into our schedule right now."

"But —"

"I'm sorry, Thibault," the headmaster said. "It's not going to happen."

I hung up the phone and sank down in my chair.

When we asked Black schools if we could build them courts, give them coaches, and take their kids on field trips to other parts of Durban to meet kids from other schools, the answer was always yes. The poorer communities that had way less in terms of money and material possessions jumped at the opportunity to let their kids participate. White schools weren't as excited or easily convinced. For one, their kids were overprogrammed and overcommitted. They had rugby practice, piano recitals, and swim meets — usually in the same week, sometimes on the same day. Plus, the white schools weren't merely skeptical about letting their kids play with poor Black kids; they were often outright opposed to it. Some schools refused to participate in the program at all.

Eventually, with lots of perseverance and thanks to charismatic guys like Bongani and Thabang, and the help of courageous leaders like Brian, we were able to get a small number of mostly white schools, like Clifton, on board. We were forming great relationships with schools of all stripes as the program kept expanding. We had our big goal in our sights: proving that sports could get kids from different communities to play together and become friends. But after more than a year in the country, with the exception of our annual citywide tournament, we had yet to really make it happen. Our basketball and life skills program were taking off within each school, but we hadn't done a good enough job of actually mixing the schools together yet. We knew we needed to push the limits if we were ever going to facilitate moments for meaningful connection between the kids.

A few days before that phone call gut punch, Brian had been singing our praises. Now, he had confirmed our fears — the game wasn't going to happen. I immediately called Bongani.

"They must not have fully understood our request," Bongani said, undeterred. "I'm coming to get you so we can go over there."

"Go over where?" I asked, even though I knew the answer.

"Clifton," said Bongani.

Before I could talk through any more of the plan, Bongani hung up.

He arrived shortly after, amped up. Bongani was not prepared to take no for an answer. He had waited too long, perhaps his entire life, for the opportunity to be involved in something so meaningful. We hopped into Vusi, our trusty VW, and headed back to the preparatory school in Morningside, the beautiful community built overlooking Durban, with its country clubs, pristine sidewalks, and sprawling views of the Indian Ocean.

We arrived unannounced. Brian's assistant wasn't prepared for us but scrambled to summon him once she saw how serious Bongani was. Within a couple of minutes, the massive wooden door to the headmaster's office clicked open. Brian, as welcoming as ever, invited us inside.

Before we even sat down, Brian began to apologize, but Bongani interrupted him.

"Brian, I grew up in the township. Because of apartheid, if I wanted to come to Durban, I needed a special pass giving me permission to do so. Basketball was the only reason I got out."

Bongani took a breath and continued.

"I hold no grudges, but I know how lucky I was to get out, to be one of the few who got to experience this world of privilege that your kids enjoy every day. I never thought the time would come where the sport I love could bring white kids to see the conditions I grew up under."

Brian was taken aback, but he kept his focus on Bongani, who continued talking.

"If we are to truly begin healing our country, Brian, we need to walk in each other's shoes. I need your kids — my kids, who I coach here every week — to understand. We will all grow stronger because of it."

I kept my mouth shut, admiring my dear friend Bongani as he did his thing.

"I will be there with you guys. You have nothing to fear. Please help Clifton step up as a leader, a pioneer. Help your school pave the way for others to follow. We must change our country."

He hammered home a point I had missed. The program had gained national attention. If Clifton agreed to the visit, they had the chance to be on the right side of the country's new history. Brian's eyes were glued to Bongani as he calmly and confidently delivered the message. Brian understood it; he always had. The problem was that when the message had come from me, it just hadn't been clear enough or powerful enough. After all, it wasn't my message to deliver, just like it wasn't my story or my program. It was Bongani's to deliver and he blew it out of the water.

Later that same afternoon, it was Bongani's turn to get a phone call.

"Clifton," the proud headmaster said, "wouldn't miss it for the world."

We didn't know where the change of heart came from — if Brian had to convince the school's leadership to see things another way, or whether it was simply a matter of prioritizing it in the schedule. But the bottom line was that *no* had turned into *yes*.

Bongani and I hopped straight into Vusi and headed for Saphinda Combined Primary School in Umlazi. We parked in the makeshift dirt lot in front of the school. The tiny one-story brick building, with its red

pitched roof and broken single-pane glass windows, had been one of
the first schools to join our program.

We walked in completely unannounced, as usual. The kids who
had seen our car pull up were sticking their heads out of the windows
in the middle of class, screaming our names. Some escaped the protests of their teachers and ran out to greet us. We found Mrs. Zulu,
the school principal, in her office. The cramped space was a huge contrast to Brian's office at Clifton. A few old teacher-size desks had been
pushed together to make some working space for her. The room itself
actually functioned as the principal's office, library, nurse's office, and
storage closet.

She wasted no time in hopping up and coming over to give us a
huge hug.

"*Ey, sanibonani.* What brings you boys out here today?" she asked
with a big smile on her face.

This time, I knew better than to interject.

"*Ngiyabonga*, mama," said Bongani, thanking her, his arm still
wrapped around her shoulder. "We are going to take the PeacePlayers
program to the next level. We want to bring our friends from Clifton
out here to Saphinda for a friendly game between the teams. Do you
think that would be all right?"

There was no need to explain to her the significance of bringing
a white school to Umlazi. There were no school leadership votes required. There was no mention of SABC. There was no talk of security.
There wasn't even a pause. She understood. There was only a big, affirmative answer.

"We will be happy to have them as our guests."

■ ■ ■ ■ ■

From the moment our bus filled with students from Clifton left the
brick buildings and iron gates of the educational fortress in the posh
Durban suburb of Morningside, the vibe was like that of any other
school field trip. Kids chatted happily and teased one another. Adult
chaperones intervened to maintain order whenever things got out of

control. Teachers and staff went over the day's schedule. Then, after a short fifteen-minute drive, something changed.

Knees bounced in crisp khaki shorts. Throats cleared uncomfortably against tight white collars. The uniforms were embroidered with Clifton's European-inspired school crest — a red-on-white English Saint George's cross featuring a fleur-de-lis styled as a fountain pen in the upper-right quadrant.

Schoolboys are noisy — talkative, playful — especially a group of forty of them. Our large assembly of ten-year-olds from Clifton School had been no different until our bus turned off the M4 freeway and continued onto what today is known as the Griffiths Mxenge Highway. Suddenly, the boys were eerily silent.

Like all townships — designed to keep the Black population isolated and easily controlled in the event of an uprising — there was only one road in and out of Umlazi. It was named after civil rights lawyer and anti-apartheid activist Griffiths Mlungisi Mxenge, who famously won a landmark case that charged four white policemen with the brutal death of Joseph Mdluli, a fellow member of the African National Congress. Seven years later, Mxenge himself was assassinated by a white apartheid death squad who stabbed him forty-five times, belted him with a hammer, and sliced his throat open — leaving the lawyer's body splayed out on a soccer field in Umlazi for all to see. His wife suffered a similar fate in the township a few years later. The white police commander who ordered the killings admitted his involvement but was granted amnesty just three years before I came to South Africa.

The cause for the boys' silence was clear: everyone on the bus, including me and the cameraman from SABC who had joined the excursion, was white.

As the bus pulled into Umlazi, we drove past the abysmal hostels for migrant workers, which had shattered windows; past thousands of Black South Africans walking in the street; past chickens roaming freely; past little boys, barefoot, selling soda in plastic baggies at the intersections; past Zulu mamas balancing clothing baskets on their heads. Everywhere I looked there was trash, piled together in some places, spread out haphazardly in others. Every home appeared to be constructed from a loose collection of bricks, metal scraps, and left-over material.

After the bus weaved its way through the narrow, crowded township streets, it finally ground to a halt at the top of a hill in front of Saphinda Combined Primary School. About five hundred Black students in faded green uniforms with tan trim gathered in the parking lot and surrounded the bus. Before the rumble of the bus engine stopped, I heard something like thunder. I looked up at the sky and all I saw was blue. Then the driver killed the engine and the source of the noise became evident.

The Saphinda students were singing.

"*Shosholoza, kulezo ntaba, stimela siphume South Africa,*" they sang. "Go forward, from those mountains, on this train from South Africa."

As soon as I heard the first word — *shosholoza* — I recognized their song. *Sho sho* was a phrase meant to resemble the sound of a train. "Shosholoza" was a kind of illegal national anthem for the struggle against apartheid until the 1995 South African national rugby team's World Cup victory made it popular at all sporting events in the country. I had always enjoyed the rhythm and soul whenever I'd heard the song, but the passion and sheer volume that day made it genuinely feel like a train was coming. I looked at the stunned faces of the Clifton students and wondered what was racing through their minds.

"*Wen' uyabaleka, kulezo ntaba, stimela siphume South Africa,*" the Saphinda students sang. "You are running away from those mountains on this train from South Africa."

I glanced over at Clifton's headmaster, Brian, who was dressed impeccably. He sat at the front of the bus near a pair of security guards the school had hired to accompany the kids on the journey. This was the first time any of these white kids had ever been to a township. For a moment, Brian and I locked eyes. The singing of the Saphinda students outside poured through the doorway of the bus as the kids from Clifton began to file nervously outside.

■ ■ ■ ■ ■

The welcome was both beautiful and intimidating. As the white kids filed off the bus, a pathway through the crowd opened up. We were greeted by a procession of high fives leading toward the court. The handful of white visitors were engulfed by the hundreds of Black children, hands extended, "Shosholoza" sung on repeat. It wasn't until we made it to the court and the Clifton boys saw Bongani and Thabang — their coaches and heroes — waiting that they finally appeared to take their first breaths.

The Saphinda boys were on their side already, warming up with their own PeacePlayers coaches: Mondli and Menzi. Bongani and Thabang, sensing the fear, quickly huddled the Clifton boys up and began to get the visitors pumped.

"Okay, listen here, boys," said Bongani. He had the Clifton kids gathered around him in a tight circle, arms wrapped around shoulders almost as if they were trying to keep one another safe. "Why are we here today?"

"To play basketball, sir," answered one of the braver boys.

"Yes, Clive, that's right," replied Bongani. "But why are we really, really here?"

"We are here to make new friends, sir," offered another boy, his voice trembling, his eyes glancing nervously over to the other side of the court at the huddle of black faces doing the same thing.

That was the answer Bongani was looking for, and he rolled with it, explaining the significance of the day in a way that these boys could understand.

After a quick warm-up, they were ready to start the game. The crowd of five hundred had left the parking area and now stood ten deep, surrounding the makeshift court we had built. Both teams sent out their starting five. A few of our coaches acted as refs, and one threw up the jump ball. The game we had spent over a year dreaming of had finally begun.

At first, both teams were scared. None of the boys looked comfortable. The Clifton kids bobbled easy-to-catch passes. It was as if "Shosholoza" still rang in their heads. The Saphinda boys dribbled the ball off their bare feet. The fear in their eyes reminded me of the kids from the soccer game in rural Drakensberg when Sean and I first charged down that hill. By halftime, the score was tied at four — only two baskets apiece.

It felt like we were failing. We'd come here with the mission to unite. That wasn't going to happen if we didn't get past the tension. We all knew that we were on the verge of something magical. It just needed a push.

During the break, the coaches came up to me, concerned about the same issue.

"We need to mix the teams, T-Bose," Menzi said.

"Yeah," said Thabang. "Having the Black school playing the white school isn't working."

"It's defeating the purpose of the day," added Bongani.

They were totally right. We were still divided on the court, and everyone could feel it. The message quickly got to the rest of the coaches. They had both teams line up at center court. Then Thabang asked them to count off by ones and twos. The ones got a white jersey and went over with Coach Menzi. The twos got a blue jersey and went over with Bongani.

The dynamics of the team huddle changed instantly. As students from both schools looked on from the sidelines, five small white hands were placed on top of five small black hands, all resting on top of Bongani's stable fist. The starting players went around in a circle and said their names five at a time: Khulekani, Jonathan, Nkosiyabo, Thomas, Phumlani.

"Boys, this is why we came here today," said Bongani. "We are doing something that has never happened in South Africa. You must learn to work together if we are going to succeed. We must learn to communicate."

After another quick minute of the pep talk, Bongani had the kids ready. They jumped up and down, arms wrapped around one another's shoulders as if they'd been friends for life. They were completely focused on the task at hand.

"On three, PeacePlayers, as loud as you can," said Bongani. "So loud that the kids back at Clifton who weren't lucky enough to come today can hear you scream."

And with one huge, cohesive "PeacePlayers!" those white and Black boys left the huddle to take their positions, feeling totally invincible.

The crowd, sensing the change, broke out into "Shosholoza" once again. It no longer scared the white visitors. They felt the power in the words too. They joined in.

"*Shosholoza, kulezo ntaba, stimela siphume South Africa / Shosholoza kulezo ntaba, stimela siphume South Africa.*"

The deep song surrounded the court and flowed into the rest of the township, into the rest of the country, into the future.

"*Wen' uyabaleka, kulezo ntaba, stimela siphume South Africa.*"

Right away, the play on the court got smoother. Techniques the coaches had been working on with the kids for months looked like second nature. The kids dribbled easily. Their passes were crisp. They nailed the mechanics of their jumpers. Shots left their hands with confidence and, whether they sank the shots or not, the kids shared high fives and smiles.

From that point on, the game and the score didn't matter. We had already won. The coaches sat on the sidelines with tears in their eyes, watching something they had created, something believed to be impossible, come to life. Both the Clifton and Saphinda staffs were witnesses to the magical transformation. Linda, the reporter from SABC, and her cameramen caught it all on video to share with the nation.

As the game continued, I slipped away for a moment, climbing to the top of a nearby hill. I stood there witnessing it all, astonished. This was a resounding *yes* to all the *no* answers along the way — the hesitant school administrators at Clifton, the racist and misguided white South Africans who warned us about visiting the townships at all, the concerned friends and family members back home who had questioned my decision to go to Africa in the first place. I flashed back to my lunch with Sean in Baltimore, to boarding the plane and leaving everything I knew, to scoring that goal in the rural village, to the challenges with HIV/AIDS in the country, and to the brave coaches who were making it all possible. I remembered the words in Bongani's email: "The most talked about thing around here since Nelson Mandela being released."

I realized in that moment that Bongani and the others were more than just coaches. They tackled more than just teaching hoops. They were actually bridging divides. These disenfranchised Black coaches were being asked to forgive, to move on, and to work with white kids whose families had been — and often still were — the oppressors. They were being asked to learn about HIV/AIDS and to deliver a curriculum that could save an entire generation from dying. They had been thrust into leadership roles where the only choice was to sink or swim. No, these weren't just coaches. It would be a disservice to think of them that way. They were change agents.

I snapped a photo from the hill of the crowd, the game, and the sprawling township in the background, but I didn't need it. That moment was already indelibly etched on my heart and in my soul.

# 6

## Finding Leadership

*"A genuine leader is not a searcher for consensus,
but a molder of consensus."*

— MARTIN LUTHER KING JR.

The barbed wire spiraling above the massive cement wall always made me think of a prison. Instead, as the blue sign with yellow lettering revealed, this formidable area was actually the township of Lamontville's swimming pool. Because of enforced segregation and lack of access to resources, most Black South Africans raised in townships had never experienced any recreational water sports, let alone learned how to swim. Those lucky enough to have grown up in Lamontville, like our coach Sifiso, had the rare privilege of the community pool fortress at their disposal. In fact, most of the Black lifeguards who patrolled Durban's beachfront were from Lamontville. That's why when Sifiso asked to join me to surf one morning, he seemed confident.

"*Ey*, T-Bose, I'm the best swimmer in Lamontville," Sifiso told me with a huge smile on his face. "I know how to surf. I'm coming out with you guys. *Sho.*"

I hung out with the coaches often enough outside the program that his request was completely normal. Most of us were young twenty-somethings. We spent many of the evenings we had off drinking cheap beers and cruising to different parties together.

The only complication about Sifiso's request to be included was that surfing in Durban wasn't for the casual swimmer. For one, there were enough shark threats at the city's beaches that nets had been installed a couple of hundred yards from the shore. Although the colder waters near Cape Town are more famous for great white sightings, it wasn't unheard of to find the massive creatures off Durban's beaches and in the harbor. The other issue was that the most practical way to get into the surf was to jump off New Pier at North Beach — the city's main surf spot, which was a short walk from our apartment — and paddle into the break from there. At low tide, the fifteen-foot drop into the frothing sea below was never easy.

Despite these barriers to entry, I'd fallen in love with surfing in Durban the moment I had arrived. I woke up every morning with the beautiful African sunrise at 4:30 a.m. and hopped off the pier to humbly chase a few waves. Even though I wasn't any good at it, surfing had become one of my favorite things to do in the city. Even when I was getting tossed by the force of the sea and my face was being pounded into the sand, it always helped to clear my soul.

I had heard lots of stories about rural or township kids on family trips to the beaches who were sucked into the rip currents and quickly drowned because of their inability to swim. I hadn't met many township-born surfers, but if Sifiso was from Lamontville and said he had it covered, who was I to tell him he couldn't get in on the action?

After Sifiso nudged me persistently for a few weeks, I agreed to his request to come along. I brought him my spare board, and he met me at the pier early one morning. We walked together down to the end.

"You sure about this, man?" I asked, laughing and strapping my surf leash around my ankle.

"*Yebo*," he answered, emphatic. "I got this."

With that, we climbed over the metal guardrail, waited for the last set of waves to pass, and hopped off the pier. After surfers hit the water on that section of the surf, they've first got to regain their board and their composure. Then they have to paddle powerfully and quickly to avoid being smacked back into the pier's massive barnacle-covered concrete pillars. I glanced over at Sifiso as I paddled as hard as I could out past the break. He didn't exactly look comfortable on the board — his arms were flailing awkwardly in a mad attempt to make forward progress — but he was moving, nonetheless. I paused, waiting to see if a rescue operation was needed, but eventually he was able to make it over to me and past the crashing waves.

He looked in my direction and gave me an affirmative head bob. That signal meant I could start chasing some waves. While I was still learning the sport, I knew how to recognize a building wave and position myself to ride it. After a couple of fun sets, I glanced back, looking for Sifiso. He was nowhere to be found.

That early in the morning, the break wasn't crowded, and there sure weren't any other Black dudes in the water. I double-checked every surfer out there. No Sifiso.

My mind started to race. I had heard some of the local old-school longboarders talking every morning; they called Black swimmers "speed bumps" and wouldn't hesitate to run one over if he was in the way of their wave.

*Is Sifiso okay? Should I have taken more responsibility to make sure he was a good enough swimmer for this?*

Then, right before I started to panic, I spotted him. He had drifted way off, some one hundred yards out, past the shark nets. He looked stuck.

Knowing that none of the other surfers would be keen on heading out there to save someone from the township, I paddled out alone to bring him back. Eventually I was able to tow him back to safety. When we got to the beach, he finally admitted it.

"*Ey*, T-Bose, I was lying," he said, cracking the first grin I'd seen on his face since we hopped into the water. "I have no idea what I'm doing, but I wanted at least to try."

We both started laughing hysterically.

■ ■ ■ ■ ■

Once the eventful surfing morning concluded, I was back in the fifth-floor one-bedroom apartment that Gordy and I shared, which over-looked the Indian Ocean.

I had just brushed the last few lingering grains of sand out of the spaces between my toes and yanked on my first sock when the phone rang just before eight a.m.

"May I please speak with Thibault," a voice asked in a syrupy South African accent.

"This is Thibault," I answered.

"Ah, Thibault," the woman said warmly. "It's Mampe calling from Johannesburg."

The only times I had visited Jo'burg were with Bongani on fund-raising missions. Bootstrapping things, we'd grab the cheapest flight we could out of Durban on Kulula, South Africa's no-frills airline. Peace-Players didn't have the budget for us to stay in hotels. Instead, we slept on the floors of Bongani's friends' apartments. While I knew I had a lifeline at home if I ever got in a jam and needed money, I was prepared to do almost anything to avoid that. We were determined to make the program work on its own. We lived off tiny stipends that didn't allow for much eating out on our travels. It didn't matter if it was time for breakfast, lunch, or dinner — most of our meals on those fund-raising journeys were cans of tuna and beans we bought from the grocery store.

As my mind raced through the several trips that Bongani and I had taken to Jo'burg, the last time I'd met up with Mampe came to mind. She worked for the Nelson Mandela Children's Fund. She was always respectful and listened to us, but after all of our encounters, including the last one, she sounded noncommittal. All foundations seemed that way. They got thousands of requests for a very limited pool of money. They can't overpromise anything, no matter how personally interested they might be. Our chances of being awarded any money from President Mandela's foundation seemed low, but she had invited us to submit a proposal nonetheless.

"Nice to hear from you, Mampe," I said. "How's everything?"

The Nelson Mandela Children's Fund was one of the latest organizations we had sought out on our Jo'burg trips, once we'd made the contacts to get us in the door. Through one of our board members, we had been introduced to many famous South Africans, several of whom had served time in prison with Nelson Mandela on Robben Island.

We were persistent. With every door we opened, two more introductions followed as people fell in love with the program. I was working diligently behind the scenes to set up meetings and then sitting quietly in those meetings, watching Bongani passionately do his thing. We had our clunky early 2000s laptop with a quick three-minute video we'd play for anyone who would watch it. It had been some time since we'd visited Jo'burg at all, much less talked to the Nelson Mandela Children's Fund. They'd never called before.

*What can Mampe from Nelson Mandela's office be calling about on a Tuesday morning before eight o'clock?*

"Thibault, Mr. Mandela loved the news segment on the basketball game in Umlazi last year," she said.

"Okay," I said, stupefied that Nelson Mandela was even aware of PeacePlayers.

It wasn't that he was simply Nelson Mandela, the man South Africans reverently called Madiba, the global symbol of freedom and resilience; it was that he was also a sports icon. In 1995, shortly after he was released from prison and became president, he came out and publicly supported the South African rugby team, the Springboks, in their quest for the Rugby World Cup. The sport had always been a white man's game in South Africa. For a Black man who had been jailed for almost thirty years by the white apartheid regime to stand hand in hand with those who had held him down for so long was huge.

"I'm sure you are aware that Mr. Mandela firmly believes in the power of sports to unite," Mampe continued.

The ripple effect of Mandela's support of rugby was spectacular. He had galvanized the entire nation around a single event, perhaps for the first time in South Africa's history. The country's Black population — nearly three-quarters of its citizens — were given clear permission to cheer for the Springboks, and that had inspired the team to play like warrior-poets, lifting the World Cup in victory that year on South African soil. The players on the team were massive underdogs and the team had no business winning, but they were completely swept up by the unified surge Mandela had started. To say it was storybook is an understatement. Movies have been made of it, Clint Eastwood's Oscar-nominated *Invictus* chief among them. That win, and Mandela's unwavering support of the team, had temporarily unified a very divided country.

"He loves what you are doing," she added.

*What?*

"Thibault, we've read your application for funding, and we are excited to let you know that the Nelson Mandela Children's Fund would like to become one of PeacePlayers' largest supporters."

I was unable to speak and felt a little dizzy. Most of our other donations up until that point were for around 50,000 rand, or $5,000. That was about enough to build a basketball court in one of the townships. Our largest donor to date in South Africa had given us 200,000 rand, or four times the usual amount. Now, according to Mampe, the Nelson Mandela Children's Fund was offering to chip in 600,000 rand, about $60,000, an enormous amount of money for us at the time.

I had to sit down.

I knew the Clifton-Saphinda game had helped raise awareness about the program. I knew we would continue to grow faster as a result. I knew Bongani wanted to be part of something that one day could be as big as Mandela's release from prison, and here we were getting the support directly from his foundation. It was all simply too much to take in.

After thanking Mampe profusely, my voice trembling, I hung up the phone. I stared once more out of the window at the Indian Ocean. I had arrived just eighteen months earlier without a clue about what to do, and now we were finding our way. I just could never have dreamed that Mandela himself would jump aboard.

I pulled on my other sock, slipped into my sneakers, and dashed out of the apartment, eager to tell the team that Nelson Mandela had just joined the squad.

■ ■ ■ ■ ■

Ever since I had made the choice to get on the plane to South Africa, I had questioned myself. When Sean and I had our disagreements about leadership styles early in my time in Durban, when he said that I'd never be more than just a number-two man, those questions and insecurities had deepened. I wasn't sure if I was a leader at all, and if I was, I didn't know exactly what that meant or how I was supposed to go about it.

I had escaped from Baltimore and the shadow of my last name. People there assumed I had access to anything because of who my parents and grandparents were. In South Africa I had the chance to be nobody, and I loved that. I was free to become my own man, to learn and make mistakes on my own.

Whenever doubts crept up about my ability to lead, which was every single day, I simply followed my instincts to stay out of the spotlight, to let others shine, to be supportive and curious. I never wavered from my fundamental belief that PeacePlayers wasn't my program — that this wasn't my idea, or Sean's or Brendan's. The idea that sports could unite had always existed. It was sitting on the tip of the universe's tongue, just waiting to be brought to life. And while we were lucky enough to be helping it come to pass, I knew the credit for the idea didn't belong to us alone. Claiming it in that way could stunt its growth. I had to remember that Bongani, and our entire network of change agents, were building on an idea that Mandela himself had played a large part in growing. We were seeing that it wasn't just possible that sports could unite divided people; it was actually happening.

With Mandela's support, we went from being a few upstarts to having instant credibility. The funding floodgates swung open. Though some major national and international corporations like Laureus Sport for Good, BMW, and Sasol had begun backing us before Mandela, his support helped us further engage with major brands like Nike and

Adidas and huge American government organizations like the United States Agency for International Development (USAID).

A South African PeacePlayers board began to come together, and it was a who's who of the country. Ela Gandhi, Mahatma Gandhi's granddaughter, joined alongside Nandi Mandela, Nelson Mandela's granddaughter. Even though he wasn't on our board directly, Morné du Plessis, who was a former rugby legend, manager of the famous 1995 Springbok rugby team, and a founding member of the Laureus World Sports Academy, became a huge supporter. These advisory angels believed deeply in our mission. They grew to have as much pride of ownership and authorship in the program as the kids who participated in it, as the coaches who carried hoops for it, and as the communities who molded and embraced it. These guardian angels surrounded us to make sure that not only would PeacePlayers succeed now, but it would also continue to succeed into the future.

By 2004, our staff had grown from the twelve original coaches I had first met at DIT to more than one hundred people, expanding through townships, cities, rural areas, and affluent suburbs at breakneck speed. There were more areas and more area managers. We had exponentially more people working with PeacePlayers as their full-time job. With that growth, I was expected to step further into a leadership role.

The truth was that my take on leadership before coming to South Africa was a lot like Sifiso's take on swimming before he leaped off the pier and into the Indian Ocean: I knew it would be difficult, but I was going to try my hardest. I was not going to give up. Like Sifiso, I sometimes found myself in more than a bit of trouble, adrift out past the shark nets. But just as over time Sifiso slowly learned how to surf, I too picked up some basics about being a leader. What leadership itself meant to me began to crystallize.

Being looked to as a leader didn't mean I was more important than anyone else or that my vision needed to be executed for something to work. It was the opposite. To me, great leadership meant creating opportunities for everyone else first. It meant setting the stage for Bongani to work his magic. All of our earlier fundraising efforts — the meetings with the NBA and other organizations back in the States — had included the right spirit but missed the real-life element. They'd missed the Bongani.

As I began to figure out the leadership piece, our staff became even more empowered to shine. And with Nelson Mandela and so many other great leaders backing us, we were ready to dive deeper into the phase we'd always dreamed about: spreading PeacePlayers' South African success to other countries around the world.

# 7

## The Power of Love

*"When we love, we always strive to become better than we are.*
*When we strive to become better than we are,*
*everything around us becomes better too."*

— PAULO COELHO

The goat was ready for me, and it was loud. It grunted and fought. Menzi had told me that I wanted the animal to make noise. That's how I'd know the ancestors were accepting it.

"It's your rite of passage," said Menzi, pointing the blade's smooth black handle in my direction.

It was a tradition in South Africa, Menzi had explained on an earlier occasion. Zulus see the goat as one of their most sacred animals. Its slaughter allows for communication with the ancestors and serves as an opportunity to ask for good luck. When a new baby is born, a goat is slaughtered and prepared as a sign of welcome. When a couple is married, a goat is again a symbolic offering to celebrate the wife being accepted into the husband's family. In Zulu culture, until a boy has slaughtered a goat, he is not a man.

The air was both thick with the gravitas of the moment and festive for the celebration it was meant to be. I pulled the knife out of its sheath. I knew there was no getting around it. After all, this wasn't the first time I'd been told to cut off an animal's head.

As I took the weapon from Menzi, my mind raced back to my first month in the country more than two years earlier. We'd been in Umlazi then too, just like we were now, and we had just finished a clinic. Not long afterward, at one of our coaches' houses, I'd been unceremoniously asked to decapitate a chicken.

"No way," I protested, watching the chicken's beady eyes dart around. "I'm not cutting off its head."

"You have to," said Thulani, one of our coaches. All the coaches laughed.

Thulani showed me how to hold the neck down and take care of business. I had never done anything like that in my life. The coaches offered assurances that the chicken would be cooked and eaten, that the act was a symbolic rite of passage. I continued to protest until it became obvious that it was futile. That day, the weapon I was given was closer to a butter knife. I mourned the chicken after the job was done, but inside, I felt awesome. Everyone cheered. They slapped my back or gave me high fives. Their pride and excitement was genuine. Just by doing the act itself, I somehow felt more loved and connected to the place and the people there.

Taking a page out of the playbook of organizations like the Peace Corps and Teach For America, we too had begun to recruit outstanding college graduates from American universities to come over and work as PeacePlayers fellows. It was a two-year commitment. We covered housing and transportation and, just like we had done, they lived off a small stipend, which for many of them was a huge sacrifice. These were smart kids, and they could have gotten any job they wanted. More than anything, it was an opportunity for them to feel like they were part of helping to better build the bridges that could unite the world.

Most of the Americans who came to work with the program as fellows chose to participate in the poultry rite of passage. Our fellows felt that the tradition was important, and they embraced the bonding it fostered. It helped to prove to both the PeacePlayers staff and the locals that we were different from most white South Africans, who were unwilling to so much as visit the townships. It proved we could hang. We weren't just spending time in the townships; we could handle the knife too.

By now I had become accustomed to the chicken-slaughtering routine, but as I gripped the knife Menzi had just offered, I felt something bigger rising inside me, and it wasn't just about the change in animal size.

"Don't look so shocked," Bongani joked, taking his position at one of the creature's legs. "It's not that much bigger than a chicken."

"But it will be a much bigger feast," Menzi added, laughing hysterically as he grabbed another leg.

My dad, who was visiting me for the second time, took hold of another leg, somehow maintaining his usual stoic demeanor despite how different the whole township sacrifice occasion must have been for him.

Gordy — who had undergone his own poultry rite of passage — took his position on the last leg.

For major occasions across traditional communities in South Africa, a sheep, goat, cow, or bull is sacrificed to honor the moment. That day, no one had died. No one was getting married, either. The occasion was that I had decided it was time to leave South Africa and focus my attention on the organization's global growth. I was leaving a surfboard and a small handful of things behind at the PeacePlayers apartment for trips back to check on the program, but my day-to-day life was transitioning to bouncing around the world.

I gripped the knife. As I pressed the blade into the animal's neck, I was intensely focused. Zulu ancestors had performed the ritual for centuries. I felt like I was being accepted as an adopted member of the Zulu community by partaking in something that had begun way before me. I focused as best I could to honor that tradition, to treat the animal with love even as I took its life.

Soon it was all over. The goat's head was no longer attached to its body. Everyone hugged me. They thanked me and congratulated me.

"Here," said Menzi, following the sacrifice. He held a strip of goatskin taken from the animal's leg, the hair still attached. "This is your *isiphandla*."

Menzi was one of my oldest and dearest South African friends. He had first welcomed me into the township, and he continued to help bring so much of PeacePlayers to life. As he tied the strip of goatskin to my right wrist, he said, "This bracelet, Thokozani, is a sign of respect, pride, hope, and security. It will connect you with the ancestors as a sign of belonging and a celebration of your time here with us."

I watched Menzi's words leave his lips. The goat flesh was still warm as he slipped the bracelet on me and pressed it against my skin. I examined it, my new *isiphandla*.

"It will smell like hell," Menzi said, choking back his tears. "But you must not cut it off on your own. It has to fall off naturally."

I thanked him, and we shared a powerful embrace. Next I thanked Bongani, whose words had inspired me before I ever left the States and who was the first person I met at the airport upon my arrival. Next I thanked Gordy. His initial work with Nathi and his current work with the rest of the team on the life skills program and other parts of Peace-Players was often so behind the scenes that he rarely got the recognition he deserved. Despite that lack of traditional recognition, Gordy would be part of the team carrying the PeacePlayers torch in South Africa now, and I was so grateful for him. Finally, I thanked my father, who beamed with that same sense of pride I remembered he and my mother having when I first boarded the plane all those years ago armed with a wild idea that had now gone global.

■ ■ ■ ■ ■

Before we even began, PeacePlayers was larger than each and every one of us. As Bongani Nkosi had proclaimed and as Nelson Mandela had proven, the time had come for the idea of sports to unite, and there was no stopping it. The best anyone could do was to join in and help it grow.

My leadership role within PeacePlayers evolved. I led an effort to help strengthen and grow the program in other countries. First, I went to Northern Ireland, the place where the idea for the program had been born. PeacePlayers was already underway there, working to bridge the

Protestant-Catholic divide, but I came in to help take the program to the next level by beginning to raise local funds and recruit local leadership.

PeacePlayers fellows were a big part of the operation in several parts of the country, including Belfast, where I set up shop in a small apartment. The daily grind of these young coaches reminded me of my trips with Bongani to Johannesburg to raise money early on in South Africa, where nothing was fancy and where we worked happily in complicated conditions because of our massive belief in what we were doing. My priority in Northern Ireland was helping the program become financially self-sustainable and operationally sound, and to help set up a board of directors like we'd done in South Africa to guide us along.

Although there was no longer a violent conflict in Belfast, the divide between Catholics and Protestants was still very real. The city featured many forty-foot-high concrete separation barriers — called "peace lines" or "peace walls" — that were constructed to separate the Catholic and Protestant neighborhoods. Those walls still stand today. The PeacePlayers approach to building bridges between groups was a new way to tackle the divides in Northern Ireland, but that didn't mean it was going to be easy. We had to figure out a way to break through.

To that end, we instituted a model called *twinning*. Using this approach, PeacePlayers paired two schools — one Catholic and one Protestant — together for an entire year. The prolonged contact allowed the students to become friends. It also allowed the parents, teachers, and administrators to realize that these were just kids and that if we reached them early enough, they might not form irreversible negative opinions about each other. It worked. The success of the twinnings in Northern Ireland inspired a similar program in South Africa.

The more time I spent in Northern Ireland, the better I understood the culture. I was able to wrap my head around the struggle. I fell in love with both the Catholic and Protestant people the way I had fallen in love with the different people who shared the country of South Africa. Slowly, the PeacePlayers team was able to implement the lessons we had learned in Africa, and the program really began to take hold.

We hired a local managing director. We began to raise local money. We implemented outcome-measurement strategies to prove we were succeeding in our work and, in the end, we were able to put together a strong board of directors.

Adding further confirmation that our Irish program was bridging religious divides as successfully as our South African program was bridging racial divides, His Holiness the Dalai Lama came to visit us. After he shot some hoops with a group of Protestant and Catholic kids at one of our school twinnings, images of the event spread around the world. In the photos, the spiritual leader of the planet, in his crimson and yellow robes, peacefully holds a basketball with kids who'd been separated by differences in their religious faiths.

Not long after my time in Northern Ireland, PeacePlayers was invited to Cyprus by USAID to study whether the program could work there. As in Belfast, where the "peace walls" divide Catholics and Protestants, the entire island nation of Cyprus is split into two halves by its own wall. Officially called the "United Nations Buffer Zone" — or the "Green Line" — the barrier is more than one hundred miles long and separates the northern Turkish Cypriots from the southern Greek Cypriots. The tensions between the two groups have a long and violent history.

For the past several years, Sean and I had each been laser-focused on completely different parts of the global PeacePlayers operation, but now we had the chance to meet up in Cyprus. While our time together in South Africa hadn't been great, we had both come such a long way as people, as leaders, as men. In Cyprus, the two of us engaged with businesses and government agencies that were curious about the program, holding meetings in basements of collapsing old buildings and using translators to passionately and confidently explain how PeacePlayers worked. As I thought about how much I had initially felt like a fish out of water after leaving the comfort of my home to join PeacePlayers, it was surreal to be here almost four years later, meeting with grown men and women who were excited to join the movement that had swept us up. They asked questions because they were curious, because they wanted to learn more, and because they trusted us to have the answers. I was only in my midtwenties, but I was already giving advice on how to bridge the kind of divides that had bothered me so much as I was growing up. It felt amazing.

No matter what meeting we were in, we were always very clear that this wasn't our idea or our struggle, and that we didn't claim to have all the answers. Instead, we were there to listen, to empower, and to help. Like the townships in Durban, the poorer Turkish communities in Cyprus were eager to be involved; like Clifton, their wealthier Greek counterparts on the other side were more hesitant. Eventually, we made progress on both fronts and helped launch a version of Peace-Players that worked on the island.

We were also invited to the Middle East to address the divide between the Israelis and the Palestinians. The success of the program there depended deeply on how well we could understand the local situation. I'll never forget walking through the town of Tulkarm in the West Bank after a coaching clinic we had just run. There were rows upon rows of posters of men holding machine guns and explosives, and when I asked the Palestinian coaches who they were, a coach explained that they were dead martyrs for the cause — people who would have been called suicide bombers on the Israeli side of the wall. The experience was another reminder of the complexities of the conditions where we worked.

With such a huge and wealthy Jewish population in the United States, our efforts in the region were well supported right away. It was easier to get funding there than in places like South Africa or Cyprus. The divide in the Middle East was on everyone's radar, and it quickly became one of PeacePlayers' strongest programs.

Meanwhile, our board of directors in the States was growing significantly. Superstars like Steve Kerr, five-time NBA champion with the Chicago Bulls (three championships) and the San Antonio Spurs (two championships) and current three-time NBA championship coach of the Golden State Warriors, joined in. Ron Shapiro, a famous sports agent and bestselling author, and R. C. Buford, the general manager of the San Antonio Spurs, also came aboard.

No matter where I went in the growing PeacePlayers network, the one constant that I found was love. There was love and passion for basketball, a newer sport in a lot of places. There was love and camaraderie within and between the branches of the organization, where people were sharing ideas and working together to solve the bigger problems in the divides. Love became the fuel for the global growth, and it is what kept me going personally.

All the while, as I was helping tweak the program in all of these different places and wrapping my head around their different circumstances, I was also darting back and forth between the United States and South Africa, which was still the closest thing I had to a home base in those years. It was exhilarating and exhausting at the same time. Despite all of our success, the lifestyle began to wear me down.

Almost five years in, I began to consider that extra leap of leaving PeacePlayers entirely. That $8,000 we started with had turned into millions of dollars of support. We'd grown from working with a few dozen schools to touching the lives of tens of thousands of children all over the planet. It had spread beyond anything we ever thought possible. But I knew that as much as I loved it, the time had come to make a change.

Living my life out of a suitcase started to scatter me. I began to feel like Ed Norton's character in *Fight Club*, hopping from plane to plane. Without much routine or consistency, I began losing touch with old friends more quickly. Holidays passed. Birthdays. Seasons. I felt like I was slowly disappearing. Just as I was starting to wonder whether I was even real anymore, something incredible happened.

After choosing Brazil for a rare, weeklong break from the Peace-Players work, I unexpectedly met the most amazing woman in the world there. Her name was Lola, and she was beautiful, passionate, fiery, and soft, all at the same time. She was untamable and she completed me. As our long-distance relationship kicked into gear, perhaps inspired by the way my parents had crossed continents to try out love, I knew I wanted to pick a city, convince Lola to marry me, and think about raising a family together.

■ ■ ■ ■ ■

In the late summer of 2006, after gathering the last of my personal belongings from the PeacePlayers apartment and saying my final goodbyes to my friends in my adopted home of Durban, I settled into my seat on the South African Airways monster Boeing 747 headed back to Washington, DC. For me, the window seat is a must on any flight over sixteen hours. This time I wasn't leaving South Africa to help the organization continue to grow abroad. I had made up my mind to leave PeacePlayers altogether. My *isiphandla* — the goatskin bracelet — still clung to my wrist. It reminded me every day of the momentum we had been a part of creating. It was my link to a chain that was playing some small role in uniting the world.

While my personal life was leading me in exciting new directions, my work life was leaving me exhausted, sad, emotionally drained, and confused. Most of all, I was scared, paralyzed by a completely different kind of fear than what I had felt going the opposite direction nearly half a decade earlier. I was no longer scared for my life. This time I was worried about what would come next. This time I had no plan, no big program or idea I was flying toward. I was about to give up the single greatest thing I had ever been part of. I was second-guessing everything, even as I sat there staring out the window.

*What good is discovering my capacity to lead if I never find anything as fulfilling as PeacePlayers again?*

Leaving meant I wouldn't be back in Africa, at least not in the same way. My decision to move on from PeacePlayers had come after months of conversations with my greatest mentors and closest friends. I didn't take it lightly. It was the largest and hardest decision I had ever faced. I was madly in love with what we were doing, but at twenty-eight years old, the travel was starting to eat me up.

The nonprofit industry is all about hustling. It's very grassroots. So much of your time is spent raising money, trying to convince millionaires and billionaires and foundations to give you the fuel for all the things you want to do. Sometimes during those years in South Africa, I would imagine what it would be like to be on the other end of that conversation. My heroes, like Nelson Mandela, Ron Shapiro, and my father, have been able to have a massive positive impact because of the respect they have as leaders as well as the financial position they are in. They could give their time, their knowledge, and their money. The idea of being able to help not just from the grassroots level but also from higher up was really appealing to me — as was the thought of spending as much time as possible with Lola.

The almost five years had been spectacular: traveling all over the world while pushing to make it a better place by tackling war, divided nations, and HIV/AIDS, and by developing leaders who could bring change for generations to come. The stakes had been so high for so long. I loved every minute of it, but I was tired of scattering myself. My life felt fragmented — the pieces of me spread out around the world across basketball courts, villages, towns, and oceans.

"The cabin doors will now be closing," said one of the flight attendants over the intercom. I looked out the window and saw the sun readying itself to drop over the western horizon.

I'm usually talkative with whomever I'm sitting next to, but that day I felt too preoccupied to chat. I wanted to put myself back together, to focus my energy and dial it in, but the questions kept pummeling me like a barreling wave.

*How will I ever find anything to replace the power, impact, and importance of what I've been doing? How will I find anything on such a large scale that will touch so many people in so many different ways?*

The ding of the seatbelt sign being illuminated was the last thing I remember as I fell asleep before the airplane even pushed away from the gate.

■ ■ ■ ■ ■

I couldn't tell if I had been asleep for an hour or ten when I heard the ding of the seatbelt sign again. The flight attendant explained over the intercom that we had hit some turbulence. Everyone needed to be seated.

My sleep had been so deep and my dreams so vivid. In my dreams I had been walking around Umlazi barefoot. Then, suddenly, I was walking around my hometown of Baltimore barefoot, wondering where my shoes were and why the poverty and oppression felt so similar to what I had seen in the township.

As I came to, I did my best to stretch out in the cramped seat. I checked my watch. I had slept only an hour. There were fifteen more to go until we landed in Washington. Sitting next to me was a kid who looked like he was about twelve years old. He was reading a thick book. He had noticed me shifting around, and our eyes locked as we nodded to each other.

"I'm Thibault," I said, extending my hand. This kid must have been the same age as the ones I'd become so used to coaching over the past five years.

"Simon," the boy responded, shaking my hand and closing the book.

These were moments I cherished. It was exactly why I had fallen in love with traveling — not for the beaches and fancy drinks with tiny umbrellas in them, but for the intimate and spontaneous conversations with a Zulu grandmother in a Kombi van in Umlazi, an Israeli soldier at a street café in Tel Aviv, a Protestant cabdriver in Belfast, a bearded basketball fan in Turkish Cyprus, or a young kid on an airplane.

My conversation with Simon, like others, began totally raw and unscripted with no judgment or expectations. Soon it was flowing. I shared a bit about my bracelet, the goat, and South Africa, and then I asked one of my favorite questions.

"Simon," I said, "if you had a time capsule that could take you back in time to any period in the history of this universe, what time period would you go back to?"

I had received some fascinating answers over the years. Some people wanted to go back to the Middle Ages to be a knight or a king. Others chose the sixties to experience Woodstock. I even remember someone once telling me he wanted to return to the Stone Age to experience life as a caveman.

Simon's eyes locked with mine. Without even skipping a beat, as if he had known I was going to ask the question, he answered.

"I'd go back to the time period of Nazi Germany."

I was sure I'd misheard him.

"What was that?" I asked awkwardly.

I couldn't think of a worse period to return to. I'd bet the majority of people alive during the rise of Adolf Hitler, including the six million Jews who were brutally murdered on his watch, would have used that time capsule to get as far away from Nazi Germany as humanly possible. I hoped I'd just heard him wrong.

"Nazi Germany," he said again, not blinking as he stared into my eyes. "If I could go back to Nazi Germany, I would have a chance to stop Hitler."

I sank back in my small seat, unable to respond for a moment, swirling in the space his response had opened inside me. In the past, I had frequently asked myself this question: If I had been born in the South during the civil rights era in America, as a white boy would I have had the strength to stand up for what was right? Would I have stood by the side of Dr. Martin Luther King and fought for justice and equality, even if the family I was raised in didn't agree? If I had been born in South Africa as a white kid during apartheid, would I have had the courage to stand up against the oppression that my fellow white people thought was right?

The truth was that even though I'd come so far in those years in South Africa, I was still self-conscious about my role in the world. Knowing how much privilege I'd come from always made me take any success with a grain of salt. It wasn't just that I was born into a family of means; it was that my parents had set a great example. Perhaps the biggest part of my privilege was being born into a family that cared about others.

There, in that instant, it hit me.

Fifty years from that day, two strangers would be traveling together. After striking up a conversation, one would turn to the other and ask some version of that same time capsule question. And the other might just respond about seizing a chance to turn around broken social systems, fight racial injustices, or discover a cure for a disease.

Whatever the problem — or opportunity, as I began to call them — whether large or small, abroad or at home, it needs champions, worker bees, and leaders. I realized then that we can't just sit on the sidelines waiting for someone else to address it. With that, Simon, this random twelve-year-old kid, had just changed my life.

All of a sudden I was no longer scared of what was coming next for me, no longer scared that I wouldn't find something as fulfilling as PeacePlayers. Simon helped me understand the immediacy of life. Right there, on that airplane, I committed to never letting a day go by where I didn't feel like I was part of the solution. Simon had made me excited to find out what that solution would be and what role I would play in finding it.

The seatbelt sign dinged again and it was settled.

I was ready to move on from PeacePlayers. I was ready to go back to America.

# Part II

# BUILD

"Carver, we are in a code red. All faculty, please assume code-red protocol. Everyone lock your classroom doors."

The message blasts out of the intercom in Michael Tobass's tenth-grade English class at Carver Vocational-Technical High School on Baltimore's notorious West Side.

At twenty-three years old, fresh out of college and dusted with a peach-fuzz beard, Michael hasn't even been on the job, or a teacher for that matter, for six months yet. And with the exception of a Boy Scout trip and a family vacation to the touristy Inner Harbor as a kid, he is also brand new to Baltimore.

This must be a drill.

Michael stands at the head of the classroom, a lone motivational sign hanging above the well-used dry-erase board bolted to the cinder-block wall behind him. The sign reads: *Write Your Own Story*.

Michael grew up in Bergen County, New Jersey, one of the wealthiest counties in the country, where just five years ago he finished his senior year at Bergen County Technical High School, ranked one of the top fifty public schools in the United States. While not a part of Bergen's elite, Michael's family lives a comfortable life. His mother is a teacher in Paterson, New Jersey, and his father runs a small industrial water pump distribution business.

As a kid, Michael and his classmates had plenty of code-red drills, starting when he was in second grade, right after the 9/11 attacks. He and his friends would calmly walk over to the corner of the room, telling jokes and waiting for the principal to jump back on the PA system and confirm that this was, indeed, just practice and that teaching should resume.

This isn't Bergen County, though, and before the alarm sounds a second time, his class at Carver erupts in chaos. Students dash out of their chairs and begin shouting. Desks screech as frantic fifteen- and sixteen-year-olds charge toward the side of the room farthest from the door, tripping over the backpacks and jackets strewn across the floor.

Michael freezes for a moment, trying to get his bearings.

"Everyone remain calm," he says, half to himself, half to the students. His usual soft tone shakes faintly against the din of activity.

He tries again a tiny bit louder, as half the students gather in the far corner of the room and begin to look at their teacher as he fumbles through the drill.

"You scared, Mr. Tobass?" asks one student, staring at her rookie teacher, who is clearly unused to life at Carver and in Baltimore.

"This ain't no drill, Mr. T.!" shouts another. "There ain't no drills at Carver."

Those words snap Michael out of his hazy disbelief and drive home the urgency of the situation. He tells himself, *I'm the only adult in the room. I'm meant to be in charge.*

Not only is he supposed to provide an opportunity for these thirty teenage kids to get a good education, something too many people had already given up on, but he is also responsible for keeping them safe from danger, however foreign those dangers might be to him personally.

"Everyone in the corner. Everyone sit down," commands Michael, uncharacteristically raising his voice out of sheer necessity over the code-red alarm messages repeating through the speaker in his room. His body quakes from the adrenaline surging through it.

Worst-case scenarios flash through his mind as he runs to shut the door, puts the dead bolt in place, and draws the blinds. In just his first month on the job, two massive fights have broken out in Michael's classroom. The first brawl sent him sprinting to find the hall monitor for assistance. The second one had him in the middle of the melee trying to break it up as a flying haymaker just barely missed his face. Fights like these and normal gang activity are far too common at Carver to trigger this level of warning. It must be something more severe.

A code red means many people's lives are in danger.

"Everyone remain calm," Michael says loudly to the students, trying to remind himself to do the same.

The school is located in the heart of Coppin Heights, one of the city's poorest and deadliest neighborhoods. It's located less than half a mile from the intersection of Pennsylvania Avenue and North Avenue, the epicenter where protests erupted in 2015 following the death of Freddie Gray, a young Baltimore man killed in police custody, only for the officers involved to be cleared of wrongdoing. Years before his death, Freddie had been a student at Carver.

Michael places the red placard over the window in the door to indicate there is a real emergency in the school. The dull thuds of the other classroom doors shutting in the hallway give him a sinking feeling in his stomach. He takes his place back with the students. All he can do now is wait for further instruction and hope nothing terrible happens.

The better Michael has gotten to know his students, the more aware he's become of just how hard their lives are. The crime, violence, homelessness, broken households, and unplanned teenage pregnancy they deal with on a daily basis can be debilitating, leading students to believe they don't have many options. Michael isn't pretending to be at Carver, or in Baltimore for that matter, with some silver bullet to solve the complicated issues brought on by generations of poverty and the impact of historical and current racism, segregation, and inequality. He is there to listen and offer what he can: his love, his commitment, and his passion for education as a way to create whatever possible future they desire.

Michael knows he can do anything in life. He has the full support of a loving family, and he was an exceptional student in both high school and college. The students he's huddled up in the corner with, none of whom look anything like him, are just kids, and Michael believes they deserve the same education, life stability, and access to social capital that he enjoys. While Michael can't immediately see how to change the conditions they were born into, he believes that with the support of dedicated teachers bringing their best, his students can open many more doors for themselves. He believes in the potential of his students to write their own stories, however they want, no matter how many people and code-red situations try to convince them otherwise.

Eventually, after what seems like hours huddled in a corner with his students, the code red is lifted and school resumes. The students pick up the things that were tossed on the floor during the chaos — jackets, pens, notebooks, tattered and outdated textbooks — and make their way to their next classes. It's clear to Michael that this kind of situation isn't unusual. For these students, it's daily life.

Indeed, it turns out not to have been a drill. A student had pulled a loaded gun on another student in the crowded cafeteria. The police had intervened just in time.

The severity of the situation for Michael and his students is real. While the young teacher is shaken, he feels even more committed to his students than ever. He is not there just as some temporary teacher killing time after college or doing something to make himself feel better. He is there to do everything he can to make a real difference in the lives of his students. This situation, hazards and all, only reinforces his desire to serve.

As remarkable as Michael is, he isn't alone. He was one of 120 new teachers to come to Baltimore in 2015 through the Teach For America program. All those young men and women were part of a simple idea that sought to challenge the status quo of how we educate the future generation. The organization was started in 1990 by an inspiring young woman named Wendy Kopp, who believed that if we as a country were going to address the inequality that had plagued America's school systems, more leaders had to make teaching their life's work. Teach For America's plan was to recruit high-performing college grads to teach in high-need urban and rural areas around the country. They weren't going after the young adults who wanted to be career teachers and who had just received their master's degrees in education. Teach For America wanted to pull America's best and brightest away from Wall Street, powerful law firms, and corporate America to give them the skills to educate our most at-risk children.

That simple idea became an enormous force that, for over three decades, has disrupted not only the public education system, but also the systems that Fortune 500 companies use to recruit our country's most impressive college graduates. All of a sudden, out of nowhere, 10 percent of Ivy League college seniors were applying to Teach For America. Companies like Morgan Stanley and JPMorgan Chase couldn't believe it. What did Teach For America have that they didn't?

Teach For America couldn't offer $100,000 starting salaries, corporate credit cards, or huge bonuses. Instead, it offered college graduates the chance to really make a difference in our world, to bridge divides and share valued resources with places that could use them the most. They offered those young men and women the chance to be a part of something very few companies could match: to serve on the front lines in fighting for the country's future.

These college graduates weren't signing up to teach because they were going to get paid a ton of money. They were signing up because they wanted to serve. They wanted to play a role in helping shape the lives of people outside their own bubbles, perhaps even having their own lives shaped along the way.

Michael and his cohort were just the latest generation of the more than 1,300 Teach For America corps members who had come to Baltimore since the early 1990s. And that group of over 1,300 in Baltimore was just 2 percent of the more than 65,000 passionate young adults who had committed at least two years of their lives to teaching in our country's poorest urban and rural communities over the past thirty years.

Sixty-five thousand young adults like Michael Tobass. That's a lot of brilliant, caring, loving, and devoted people wanting to bridge the educational divide that our country had created. If only society could find ways to care for these young adults as much as those young people care for future generations.

# 8

# Uncomfortable

*"Before anything great is really achieved,
your comfort zone must be disturbed."*

— RAY LEWIS

I stared at my old bedroom ceiling; my mind wouldn't turn off. My first night back permanently on US soil after close to five years spent living in fascinating countries around the world couldn't have felt more foreign. My parents' stone farmhouse stood in the cushy suburbs of Baltimore County. Here there was no twenty-four-hour symphony of blaring car horns, hustling street vendors, and raucous kids. There was simply a sharp silence. Even the late-summer breeze pushing around the branches of the white pines outside my window refused to be heard. The large queen-size bed and soft, clean sheets I lay on — an epic departure from the secondhand mattresses, couches, cots, sleeping bags, and hard African earth I had become used to as bedding — only unsettled me more. I had grown up in this stillness and softness. While I had visited during my years with PeacePlayers, I had never felt so uncomfortable in my own home as now, when I had prepared myself mentally to be back for good.

Once the edges of dawn began to splash my family's sleepy wooded suburb with light, I gave in to the restlessness. I had stared at the ceiling long enough. I hopped out of bed, threw on a pair of shorts, grabbed the keys off the nightstand, and headed outside. There it was possible to hear some of the swaying branches, rustling leaves, even the chirps of morning birds, but I needed much more. I hopped in my beat-up, old Toyota truck and, without a destination in mind, I sped south down Interstate 83 — the Jones Falls Expressway — in the morning traffic toward Baltimore and anything that might bring back that commotion I'd grown to value.

As I drove on, my foot unusually heavy on the gas, my jet-lagged mind began to catch up to my body. There was still so much uncertainty surrounding my permanent reentry into America: what my life would look like, how long I'd stay in my hometown. There was a new curiosity too. It had begun during the visits I'd made over the years flying in from divided countries, and now that I was home, even on that first day I felt it deepening.

In South Africa, the divisions between people were as stark as day and night, black and white. In Northern Ireland, Cyprus, and Israel, the issues that tore people apart were equally front and center. There was a frankness I appreciated about how real and open the problems in those societies were.

*Why was the United States so good at sugarcoating and hiding its problems?*

This was 2006, nearly a decade before Black Lives Matter and Freddie Gray, two years before Barack Obama was elected president. Except for the time when Islamophobia had bubbled up nationally in the wake of 9/11, there didn't seem to be enough public discourse about division. Everything happened in private bubbles, or it was unfairly swept under the rug, filtered through so many media outlets that honest conversation felt impossible. Poor people of color had been shouting about these things for generations, but the rest of the country did everything possible to mute them out. I witnessed the phenomenon every time I visited home in the mid-2000s, but the truth was that it had been right in front of me my whole life.

So many years had passed since I'd watched *Mississippi Burning*

and participated in the Hands Across America moment as a boy —
those initial experiences, and so many others along the way, that helped
pierce my own bubble. Still, the fact remained that people rarely talked
openly with one another about race in my home country. So much
of America simply ignored the issues facing its most vulnerable citizens. It was this inability to be frank about division with those on the
other side of the divide — the way people could be frank in all the other
countries where I had spent time — that I saw as a ticking time bomb.
The more I noticed how infrequently we were discussing the division,
and the more I realized how voiceless our country's disenfranchised
were, the more I questioned whether we were united as Americans at all.

It was those thoughts I'd wrestled with as I had tossed and turned,
fidgeting all night in a bed I had slept in comfortably thousands of
times before. Those thoughts had gotten me out of the house, onto the
highway, past Druid Hill Park, and they were now leading me west-
bound on North Avenue, toward what I had heard was one of the city's
roughest areas. The question presented itself clear as that Baltimore
summer morning: How divided was the United States?

This idea that the United States was perfect, that we were the model
of a democratic melting pot that other countries should strive to em-
ulate, had stopped resonating with me long ago. I was home now, and
even if I didn't know for how long, I understood that it was time to stop
wondering. I had pushed aside my questions for far too long. I needed
to see how divided we really were.

I piloted my old truck into the Penn-North neighborhood, eventually pulling over at 2533 Pennsylvania Avenue. I stopped less than
a block away from the CVS drugstore that would be burned to the
ground nine years later in the wake of the brutal death of Freddie Gray.
I hadn't planned to stop there, but I felt a buzz in the air there that
reminded me of Durban. The community stirred to life with the same
gusto. There were similar wafts of quick, affordable meals for folks on
the go. Rhythmic music floated from nearby. I reached for the keys
in the ignition and remembered the day Sean and I had stopped in
the Drakensberg village all those years ago above the field full of Zulu
kids. I didn't have a ball with me this time, though. I wasn't sure if I

had anything besides a desire to better understand Baltimore's great divide.

I glanced to my right. Overgrown weeds jutted out of the foundation of an abandoned two-story townhouse. Fast-food wrappers blew past the front of the building, carried by a warm morning breeze.

Hip-hop blasted out of an approaching sedan to my left. The driver stared at me as he slowly rolled by, the boom of his subwoofer rattling everything around me — mirrors, windows, license plate covers. I felt it in my spine, and I smiled. It reminded me of the deep beats that pumped out of the Kombi vans that shuttled people through the overflowing streets of Umlazi.

I flicked my wrist, turned off the engine, and took a deep breath.

Statistically speaking, I knew I was in one of the most dangerous neighborhoods in Baltimore, maybe the country. Even with this knowledge and without a concrete plan to follow, a person to meet, or an end destination, being there just felt right.

I reached over to unbuckle my seatbelt to get out and take a walk through the neighborhood, but then I froze.

*Will I be safe?*

I gazed out as the street became more crowded in the growing morning. The people there looked nothing like me. It was an open question whether it was okay for me to be here at all.

Once, during high school, I had taken a shortcut down Reisterstown Road and inadvertently found myself in the same part of town. I stopped at a red light on Pennsylvania Avenue and a few young guys on bicycles started swirling around my car. It was the late afternoon, with plenty of people on the streets, but the tension was palpable. One guy banged my car with his hand, another stared at me. It was clear none of us thought I was welcome there. As soon as the light flipped to green, I raced away before things could escalate.

All those years later, despite that memory, my instinct to flee caught me off guard.

*Can this really be happening to me?*

After almost five years of living and working alongside people of different races, cultures, backgrounds, and socioeconomic groups, of pushing myself way outside my comfort zone and always challenging the status quo way of thinking in some of the most divided countries in the world, I was suddenly torn myself.

*Am I really this nervous to get out of my car in my own city, less than five miles from the house I grew up in?*

In South Africa, we were sure that the avoidance mentality was the wrong approach. We understood that people on both sides of a divide were immersed in a cultural way of thinking brought on by generations of bias, real-life horror stories, and devastating personal experiences. We as outsiders had some objectivity, though. Distance gave us a chance to see the shape and thickness of the dividing lines more clearly. It's what got us out of our car in the Drakensberg village to play that game of soccer, brought us into townships and rural areas, and allowed us, ultimately, to help prove there was a way to bridge a seemingly impossible divide.

Here in West Baltimore, though, there was no Sean with me. I was all alone. I wasn't an outsider. The objectivity that allowed me to see past the deeply rooted beliefs of others overseas was replaced by twenty-eight years of accumulated stories about this neighborhood and others like it. The stories had one message: I was not safe or welcome.

These were the same stories that white South Africans had told me about Black townships. They were stories that reinforced and created separation. But that was the fiction. The truth was that I was judging the neighborhood without having listened to the people who actually live there. That bothered me profoundly, and I felt a quick bolt of anger at myself. I grabbed the plastic door handle and shot out of the car, as if to escape the embarrassment I was feeling for having paused.

*What would Bongani say if he saw me flinch like that?*

He was the one who had taught me that the way I approached any situation, especially an uncomfortable one, directly impacted its outcome. I had come to understand that we create situations by the way we perceive them — that if we go into a place afraid, it makes it very hard to initiate and produce a meaningful, loving connection. In contrast, if we approach uncomfortable situations with an open mind, a huge smile, unflagging optimism, a warm hug, and as much generosity and love as possible, we can create a platform where powerful interactions can occur.

Like the places I was warned not to visit in South Africa and the Middle East, West Baltimore carried connotations of danger — and not much else — for most outsiders. In fact, while I'd been away, HBO's hit drama *The Wire* had captured the country's attention and put the sometimes-violent parts of Baltimore at the very top of the list of places Americans should stay away from. I hadn't watched much of the show myself, but it had been running for four seasons by the time I began to walk down Pennsylvania Avenue that day. The show was only the latest thing that had helped to make Baltimore, and the part of town I was in, famous for all the wrong reasons.

Despite the narrow lens it pointed at the city, *The Wire* has a lot of memorable dialogue, and one bit in particular resonated with me. Avon Barksdale, the king of West Baltimore's underworld, and Proposition Joe, his East Baltimore counterpart, coach teams from their respective sides of the city in a basketball game in season 1. At the end of the game, after tempers have flared and died back down, Proposition Joe asks Avon if they are cool. Barksdale says they are, but with one caveat.

"Of course, you come on the West Side again, without a ball," says Avon, "I'ma light your ass up."

Today, I didn't have a ball. I didn't have a specific reason for being there. I didn't have anything but questions.

*What is daily life like beyond the one-dimensional news stories about the violence and destitution of Baltimore's inner city? What are the experiences of those who actually live here? What truly causes these divides that separate races and communities, and how can we channel the diversity and vibrancy of our city to bridge them? How can we counteract the years of neglect and lack of access by leaning into all the things that are already Baltimore's greatest strengths?*

I had asked versions of those questions hundreds of times all over the world, and I was now ready to ask them here, at home.

■ ■ ■ ■ ■

I hopped onto the pavement, slamming my car door shut. A city bus raced past me, belching a thick cloud of black diesel fumes into the air as it accelerated one last time before pulling into its designated stop farther along Pennsylvania Avenue. I scanned the already bustling intersection and stepped onto the sidewalk.

Standing on the uneven surface, I picked a direction and walked. I noticed the visible markers of the challenges this underserved community faced. I walked past blocks and blocks of boarded-up townhouses and collapsing row houses. In the growing morning daylight I could see the intense blue sky through the blown-out windows and caved-in roofs. I walked past corner stores selling alcohol and cigarettes behind bulletproof glass. I saw teenage kids in oversize white T-shirts and baggy jeans dealing drugs on the corners, giving me suspicious looks as I nodded their way and walked past. I walked by their customers, drug addicts, huddled in abandoned doorways or dozing off, temporarily incapacitated.

I made my way down Presstman Street, past the three- and four-story Gilmor Homes public housing project. The buildings reminded me of the cheaply built migrant workers' housing in Umlazi. Both of those communities had been constructed by the government to house poor people of color so they could be concentrated in one area.

The more I walked and the more I observed, the more deeply I began to understand that nagging feeling. No, America wasn't as united as we claimed. The townships of South Africa, with their one road in and one road out to isolate Black people from white people, the forty-foot-high "peace walls" along Shankill Road in Belfast that separated Catholics from Protestants, and the heavily guarded border crossings with soldiers holding machine guns between Jerusalem and the West Bank all seemed so much more overt, but honest. The unspoken divide in America was stark and profound in its silence.

As I came to the corner of Presstman and North Fulton across from a liquor store and waited for the light to turn green, something started to come to me, something that until that moment I'd never understood before. In this part of the city, about two and a half miles from Baltimore's touristy Inner Harbor, in an area that didn't show up in any glossy brochures promoting city living and that most outsiders pretended didn't exist, I was at the center of an American township.

*An American township. Can that be true?*

Those words struck me with such impact that I had to pause for a moment. I was at the edge of the sidewalk, still waiting to cross the street, but when the light turned green, I didn't walk. I stayed there, letting those two words sink in.

*American township.*

Just like the townships in South Africa, I was in a place that had been built so that poor Black people would live in a segregated community that kept strict divides along race and class lines, while separating them from the resources and infrastructure offered in other communities. Though there were no walls or checkpoints, there was an imaginary line that as an outsider I had been made to believe I shouldn't cross. It was the same line that the poor people who lived here were made to believe they would not and should not ever make it past.

I waited on that corner through several more traffic light cycles, unable to move. The streets were full of cars and buses, and the noises of their engines filled the air. Just like in the townships, there was so much activity around me.

*How could I have missed this for so long? How could I have overlooked the glaring reality that there was something so close to a township in America?*

I vaguely remembered learning about redlining in my high school classes, but in the comfortable suburban bubble where I had grown up, I understood the issue to be more of a relic of the past than a reality of the present. But here was the legacy, right before my eyes.

I felt myself getting angry. I was angry for having gone this long without understanding this part of my city, for having unintentionally ignored the divide that existed here in my own country. I was also angry that these physical conditions even existed. With the affluence in Baltimore, the juxtaposition between this area and the one in which I had started the day was stark.

*My family has been a part of the real estate business in the city for generations, so why have I never seen this part of Baltimore? Why have they never taken me here? Why aren't they helping to build in this part of town?*

Somewhere in that anger came the realization of where to direct it. There was something about the ownership and control of land that was contributing to holding poor communities back. In Baltimore, I was just beginning to see this separation in the abandoned houses, the collapsing infrastructure, and what appeared to be a lack of resources. None of those challenges existed in the neighborhoods where I had grown up, yet they seemed to be crippling this part of the city by depriving people who lived here of the access to the choices and options that allow for upward mobility.

As I walked past a car wash that was bustling with shiny vehicles getting their summer coats of wax, that initial wave of anger began to subside. I had seen far worse conditions around the world than the ones in this neighborhood. I had also heard many people tell me it was a waste of time to discuss the problems or seek solutions. Yet I had also seen the enormous shifts when improvements were made and barriers crashed down.

I was quickly realizing that Baltimore was as foreign to me as Africa had been when I first showed up. I now understood that I hadn't fully grasped the city yet. I hadn't even begun to listen to people's stories. All the same, I started to feel a sense of possibility. I started asking myself the big questions.

*What is a new way to unite, empower, and serve here in America? If it isn't basketball, what would help level the playing field? Is it sports at all?*

I wanted to utilize my newfound confidence in my ability to listen to people on both sides of a divide. I wanted to take my understanding of the importance of empowering communities and apply it to my hometown.

*How can these underserved communities get a seat at the table in shaping their own trajectories and writing their own stories instead of enduring the ones society has imposed on them?*

As these thoughts and questions consumed me, I felt my pace quicken. I was hurrying back to my truck, an hour after I had first gotten out of it. I needed a pen and paper to write down some notes to explore the urgency growing inside me. While I had been observing that day, not actually listening, I had begun to feel the start of a connection to the people in this challenging environment, to people struggling to create something out of the hard concrete all around us. I was ready to figure out how I could play some role in empowering and uniting the city and country I grew up in. I felt an idea begin to explode in my heart.

# 9

## Purpose Refined

*"Reimagine what's possible."*

— QUENTIN VENNIE

I had no more small talk left in me. I had stalled as long as I possibly could. It was time to make my move.

I sat across from my dad at an unremarkable table at the Outback Steakhouse not far from my parents' home. The place was packed. I had hoped the chaos of the chain restaurant — the TVs blaring behind the bar, the loud conversations over drinks — would provide enough cover for the uncertainty and anxiety I felt.

*This isn't going to be an easy conversation.*

I took one final swig from the oversize glass that sat directly to the right of the soup bowl in front of me. As the cold Australian beer hit the back of my throat and rushed to my stomach, I braced myself for the big ask.

"Dad," I managed to blurt out in a shaky voice.

He glanced up at me.

"Can we ..." I paused as a bead of sweat rolled down my forehead. "Let's start a company together."

My heart thumped so loudly, I thought others in the restaurant might hear it.

"Let's start a real estate development company," I clarified.

I had become pretty good at pitching ideas I found exciting, and I had so much more I wanted to share with my dad, but for some reason I was petrified to ask him to team up with me. I was convinced the guy could move mountains and walk on water. He was my hero, the greatest and most humble man I had ever met. I couldn't get another word out.

Without saying anything, my dad leaned back a bit in the stiff wooden seat.

As endlessly kind as he had always been to me and others, the thought of being turned down by him was enough to overwhelm me. I fidgeted nervously on the other side of the table. My tongue was tied, my stomach in knots.

My dad took his napkin and spread it across his lap; still not a word.

I had planned to tell him about my experience on Pennsylvania Avenue and how it had reinforced my desire to help unite the world and bring people together. I wanted to share how there was something appealing about doing that work in my hometown of Baltimore. I needed to ask him for help in harnessing the power of real estate to do it. I had so much more I wanted to say, but I remained frozen.

He simply sat in silence, looking across at me with an expression of cool surprise on his face.

Even though it may have come as a shock to my dad in that moment, and even though I had been incapable of properly articulating exactly what I wanted to do, my draw toward real estate as a tool to unite wasn't random. Real estate was literally in my blood.

In 1972, when my dad was twenty-one years old, he went to work with my grandfather in the small business my grandfather had begun creating right after World War II. I grew up watching my grandfather and father develop this enterprise into a formidable family-owned real estate development company in Baltimore. The industry was different then. Brand-new cities were getting built. There was so much work to go around. The projects, and the capital behind them, were mostly local. While it was important to make money, the well-being of a community was front and center in many developers' minds. Accordingly, profits came primarily as a result of that focus.

Long before our dinner that night, my dad had told me stories of the early days. Back then, he would do deals off a handshake and a hug, without a single contract or signature. On hot summer afternoons, with his old brown mutt, Woody, riding shotgun, he would rent an ice cream truck and drive it around to the different office parks his company had built, surprising his tenants with an unexpected cold treat. The opportunities seemed endless, and the work was so pure. My dad's entire focus was on deeply connecting with and understanding his clients so that he could find the best ways to serve and support them. He wanted to provide them with efficient places to work, allowing them to concentrate on what they did best.

But when major national and international companies began to flood the markets with their capital, the real estate industry began to shift even further toward a focus on making as much money as possible as more and more companies jockeyed for a slice of an ever-shrinking pie. Too many developers did whatever they needed to do at all costs to move projects forward.

That competitiveness and shortsightedness weren't things my dad was interested in. The industry he had grown up with, the one he had fallen in love with because it let him serve others, had changed dramatically. It was no longer a world he wanted to be in. His real passion was in helping communities, which is why by the time I initially boarded that plane to South Africa, my dad had already embarked on an epic and life-changing journey of his own.

In late 2000, totally out of the blue and twenty-three years after he had first started in real estate, my dad was invited to become the chief operating officer of the struggling billion-dollar-a-year Baltimore City Public Schools. He had always been passionate about helping children. His college degree was in early childhood education, and he had briefly worked as a student-teacher in Baltimore City before going to work with his dad. Without a second thought, he took the position. Before I left the United States to help build PeacePlayers, my dad left the family business and everything he knew to jump headfirst into the administration of public education, a world he knew very little about. Armed with an insatiable determination, love, compassion, patience, and the ability to listen deeply in order to help others, my dad dove in headfirst to help reorganize what he believed was one of the most important institutions on our planet. Public education had the awesome responsibility of preparing the ambassadors of our future, our children, with the skills needed to live meaningful and productive lives.

In the days that followed my brief walk around West Baltimore, these highlights of my dad's career, especially of his desire to do meaningful work for the community, ran through my mind. During my time in South Africa, thoughts about real estate had come to me occasionally. Although it was the industry I was born into, I had always had an aversion to it. As a kid, and for as long as I could remember, I wanted nothing to do with the family business, or real estate itself for that matter. For one, I disliked the insanely long workdays that had taken my dad away from me and my three younger sisters. He would often leave the house before we woke up and come home well after we were asleep at night. Before I was old enough to be grateful that I had a dad who was driven and passionate about the work he did, I just simply missed him.

I also knew I wanted to be my own man and pave my own path without feeling like I had to follow directly in my father's and grandfather's footsteps. While I had tremendous love and respect for them, there was something too conventional for me about the work they did. I believed that my personal journey was meant to be different, and I needed to prove that to myself, which was one of the reasons I had ended up close to ten thousand miles away in South Africa. I was busy on a quest to become my own man, and I felt real estate would be a cop-out, the path of least resistance, the comfortable and easy choice that everyone expected me to take because it was there on a silver platter. Yet as much as I tried to push it away, there were moments in South Africa, and all the other countries where PeacePlayers worked, when it was impossible not to think about physical space, about land, and about how both had been used to oppress and divide. It was impossible not to think about my dad and about being a leader.

I had come to realize that real estate is the largest, most powerful, most expansive, most encompassing industry on our planet. It is inescapable. It touches every single one of us every single moment of every single day. And 99 percent of the time we don't even realize it. We take it for granted that it is there, and we never stop to truly understand it. We wake up in the morning in a house or an apartment, a place that someone, at some point in time, carefully thought out, designed, financed, built, and leased or sold. We walk and drive down sidewalks and roads that municipalities own, all of which have also been painstakingly planned and scrutinized so that they work in the most efficient way possible. We pop into cafés, we buy groceries in stores, we play in parks. All of that is connected through the amazing and mostly silent web of real estate.

Yet, even though it is the most connected industry on the planet, the control of land and the manipulation of it by a small handful of privileged people, companies, and countries has always been the largest divider of the human race. The real estate industry itself was born out of our desire to control land to gain power. In fact, that control can be traced back as the cause for so many major conflicts on our planet. While religious and racial differences have fueled many wars, often what countries and people are fighting for most is land and what happens on it. They fight for what we now call real estate. They fight for imaginary lines drawn in the sand by whoever has the biggest guns, the most money, and the greatest power at any given time.

As a result of its reach, connectivity, and power, real estate has set the stage for how our countries, our communities, and our people either do or don't work together. While governments make decisions that affect us all, often they use real estate as their tool to carry out their visions, whether just or unjust. White people used real estate to create townships in South Africa that isolated Black people from the rest of the world. Similarly, real estate created redlining in American cities, a practice that intentionally created segregated neighborhoods.

Real estate caused "peace walls" to be built in Northern Ireland, and it has been at the heart of the Israeli-Palestinian conflict.

If anyone could see how we might flip the traditional notion of real estate on its head to use land and physical space to empower and unite, it was my dad. I wished I could find a way to articulate all of what I had hoped our new company might do, but I couldn't, and he hadn't spoken once since the moment I had asked him to team up with me.

As I stared into my dad's eyes, it felt like a lifetime of relationships and transactions were flashing through his memory — the thriving companies he and my grandfather had built space for; the subcontractor parties with coolers of beer, which went on late into the night; the real estate crash in the early 1990s, which few companies survived; the corporate crab feasts in the summers. Unfortunately, the simplicity of those early days in real estate were long gone, which is why he had left the industry.

*And here I am selfishly asking him to jump back into a world that he had happily left behind.*

While I tend to be pretty impulsive, my dad has always been thoughtful and deliberate, a contrast that only contributed to the pressure building in my chest as each moment drew on in silence.

"Thibault," my dad started eventually. His serious tone immediately pulled my attention back to him.

I held my breath. We had never talked in a straightforward way about real estate up to this point. He wasn't the kind of father who came home and talked about work. He left it all in the office. Now, it was suddenly on our dinner table.

He paused for a second, straightened his navy-blue, button-down shirt, and then continued. "I'm not interested in starting another real estate company."

My heart sank.

I tried to hide the wince that shot across my face. I cleared my throat and adjusted in my seat, which creaked underneath me. I turned my eyes down toward my dinner roll, which was sitting like a lump on the side plate. It had taken every ounce of courage I had to even ask the question, and in a few short words my dad had confirmed that my plan wasn't worth the investment of his time or energy.

Having successfully completed his commitment with the school system a couple of years before, for all intents and purposes my fifty-five-year-old dad was retired and living the dream. He was happily married. He had enjoyed a spectacular professional career. He was comfortable financially. His four kids had left the house and were either finishing up college or out in the workforce.

*Of course he didn't want to go back into real estate.*

My mind started reeling about what I was going to do. This was my plan. I didn't even have a backup.

*I have a little bit of savings from South Africa but not the kind of money or connections needed to start a company on my own.*

I saw him shift slightly, and I braced myself for his kind letdown.

"What if real estate could play a role in helping inner-city kids get a better education?" he asked, his eyes lighting up for the first time that evening and his voice becoming animated as he sat up straighter in his seat. "What if we could reinvent what it means to be a real estate developer?"

I sat stunned as he continued.

"What if we focused on empowering the communities we work in and the tenants we work for?"

I felt myself lighten, the adrenaline rushing through my brain.

"What if we focused on rolling out the red carpet for those individuals and organizations who are doing the most important work in our cities?" He paused. "Let's say anyone focused on kids and education?"

Something magical was happening. He was opening my imagination to new possibilities. I was fresh off the experience of taking something the world had understood in one way — sports — and shifting it to achieve more socially conscious objectives. I felt strongly that evolutions like these were my generation's responsibility. I had seen it work with basketball and had wondered what else could be reimagined. Now my father was showing me an industry that was ripe for reinvention.

"What if real estate took the control out of the hands of those who were just looking to make money and disregarding community interests?" he asked.

Of course real estate development needed to be reinvented, and of course my dad knew that. He had watched the industry change dramatically over the last three decades.

"What if that control shifted into the hands of the people who would be living and working in the buildings?" my dad continued. "Into the communities we wanted to serve and the passionate neighbors who represented those communities?"

"What if it existed to help those groups bring their own ideas to life?" I added.

It was like we were daring each other to leap off the cliff together.

Often it's the things that seem the most broken that have the most potential for change. Perhaps real estate could be the link that pulls a city together, rather than something that further keeps people apart. It could be the catalyst that provides space for purpose-driven people to collaborate when placed all under one roof. It could be the industry that allows the people who actually live there to shape their cities and communities in ways that work for them.

"What if real estate could be a launchpad for inspiring new ideas to come to life?" I asked. "Especially for people who didn't know anyone would listen to their ideas in the first place?"

"What if that platform paved the way for ideas that would bring about massive social change?" said my dad.

The somber, anxious silence around our tiny table had been replaced by a powerful and invigorating conversation. My dad and I shot exciting ideas back and forth. It was as if we were condensing, out loud, all of our years of meaningful work to support people and communities into the early stages of a single, inspiring new idea.

This was exactly how I had felt when I first read that email that Bongani had sent, where he had dreamed of PeacePlayers mattering as much as Nelson Mandela being released from prison. It was that inexplicable feeling of being at the beginning stages of something so large and revolutionary that it could change the way the world turned — something so important, so critically needed at that moment in time, it could pave its own way forward.

"Instead of feeling constrained by real estate, what if people felt freed by real estate to focus their time and energy on what they were great at?" my dad asked.

The more he and I talked that evening, the more I understood that this was the cause I was looking for. This was the answer to the questions that had begun with my conversation with Simon on the plane out of South Africa. It was the answer to the questions I'd asked myself walking around West Baltimore. We were going to find a way to put the most powerful and connected industry in the world to work for and on behalf of all people.

"What if every building was built out of love? What if it was built to connect people and bridge the divides that we have spent too long pretending didn't exist?" I asked, finally.

Neither one of us had any idea what we were getting ourselves into. We had the beginning of a cause that deeply inspired us. With my dad's unwavering commitment to public education and to helping communities, and with my own naive and enthusiastic belief that the world could be creatively united, we had enough to get started.

# 10

## Can't/No as the Teacher

*"Impossible is just a big word thrown around by small men
who find it easier to live in the world they've been given
than to explore the power they have to change it."*

— MUHAMMAD ALI

Clouds hung low and heavy in the sky. My dad and I parked our car on an empty Baltimore street. A massive 100,000-square-foot factory building dominated the entire city block. Its four stories cast an enormous shadow over the row houses hugged up next to it. We got out of our car and inched uneasily closer. The sheer volume and deplorable condition of the looming structure consumed me. Like too many old factories in Baltimore's forgotten neighborhoods, it was abandoned. Every window had been blown out and boarded up with plywood. Bricks were falling out all over the place. There were even huge trees growing through decaying walls, window frames, and what little was left of the roof.

As we took in the surroundings — some vacant houses, an old tire shop, a lightless street with cars whose windows had been smashed out, and massive parking lots with overgrown, fifty-foot weed patches — I

120

tried to reignite the excitement I'd felt on the phone a few days earlier when I'd received a call with a tip about the place.

"I know you guys have been looking for a building," said my buddy Sam Polakoff on the other end of the line. "Think I spotted a decent option."

Sam was a local developer and hometown hero with an insatiable passion for connecting people and ideas. He continued. "Every developer in town has looked at this place, and none of them want anything to do with it. It's actually being foreclosed on by the bank. Some Washington, DC, developer couldn't get past the community and ran out of money. You might be able to step in and buy the note from the bank for a big discount and get control of the building."

"Awesome," I said, eager for a chance to find a site for our first project. I was also trying to hide the fact that I was so new to real estate that I had no idea what he meant by *foreclosed on*. "Where is it?"

"It's in Remington."

I paused, trying to pull up a map of the city on the computer.

"But don't let that deter you," Sam added, as if he'd noticed my hesitation. "I think it's perfect."

"Remington?" I repeated, unable to locate it. "Where's that?"

Turns out I had heard about that neighborhood, just not by name. When I was in high school, I spent my summers working for a commercial painting company whose offices were in this industrial, blue-collar community. The guys I worked for carried loaded guns with them because of the number of times they'd been jumped walking back to their cars at night.

Soon my dad and I were down in that small, glove-shaped northern Baltimore neighborhood, which was split between Districts 12 and 14. We were on the corner of Howard and Twenty-Sixth Streets, looking at the place Sam had recommended, and I began to understand why developers had passed not just on this building but on so many like it around here.

As we made our way down the trash-filled alley that ran behind the building, I wasn't even able to speak. By that point, my dad and I had looked at dozens of buildings all over town, but we hadn't found anything that worked for the unique concept we envisioned. The amount of patience required in the real estate world began to dawn on me. In South Africa, I got off the plane and started coaching. Several months into PeacePlayers, we were running a citywide tournament with thousands of kids. The same time had passed since we started our ambitious new company, but we had nothing to show for the work. I had begun to worry whether the exciting ideas we'd dreamed about over dinner were even possible. Seeing the skeptical look etched on my dad's face convinced me that he was wondering the same thing as we continued to circle the block.

Two rats the size of small dogs scurried past us and darted through a large opening in the brick wall. One poked its head back out of the hole, staring at us briefly before disappearing again into the dark. I couldn't help but think we had struck out again.

We rounded the last corner on the block. Down the sidewalk stood Sam and the representative from the bank who had come to open up the building for us. Sam's tall and skinny six-foot, three-inch frame towered over the shorter banker as they waved us over to what appeared to be the only working entrance to the old factory. Both men were dwarfed by the imposing building.

"You guys sure you want to go in this place?" asked the banker. He appeared to be struggling to read our expressions.

I couldn't tell if he was joking or not. The prudent response on our end was to say no and continue searching for smaller, more manageable sites. However, there was something intriguing about the massive structure and the apparent lack of human life or activity surrounding it. We had already come this far, so we asked to go in.

The banker turned to the huge wooden door. On it was a massive rusted chain that must have weighed fifteen pounds, not including the weight of the apple-size lock joining the two ends. He struggled with the key, cursing under his breath, until the latch finally clicked open. The banker then gave the door a solid kick with the heel of his black leather dress shoe, leaving a small mark on the heavy, worn wood.

The door swung open, startling a group of flying creatures. Wings flapped violently as they fled to an even darker part of the building. We didn't know whether they were bats or pigeons. Neither would have surprised us. The banker switched on the one flashlight he had brought and peered in.

*Are we really gonna do this?*

I scanned the rotting wood floor immediately in front of us, making sure there was nothing to trip on or fall through.

We walked into the hazy blackness, the lone flashlight beam like a tiny candle in the pressing dark. It looked like a bomb had gone off inside. The trickle of natural light that snuck through cracks in the boarded-up windows made the interior even more eerie than the exterior. The needle-thin rays of light spotlighted millions of dust and dirt particles that danced in the air. The floorboards were so rotten that we couldn't walk on most of them, and large parts of the roof had caved in. Inches of pigeon excrement blanketed the already filthy surfaces.

As we continued walking, it was clear that the building wasn't as abandoned as it seemed. People lived there, at least in spurts. Soiled mattresses were strewn throughout the dark space, each surrounded by a halo of empty booze bottles, convenience store food packaging, and heroin needles. Elaborate graffiti decorated every square inch of the interior walls, a twisted underground art show.

A passing freight train whistled by so loudly that it felt like it might shatter through the collapsing building. The track was less than a hundred feet from the front entrance. In the commotion, I could barely hear the banker.

"I can't believe you guys met me here," he shouted, cautiously tiptoeing forward, careful not to scuff his shoes. "Can you believe that this eyesore was built in 1890 and that it is still standing?"

He continued on, telling us that the factory was the original home of the H. F. Miller and Son Tin Can Company, the fourth-largest tin can manufacturer in the country at one point. The banker explained that the Miller building was part of what made Remington, all those decades ago, a booming factory town. The hundreds of row houses that surrounded the old factories and mills there came because the industry created great working-class jobs. When those hubs closed down and left the city in the 1960s, the jobs and people left with them. H.F. Miller himself vacated the building at that time, and with the exception of a handful of brief tenants, it had sat completely vacant ever since. According to the banker, for the better part of fifty years the building and Remington had been left to fend for themselves, suffering declining population, rising drug use, increased crime, and near-zero investment.

"This neighborhood is hopeless, and you wouldn't catch me here after dark," he said, pausing to turn back to face us for dramatic impact. "Ever."

Even though the banker kept going on like that, I stopped really listening. He had no doubt given this tour many times before but couldn't have seemed more out of place. His clean, pressed suit and carefully arranged hair — combed over to the side with a perfect part — contrasted with everything around us. For him, this was just another transaction. He was there to help clean up a bad loan his employer had made. There was no upside for him or the bank. They were going to lose money on this one.

While I realized that the building was totally trashed and uninhabitable, something strange was happening inside me. The more negative comments the banker made about the place and the neighborhood, the more my view shifted. It was as if he was looking at the building the same way basketball scouts had looked at Thabang's lack of ball skills. The problem in both cases — with the banker and the basketball scout — was that they were only considering the surface, skipping the deeper possibilities and future hope. As I walked further into the musty space and the banker's voice faded into the background, I realized that with this building, just like with Thabang, there was the potential here for something much greater.

■ ■ ■ ■ ■

Several months after that dinner with my dad, we had agreed to launch a company, called Seawall, that sought to reinvent the real estate industry. Choosing the name didn't require a full brainstorm session; the only thing we knew was that we didn't want it to carry our last name.

Right away, we began engaging closely with those we wanted to serve. Naturally, because of my dad's recent work in education and with the Baltimore City Public Schools, one of those first communities was teachers. Every year, our inner-city school systems across the country find themselves short thousands of teachers based on attrition — retirements and resignations. A midsize city, Baltimore alone needs to hire more than eight hundred new teachers every single fall just to open its doors. As a result of that demand, hundreds of teachers move to Baltimore each year. Many of them come through Teach For America or similar programs, like Baltimore City Teaching Residency. The shortage of teachers each year in Baltimore is so significant that the city school system would struggle to survive without those programs.

For years, in his role as the COO of the school system and as the chair of the local board of Teach For America, my dad met hundreds of young, well-meaning teachers just like Michael Tobass. Each year he witnessed these young adults showing up in Baltimore, usually for the first time, full of adrenaline, passion, and excitement. Months later he saw that energy being sucked out of too many of them as the harsh realities of inner-city public education set in.

In addition to the difficulties in the classroom, one of the many challenges for these teachers new to Baltimore was that from the time they first showed up to town in the summer ahead of a given school year, they only had a few days in the city to figure out where their schools were, how to get fingerprinted, where to go to the gym, what neighborhood to live in, and who to live with. As a result of these rushed decisions, combined with the general lack of quality affordable housing, too many new teachers were making poor living decisions because they just didn't know Baltimore.

They rented run-down houses or apartments. They found roommates online who were less than suitable. They moved to neighborhoods where just finding a parking spot after work could add another forty minutes to an already stressful day. These living conditions accelerated teacher burnout. Worst of all, those new teachers lacked that sense of community and sanctuary at home that is so crucial when we are faced with challenging situations.

The more we listened, the more we understood why they were having such a hard time acclimating. They kept telling us that it would be

amazing if there was a centrally located, safe, cool, funky, and affordable apartment building just for teachers. They craved a place where
they could live with like-minded people who inherently understood
what they had gone through on any given day, a place where they could
cry together and laugh together. In turn, this support would help them
keep one another focused on the importance of the task at hand: educating the future generation.

My dad and I had asked ourselves whether real estate could play
a role in helping to give the children of Baltimore City a better education. Our questions were starting to get more specific.

*How can real estate not just attract brilliant young teachers to Bal-
timore but actually help retain them? When they go through a code-red
lockdown for the first time, can we ensure they have the support system
in place outside of their jobs that will help them stick it out and use the
experience to make them better educators? Is it possible for their living
environment to empower them to avoid quitting on the kids who need
them the most?*

We knew exactly what we wanted out of one of our company's first
projects. We wanted to prove that real estate could play a role in supporting those passionate individuals who were actively bridging the
educational, socioeconomic, and racial divides society had created. We
at Seawall wanted to help ensure that the change agents of Baltimore,
like Michael Tobass, had an affordable, welcoming, and collaborative
place to live. If we could provide that, then they could focus all of their
energy on the kids and the classroom.

The more we listened, the more the plan continued to evolve. It became much bigger than just teachers. The idea was to create a building
where we could roll out the red carpet for anyone focused on kids and
education, whether that meant teachers in the classroom or those nonprofits that were quietly helping to underpin the success of the school
system.

Our trajectory had been set years before we even filed the paperwork to incorporate our company. The idea of affordable, welcoming,
and collaborative housing and office space for the people doing the
most important work in our cities wasn't ours. It already existed and

was on the tip of the universe's tongue. Our role was to help continue to bring that idea to life.

■ ■ ■ ■ ■

As I continued to creep along the creaking floorboards in the bowels of the Miller building, I began to see just how wrong I had been when I had first judged it. I was actually starting to fall for the building. The old four-story factory was gorgeous. Focusing the banker's flashlight into several corners, I began to see through the mess and the grime, noticing the exposed brick walls. I clicked off my light and saw how the tiny strands of natural light that had snuck into the building illuminated enormous timber beams and columns. I explored more, finding old fire doors and wide factory window openings. Every new pocket bulged with the potential to reimagine the building without ever losing touch with its beautiful, endearing history.

An hour after we had first walked through that massive wooden door, we finally made our way back out to the street. The building was so dark and intense that stepping outside felt like walking into a cascade of fresh air. I glanced over at my dad. He flashed a knowing smile. As my eyes adjusted to the daylight, I suddenly knew that the old Miller building could actually work in our effort to reimagine the real estate industry.

Over the next few days and weeks, we brought our family, our most trusted advisors, and some of our best friends for a walk-through of the building and the neighborhood of Remington itself. They all told us that what we were proposing made no sense and that we should run from this property as fast as we could. They told us we'd never get our investment back, that a for-profit company could never make affordable housing for teachers work financially, and that we'd never get enough people to live or work in the building or in the neighborhood.

My mom even threatened to not sleep in the same room as my dad for a week while we were exploring the opportunity. She knew that my dad wasn't a traditional developer, that he didn't have the expertise to put together a spreadsheet to analyze a deal. In his past work, which was mostly suburban, he had big teams around him who knew the ins and outs of the development industry. She was hesitant to see him putting up their savings, not to mention so much of his time, toward something so uncertain. After all, this was happening without the infrastructure that he had counted on for so many years.

"Donald," she said, "of all the senseless things you have done since we have been married, this would be the worst."

Coming from my mom, that was a sobering statement, because she had always encouraged us to push the limits and take risks. She was the one who had been the driving force behind Charlie, who was still living with my parents more than a decade later. When she had cried as I departed for South Africa, she had done so in full support of the journey. For her to question me and my dad on this one meant there was something almost insurmountable about the challenge in front of us.

While my dad had years of suburban real estate experience, I had none. Neither of us had ever done any urban development, let alone undertaking the adaptive reuse of a 117-year-old collapsing factory building in a part of town few people even seemed to want to visit. On paper, my mom was right. We had no business messing with that building. But we had fallen in love, so all the advice we got, well-intentioned as it was, went in one ear and out the other. It's almost like there was a larger force guiding us to that specific building, in that specific neighborhood, for one specific use, and at that specific moment in time.

As my dad and I met over the following weeks, we understood that pulling off this project would require a drastically different approach than traditional real estate development. We weren't just renovating an old building. If we tried to push this project to completion by ourselves, it would never work. We needed to build it in a way that allowed the people it would serve to take ownership of it. Like in South Africa, we needed to find our change agents, our community, and our team to help bring this idea to life. What we needed most was a pioneering group of teachers and nonprofits who might be daring enough to take an enormous leap of faith, and a community that was ready to join in.

# 11

# Group Ownership

*"Alone we can do so little; together we can do so much."*

— HELEN KELLER

A few pieces of trash scooted across the cracked asphalt parking lot. My dad glanced at his watch. I clicked open my cellphone.

It was 9:00 a.m. on the dot.

The Miller factory, our newly purchased behemoth of a building, stood imposingly beside us. We'd blasted out an invitation to hundreds of teachers in Baltimore. I began to worry whether our guests even knew how to find Remington.

"Any teacher interested in creating stunning class-A apartments for themselves at discounted rents should meet on the corner of Howard and Twenty-Sixth Streets in Remington on Saturday morning for a tour of an exciting project and a focus group to discuss it," our email had read.

Given the number of people the message had gone out to, we had anticipated seeing up to dozens of teachers lined up and excited to participate in the experience. The fact that no one was there yet was a reminder of the uphill battle the project faced.

My dad and I were no longer uncomfortable pulling up to the

abandoned warehouse. If anything, it was starting to feel like home. We knew every nook, cranny, and unsafe floorboard in the building, but our familiarity and optimism didn't always transfer to outsiders. In fact, those who lived closest to the site weren't sure if bringing it back to life was even possible.

"Morning, Randy," my dad said, waving at a man a few houses down the block.

Randy waved us down to his stoop. He sat there every morning, watching the streets like a hawk, and for good reason. Remington looked nothing like it had when he was a kid growing up in the neighborhood fifty years earlier. He didn't believe there was anything he could do to bring things back to how they once were, but he was right to assume that the presence of his massive 250-pound frame atop that front step for hours each day kept some things from getting any worse.

"Mornin', guys," Randy greeted us, his eyes scanning the largely quiet Howard Street to the north and the south.

The Remington that Randy remembered from his childhood was a place where families like his walked around without fear of violence or hassle. It was a place where people knew their neighbors. These days, Randy told us, sometimes folks were lucky in Remington if they even had neighbors.

"Y'all be careful in there today," he warned, pointing toward the old Miller building. "Saw some junkies climb through the fire escape last night, and I ain't sure they came out. I yelled at 'em and told 'em to beat it, but they had already disappeared inside."

Hanging with Randy for a little bit every day had become a routine on our visits to the building. We befriended him and many of the other neighbors. They were the best sources for the latest happenings.

"Not safe around here no more," continued Randy in his raspy voice. "Too much crime and drugs. No wonder this building is still empty after all of these years, but y'all better get to doin' somethin' with it quick because every day it gets worse."

My dad looked at me.

"That's the idea, Randy," I said, smiling. "We've got some teachers coming to check out the building today, actually."

· "Teachers?" Randy sounded incredulous.

I took a deep breath.

Randy then repeated what so many others had told us over the last couple of months: "The hell you 'spect teachers gonna think of a place like that?"

■ ■ ■ ■ ■

Just before 9:30 a.m., as Randy was telling another story to me and my dad about how Remington fell apart, the three of us noticed an old blue Honda Civic slowly inching down Howard Street. The driver peered out of the window. She looked lost. Then, as she saw the building itself, her expression changed. The car stopped, started slowly, and stopped again as it pulled over to the side of the road.

From where we stood, we could see a young woman with brown hair tied up in a ponytail. She was wearing a thick wool sweater, and she was sitting in the driver's seat, hunched over as if desperately checking for an address on a slip of paper. She looked up again out of the car window, appeared to double-check the address, and then stared back at the paper in her hand, as if in disbelief.

"That lady ain't from around here," Randy chuckled, temporarily abandoning his verbal barrage about Remington.

I walked across Howard Street toward her car, motioning for her to roll down her window as I got closer. Behind her thick glasses she looked even more unsure now with some stranger standing in the middle of the road gesturing at her.

She cautiously cracked her window.

"You here for the teacher tour?" I asked enthusiastically, trying my best to make her feel welcome with a genuine smile.

"I am. Is this the right place?" Her reluctant tone indicated that she was half hoping I would say no.

I introduced myself and explained where to park around the corner. After one more glance up at the building, she nervously putted along in that direction.

My dad and I told Randy we'd catch up with him later, and then we walked back toward the factory. On the way, a few more cars filed past us and parked. The drivers got out, and it also looked like most were checking their directions and the address twice to make sure they were in the right place.

"You got the email invitation too?" I heard one ask.

"Yep," another responded. "Isn't what I expected when I read 'exciting project,' but I think we're in the right place based on the directions."

For probably the first time in years, the abandoned Twenty-Sixth Street that flanked the old factory to the south had a caravan of ten working cars parked along its sides. Ten twenty-something-year-old teachers had shown up, each looking somewhat uncomfortable in the presence of this massive building bearing down on them in the chill morning air.

I was a little upset at the low turnout. I had expected one hundred teachers to come out for the tour. However, as the clock ticked on and it became clear that the group wasn't going to expand to meet my dreams, I accepted it. Ten was our number.

Each of the teachers had wandered hesitantly forward to form a small group at the southwest corner of the building. They were milling around and greeting one another, exchanging small talk. Few appeared to really know one another at that point, and they had clearly shown up as ten individuals with no sense of cohesion or unity. They also had no idea who we were or what we wanted from them. They were there with the vague promise of an affordable place to live.

My dad and I chatted with a few teachers as the group moved toward the door. Then, with an inspired burst of energy, my dad hopped up on the front step to officially welcome them. Decked out in a thick blue winter jacket, he blew once into his cupped hands to try to warm them up before starting into an impromptu speech I'll never forget.

His voice was steady and confident, the way it had been that night at the restaurant when he had told me he wasn't interested in starting a real estate company but that he was interested in helping to reinvent the industry as a whole.

"Thirty-five years ago, I was a first-grade teacher's assistant in the same public school system you currently work in. Five years ago, I was the chief operating officer of the Baltimore City Public Schools. Today I am the chair of the local board of Teach For America. In all three of those roles, I have had the honor and privilege of getting to see education from the inside out. Because of that, I have an enormous appreciation for the heroic work that each of you do every single day."

I had heard my dad's passionate speech about the importance of investing in kids and education what felt like hundreds of times by that point. He always said there was no greater economic investment than in the success of our future generations. Each time I heard it, I got chills up my spine, but this time, in front of a group of actual teachers, my response was different. As I watched him speak, I realized that his piercing blue eyes held fifty-five years of experiences and life lessons. He had earned those lessons in the trenches, and his eyes were now locked with the young, ambitious gazes of teachers who were in the process of learning lessons of their own. I was only a handful of years older than they were, and I knew what they were going through. From that point of view, everything my dad said suddenly seemed so much more relevant.

While the teachers were totally focused on my dad, I found myself surveying the unassuming group of millennials who had come out that morning. They were all recent college graduates. Baltimore was uncharted waters for them.

"We have invited you here today," continued my dad, "because for years while I was working in public education, I heard from your peers about how hard it is for you all to find quality affordable housing. We are hopeful that this building, reimagined by you, can provide all of the things you need so that you can focus one hundred percent of your energy on the kids and your classroom and not have to worry about where you live or who you live with."

The worried expressions of those ten teachers, who had clearly wondered what they were getting themselves into when they had first pulled up moments before, began to shift into smiles as my dad continued talking.

"The idea for this building — it isn't ours. It came from you guys, from your peers and colleagues, and it belongs to them and to you.

Our role is to help you bring the idea to life." He paused, and one by one he looked every young teacher in the eye, as if to emphasize how committed he was.

"If you like what you see today, then we want to invite each of you to join a working group that will help imagine, program, and design this project."

It was amazing watching my dad in action that morning. This moment hammered home the abstract idea that even though he really wasn't a traditional developer, he had the confidence and glow of a leader. Whatever uncertainty existed within him didn't slow him down. Instead, he presented the idea in a way that made it moldable. It was as if he used the uncertainty to build momentum. There was room for interpretation, a sense that everyone could be involved in the creation. The ability to strike the balance between leading with confidence and welcoming real participation was a kind of mastery I didn't feel I'd fully acquired yet.

My mind flashed back to my time in South Africa, Northern Ireland, Cyprus, and the Middle East, where, without realizing it at the time, we had successfully transferred power into the hands of the children, the coaches, the community, and the team — those who would be most affected by the work that was taking place. I now realized that approach had originated from my dad. It wasn't genetic, but it was deeply ingrained in my subconscious.

"Ready to go in?" he asked at last.

The cries of "Hell yeah!" and "Let's do this!" that came from the teachers were the sort you might expect from players after a motivational pep talk from a coach with the team trailing in the championship game at halftime. The chilly fall morning, the intimidating factory, and the garbage and broken glass on the street were no longer obstacles. Everything was now an opportunity. The drawbacks were suddenly possibilities for us to help create something to change the lives of teachers and, indirectly, the students they served.

I was more excited for this tour than any other we had given. For my entire life I had watched my dad enable and empower those around him by helping them understand that they too had ownership and authorship of what was being created. My dad never taught life lessons by lecturing. He taught us by just being himself. While none of this had ever clicked for me before, all of a sudden it smacked me right in the face. His way was the hard way, the long road, but there, on that abandoned corner with these random teachers and this collapsing building, it all started to make sense.

We distributed flashlights, kicked open the front door, and proceeded to give the same walking tour through the building we had given a dozen times by that point. We knew the place intimately now, pointing out our favorite graffiti, showing people where not to walk, and telling the story of the old tin can factory as if we had actually worked on one of the lines.

Right from the beginning, the energy on this tour was so different from the tours we had given to our advisors. Instead of looking for reasons the idea wouldn't work — which were readily available — these teachers looked for the reasons it would. They pointed out how cool the old brick looked, how high the ceilings were, and how convenient the parking was. Where others had cautiously inched through the building, these teachers appeared to be effortlessly skipping through it, practically leading the tour as my dad and I did our best to keep up. As we weaved through the maze of floors and old partitions, we talked briefly about helping them create a one-of-a-kind space, but for the most part we just listened.

When we reached the top floor of the old factory, several teachers, all of whom were fully engaged by this point, noticed the twenty-foot, rickety, wooden ladder whose top rungs seemed to disappear into the blackness of the massive ceiling.

"Where does that go?" asked one of them. He walked over to the foot of the ladder and squinted upward, shining his flashlight into the dark abyss above.

"That's the ladder to the old cupola," I explained. "Wanna check it out?"

By the time my words came out, he was already five steps up. The other nine teachers followed one after the other. Of course they were going to climb the terrifying ladder. This was their building now, and they wanted to see every square inch of it with their own eyes.

The passion that comes when someone takes ownership of an idea is palpable. It doesn't remove the obstacles that stand in the way of bringing the idea to life, but it does make them conquerable. These teachers weren't about to let rats, pigeon droppings, collapsing roofs, or buckling floorboards get in their way of making it to the top, nor would they let the decrepit nature of the building stand in the way of their quickly crystallizing dream.

Once we were all up in the cupola, we pulled off a sheet of plywood, which had been covering an old window, to let in more light. Then we walked out onto the catwalk surrounding the room. It hovered dangerously seventy feet above the street where we had parked our cars. The dilapidated, 200-square-foot room, which was perched high above the roofline, appeared to sway in the stiff morning wind, but the 360-degree views of the city were breathtaking and worth the courage it had taken to get up there.

We paused a few moments as we enjoyed the views, each of us tightly gripping the cold metal railing. No one spoke. We just stared off at the horizon, Baltimore's skyline standing proudly before us. These brave young teachers weren't afraid of a little risk. In fact, they seemed as inspired by people telling them that they couldn't or shouldn't do something as we were.

"This building is amazing," said one of the teachers, breaking the silence.

"Yeah, this is perfect," added another. "Imagine how cool this will be when we pull it off."

My dad and I stood there and listened as those ten teachers planned for the success of their project. They were no longer ten relative strangers who had wearily parked their cars on a deserted street. They were now a united group, perhaps even a family, who had taken the power my dad had offered them and were running with it. They too had fallen in love and were able to close their eyes and see how spectacular the finished product was going to be. They owned it.

■ ■ ■ ■ ■

We spent the next twelve months in numerous focus groups with those ten teachers. We grabbed pizzas for the group whenever we could, but there was no stipend. All of the participants were volunteers. They were doing it out of love and excitement about the idea. They met with our architects and helped design their apartments. Rent was among the most pressing issues. We asked the teachers what they thought an affordable and fair price would be for the apartments they had dreamed up, given what their salaries were. It's amazing how honest people are when you give them such a large responsibility. The rent they chose was $300 to $600 less than market rate at the time, but it gave us a baseline from which to go out and finance the project so that it would work for the teachers.

They also picked their own amenities, like a fitness center, a lounge, free gated parking, and our favorite: a resource room with high-speed copiers, staplers, hole punches, and everything else needed to prep for the next day's lessons. They told us that our idea of having a washer/dryer room was terrible, explaining that they were tired of living in dorms and wanted their own washers and dryers in their apartments. They even helped design the website in a way that would resonate with their peers.

As we were having these inspiring conversations with the ten teachers, we did the same thing with the dozen or so nonprofit organizations involved with kids and education throughout Baltimore. In these focus groups, we heard time and again how they were crammed into substandard office spaces that weren't built for them or their needs because it was all they could afford. We heard the frustration of how they were all focused on the same thing — supporting students and the school system — but since they were spread out all over town, impromptu opportunities to collaborate and share resources and ideas were nonexistent. We heard that they all needed conference rooms and training facilities, but that they didn't need them all the time. They wanted to share that kind of space.

Through all these conversations, I marveled at how my dad led. He was so good at drawing people in and making them feel both involved and special. He had invited everyone to feel like they owned both the idea and the project from the very beginning. Most important, he had flattened any perceived hierarchy that would have otherwise existed in a startup organization. This wasn't Donald Manekin, former chief operating officer of the Baltimore City Public Schools, telling these teachers what he wanted them to do for him. This was Donald Manekin, passionate believer in people's ability to make this world great, turning those teachers into the decision makers and setting it up so that he worked for them, not the other way around.

My dad had made it crystal clear that this wasn't his project and that it would never be successful or useful to those teachers and nonprofits unless they grabbed the idea and carried it forward themselves. He also transformed himself from a real estate developer, which many people are suspicious of, into a listener and an enabler. He wasn't there pushing his own agenda for his own benefit. He was there because he had seen that a brilliant idea, one that would take great care of the people he believed were doing the most important work in our city, was ready to be brought to life. He knew he couldn't do it alone, nor did he want to, so he began to allow the project to grow naturally.

With the incredible buy-in from the teachers and nonprofits, the momentum needed to make the impossible possible was well underway. The end users took ownership of the project and made it their own. They were the ones who were molding it to meet their needs.

# 12

## Inside Looking Out

*"An individual can't create anything itself.*
*All of our dreams come true·with the cooperation*
*and cocreation of other souls."*

— HINA HASHMI

My dad and I were seated in the back of an old cinder-block building on Huntingdon Avenue that had been recently converted into a church. Bad linoleum tiles covered the floor, fake wood paneling from the 1980s sagged on the walls, a well-used drum set sat perched on top of a homemade plywood stage, and regal purple curtains covered the windows. The one-story building had once been the home to an auto parts store before they, like many other stores in Remington, had gone out of business. A small thirty-member Baptist church congregation had bought the building for practically nothing, and they were using it for their weekly services.

We waited for our turn to be invited forward. This type of neighborhood community meeting was a first for me in the United States. I briefly glanced over at my dad for reassurance; he appeared as calm as ever. There were about fifty other people in the church with us that evening, including Randy and several of the other neighbors we had met as a result of spending all that time in Remington.

There are crucial junctures in every project that can turn it from a dream into a reality or force it back to the world of ideas from which it came. For something we were thinking of tentatively calling the Center for Educational Excellence, our very first community meeting was one of those junctures.

We sat on folding metal chairs facing the front of the room. Everyone had come to get their monthly dose of community updates from the United Citizens of Remington (UCR), one of the two rival community associations active in Remington. People familiar with Remington had told us that we were walking into the proverbial lion's den. They said that no developer had ever come out of a UCR meeting intact. As a matter of fact, many people in Baltimore cited the UCR — not the crime, vacancy, or drugs — as the single greatest reason why development was stalled in Remington.

Members of the community had come out that evening to hear more about the swirling rumors of the potential redevelopment of the old Miller building. The building was by far the biggest eyesore in the community and most people living in Remington wanted to see it redeveloped into something positive.

By this point, we had come to understand — through our many conversations on the streets during our first few months exploring the old factory — that we weren't the first to try to redevelop the Miller building. Years before, two real estate developers from Washington, DC, and northern Virginia had made runs at it and tried to convert the building into high-end apartments. They came in and told the people of Remington what they were going to do without ever giving the community a chance to weigh in and provide feedback. That less-than-inclusive approach to development, coupled with the UCR's strong opposition to the idea, created a lose-lose situation.

It was my understanding that the first developer fought the UCR for two years before he lost the building and ended up in jail for tax evasion. The second guy put up a similar struggle for three years before declaring bankruptcy and losing the building back to the lender.

That was when we had eventually bought it and, oddly enough, we felt galvanized by how a different approach might just be the difference between success and failure. The lingering nervousness swirled only around getting the UCR on board, a task so many others had told us was impossible.

From what I could tell, the previous developers had not included the community in the process. In that respect, they deserved to be run out of town. It was time now to invite the community to take ownership, to let them help mold the idea into something that worked for them too, which is what my dad and I were doing there that evening.

Promptly at 7:00 p.m., Earl Bell, the president of the UCR, stood up in front of the crowded room and called the meeting to order. We had met with Earl several times by then. He had a reputation of being firmly anti-change, which explained how hard he had fought previous development projects. With us, however, he seemed genuinely engaged and excited about the opportunity to work together on what was now known as Miller's Court, the name of the building that would hold the country's first Center for Educational Excellence.

Several routine announcements were made as Earl paced in front of the crowd. A firefighter got up and explained how important it is for people to check the battery on their smoke detector. A police officer from the Northern District answered questions about a string of robberies in the area that the police department was tracking.

Then Earl turned to us. I swallowed hard, mentally preparing for our turn on the podium. While Earl had been nothing but helpful to us so far, it was clear he took his title and role as president of the UCR very seriously.

"Many of you have followed the numerous redevelopment attempts of the old Miller building on Howard Street," Earl began, adjusting his glasses on his nose as he glanced over at us. "We have all watched it deteriorate over the years as it has continued to sit vacant and cause safety issues in the community. Well, it finally looks like there is a path forward for the old factory. I am really excited to introduce you to Donald and Thibault Manekin, who are here to tell us about their plans for the building."

Once up at the front, my dad thanked Earl and began.

"We are honored to be here with you tonight. We want to start off by saying that we understand that this is your community and that we intend to be neighbors here and not guests. As Earl said, we are excited to talk about the Miller building."

My dad then stepped forward and did what he does so well. He outlined the plans for the project and talked about the teachers and education-focused nonprofits who had come up with the idea and would benefit the most. He acknowledged that the community members were the real owners of the building, that they had been staring at the decaying factory for decades, and that they needed to have a seat at the table in dreaming up what it could become. His words and body language were soft and engaging. He leveled the playing field by giving ownership and authorship back to the people.

When he was finished, hands flew up all over the room as everyone scrambled to get a comment in. People shouted out how great an idea it was that these teachers and nonprofits had come up with. My dad pointed to a woman in the front row who had patiently raised her hand.

"Thank you so much," she said. "This is much more appropriate than the fancy apartments those other guys tried to build."

Another gentleman stood up and described the collapsing factory as the most significant thing holding Remington back.

"If you and those teachers fix it up," he continued, "it will make Remington so much safer, and it will be the beginning of so many more great things to come for our neighborhood."

Amid all the praise for the teachers and for the idea, a young man in jeans and a T-shirt raised his hand and confidently stood up. He looked bold and defiant. The serious expression on his face made me worry that the mountain of compliments the project had just received was about to come crashing down.

"This is great and all," he started, staring right at my dad, "but what about putting a café on the corner of Howard and Twenty-Sixth Streets? There is no place to get a decent cup of coffee or a healthy sandwich here in Remington."

*A coffee shop in the Miller building?*

We nodded as we listened, but I couldn't help but shoot the idea down in my head.

*How terrible is that idea?*

"If you don't include a café or some sort of retail shop, then only people who live or work in the building will ever get to go inside once it is complete," he continued. "The café can be the place that allows all of us who have lived here forever to actually use the building. It could be the gathering place that actually helps bring Remington together. My only request is that it be locally owned. If you bring in a Starbucks, we'll throw rocks through the windows at night."

The crowd loved the idea of the coffee shop. The rock through the window comment had drawn laughter from the crowd, but it was clear to me that there was a bit of truth to that threat. Another wave of excitement blanketed the tiny packed church as people nodded their heads in approval.

Still, I resisted internally.

*Is this guy talking about a different corner than the one we knew?*

The intersection of Howard and Twenty-Sixth was not a place for retail. It was dark and intimidating. I couldn't ever imagine anyone walking there to get a cup of coffee. Plus, we had already planned to put a two-bedroom apartment on that corner. Replacing it with a coffee shop seemed far too risky financially.

Then it hit me.

The negative talk in my head — the language of *can't, won't, couldn't* — was really just different ways to say no. Just as our advisors had told us they couldn't see how this project could work, I didn't see how a coffee shop made any sense in this building. It reminded me of approaching the principal at Clifton School in Durban with the idea of a white school visiting a Black school in the township to play a game of basketball together. The idea was shot down right away. It didn't make sense based on what we knew today. It wouldn't work — no.

*Now I'm doing the same thing with this coffee shop idea.*

The community had spoken, and they were beginning to take ownership of the idea. If they believed a coffee shop was needed, then who were we to stand in their way? We thanked the young man for the suggestion and promised him we would look into it.

Seeing that there were no other comments, Earl thanked us for the presentation and concluded the formal part of the meeting. We ended up staying for another hour, talking with neighbors and answering more of their questions. People were thrilled, and the feedback was amazing. It's hard not to get excited about creating great and affordable space for people who are doing the most important work in our city. As my dad and I drove home that evening, we once again were carried forward by the energy and enthusiasm for the project, this time from the community.

■ ■ ■ ■ ■

Over the course of several more meetings, it became clear how badly Remington wanted to have this project. The same community that had fought tooth and nail against development was now actively participating in the redevelopment to make sure that it happened. For the next few months, we gave the neighbors tours through the old factory, adjusted the plans to include a coffee shop, and continued to listen.

Little by little we built up trust and developed solid relationships. As my dad had said, our whole philosophy was to come in as neighbors and not as guests, as contributors, as a company whose profit only came about as a result of harmonious and altruistic connections with the community and the end users. This wasn't just our building. It was also the community's and the teachers', and it was up to them to determine and bless what it would become.

Earl and the UCR, the group everyone had told us would never support any development in Remington, provided the city of Baltimore with this heartfelt letter of endorsement:

Dear Madame Chair,

The United Citizens of Remington (UCR), acting through our Board of Directors, is pleased to inform you that we heartily support the plan of Seawall Development for rehabilitation and adaptive reuse of the historic Miller Building at 2601 N. Howard Street.

Remington residents have waited a long time for something good to happen with this building. The success of the project is very important to the community.

Therefore, we are happy to respond to developer Donald Manekin's request for this letter of support from the UCR.

Sincerely,

Earl Bell, President

With Remington's support, the only thing we had left was to figure out how to pay for it all.

# 13

# Effective Leadership

*"I often say that leadership is deeply personal and inherently collective.
That's a paradox that effective leaders have to embrace."*

— PETER SENGE

A few months after those first tours with the teachers and those first
community meetings, my dad and I stood bundled up at our usual
meeting spot on Twenty-Sixth Street in front of the Miller building,
waiting for our next guests to arrive. A bone-chilling East Coast freeze
had kept people inside for weeks. A layer of snow blanketed the sidewalk, and the plywood from the boarded-up windows shook violently
as arctic winds howled by in massive gusts.

"Here they come," said my dad, nodding his head in the direction
of two men walking toward us down Howard Street.

*Is that really Bart Harvey?*

The men moved quickly down the snow-covered sidewalk, wearing huge winter jackets, wool hats, and thick gloves.

*It can't be.*

Bart Harvey was a national legend. In my mind he was seven feet
tall. I had heard about Bart my entire life. He was often described as
a folk hero — a banker for the poor who helped build hundreds of

thousands of units of affordable housing across the country. Neither of the approaching silhouettes fit the larger-than-life image of how I imagined Bart would look in person. I strained my eyes through the bitter cold to try to make out any details about the two bundled-up souls who were now crossing Twenty-Sixth Street.

*Which one is Bart?*

Both my dad and I knew that if the idea for the Center for Educational Excellence was going to come to life, it would need an amazing team that believed so deeply in the purpose and concept that they too would take ownership and authorship the way so many others had already done. Like our board did for PeacePlayers, the right team of guardian angels could guide us forward through these uncharted waters.

The taller of the men walked right up to my dad, and the two of them exchanged a powerful hug.

"Good to see you, Bart," my dad said as they embraced.

While not quite the giant I had imagined, Bart, with his broad shoulders and six-foot, one-inch frame, had a commanding presence.

"You must be Thibault. I've heard so much about you," said Bart. He released himself from my dad and turned to greet me.

I forgot about my frozen feet and fingers, eagerly shaking Bart's hand.

Bart was a protégé of the late Jim Rouse, whose Rouse Company had literally built cities from scratch based on the idea that real estate could be a tool to make communities more equitable. Together, Jim and Bart had paved the way for companies like Seawall to exist. I had recently read Jim's five-hundred-page biography, *Better Places, Better Lives*, practically in one sitting. Jim had passed away, and Bart was proudly carrying his legacy forward.

"Donald and Thibault, meet Joe Wesolowski," continued Bart, warmly introducing the slightly shorter man by his side. "Joe is a good friend and colleague who has never met a challenge he couldn't overcome." Joe's eyes were all that I could see between the winter hat, scarf, and massive jacket. As he reached out to greet us, Joe pulled the scarf away from his face, revealing his warm smile.

Bart ran Enterprise Community Partners, and Joe was a key leader in Enterprise Community Investments, its financing entity, which were both community development organizations Jim Rouse had helped create. Among other things, they specialized in creatively financing complicated but impactful projects. We had invited them to tour the Miller building to learn whether Enterprise could help bring the teacher-housing idea to life. If nothing else came of this, simply having Bart Harvey in Remington was a huge deal.

*But what if he doesn't like the building, or the neighborhood? What if he can't see what the teachers and nonprofits could see? What if he hates the idea?*

"You guys ready to do this?" asked my dad, unlocking the rusty chain and forcing the massive door open by leaning into it with his shoulder.

We gave each of our guests a bright-blue flashlight and proceeded with the tour.

It felt even colder inside than outside. The wind somehow managed to find its way through every crack in the building, stirring up dust and the few snowflakes that had gathered along the walls in the dark space. While my dad led the tour, I examined Bart and Joe's facial expressions as they navigated the soiled mattresses and curling floorboards. I searched for any signs of disappointment or indifference.

*Are we wasting their time?*

Neither gave anything away as we led them on a condensed version of the tour, making sure not to skip the fourth-floor cupola. Like the teachers, Joe and Bart had no problem with climbing that ladder to take in the views. We were too bundled up and it was too cold to converse fully, but the lousy condition of the building didn't require much explaining.

Twenty minutes later we were back out on the street. I fed the chain through the door handles and pulled the hanging ends together on the massive lock.

"Let's find a place to warm up and chat," said my dad, gesturing away from the building with his gloved hand, his breath shooting out of his mouth in a puff of white in the freezing air. "There's a nice little diner a block down the street."

As the four of us moved toward the warmth of the restaurant, eager for something to thaw our frozen bodies, I wondered what was going through Bart's mind.

*What if he doesn't want to be bothered with a risky project in a wretched warehouse? What if Bart, a leader I respect from the bottom of my heart, thinks it's a bad idea? What if he can't help us fill the massive $16 million gap in the financing?*

■ ■ ■ ■ ■

By the time we had invited Bart and Joe to visit, we were already a few months into peeling back the complicated layers that came with the project in the abandoned warehouse. Most developers do their due diligence before they buy a building, but our excitement about the opportunity had propelled us forward faster than expected. In truth, we were doing it all a bit out of order for a traditional real estate project — something I knew only whiffs about at the time on account of my dad keeping family and business separated as I was growing up. In fact, even he hadn't realized that the building would require special zoning variances, or that our parking plan wasn't fleshed out, or how the environmental testing process worked. There were so many things we could have better prepared for but, somehow, despite our recklessness, the project was moving along.

The teachers, nonprofits, and the community were all in. While unconventional, an epic plan for what we thought would be the coolest factory conversion in the world had emerged. Now all that was left to do was design, build, and — most important — pay for the project. The first two things we believed we could figure out, but we had no idea how to finance the idea.

Thankfully, while my dad didn't have millions of dollars in liquidity to pump into the project, we did have other advantages. Because he had been cautious with his finances over the years, we were able to convince Howard Bank, a small community bank, to give us a $3 million short-term loan to buy the building. A loan of that size would have been impossible for me, a young developer with zero experience who had never built a building before, because all I had to lean on was my modest savings from living on the cheap while working with Peace-Players. But it wasn't my dad's balance sheet that got us the meeting with Bart for a shot at really funding Miller's Court; it was his reputation. That was an advantage of unquantifiable value for a new company in this space.

After we bought the collapsing structure, we discovered the cost of fixing it up was actually about seven times the cost of buying it: $22 million. That was $21 million more than we thought our first Seawall project would cost, considering that we had initially figured we might begin with little row-home conversions for a couple of teachers. The cost of the development wasn't even the biggest problem. Because we were committed to keeping the teacher and nonprofit rents so low, the project could only support a $6 million permanent bank loan for the actual development. That meant we had a $16 million bust in our model with no real idea of how or where we would find the money to fill it.

Before we met with Bart, I thought back on all the meetings Bongani and I had arranged to raise money for PeacePlayers. We had believed — perhaps naively — that if we developed the program inclusively, the momentum would carry the idea forward and we would have no trouble finding the financial and programmatic support we needed to grow and strengthen the organization. Of course, it didn't happen right away. It built slowly over time.

To me, $16 million didn't seem like a slow build. The teachers didn't have five years to wait around for us to ramp things up. The situation was also different from PeacePlayers. Seawall wasn't a nonprofit organization that could go out and get grants to plug funding gaps. This was the private sector. The deal had to pencil out economically if it was going to move forward.

Still, the same naive hope began to pop up for me in Remington as it had done in South Africa. When I got off the plane in Durban for the first time, we had $8,000 in the PeacePlayers bank account. We had no real idea where any more money was going to come from or how to build a sustainable organization. What we had was an unwavering belief in the idea that sports could unite war-torn countries and an unparalleled commitment to making it work.

When my dad took over as COO of the Baltimore City Public Schools, he had no experience in academic administration or running a billion-dollar school system plagued by massive shortfalls. He was faced with an enormous deficit, without a clue about how to begin erasing it. However, he did know that the kids of Baltimore deserved a great education, which meant that the teachers who were committing their lives to educating those kids needed to be cared for too.

There were significant obstacles with the Miller project, but we didn't let them faze us. They motivated us. We were not at all intimidated by that sticker price, the massive gap in our funding, or our lack of knowledge about how to renovate this old collapsing factory. In the end, there was one simple question, and it wasn't about $16 million.

*Would Bart Harvey want to be the guardian angel for the Miller building?*

■ ■ ■ ■ ■

The warm air smacked us in the face as soon as we walked into the New Wyman Park Restaurant. The tiny neighborhood breakfast spot had been built into the first floor of a corner row house. It oozed Baltimore charm and authenticity. John and Bruce, the two cooks, were at their usual stations, sandwiched between the small counter where the regulars ate and the enormous eight-foot-long griddle where they flipped eggs, sausages, pancakes, and scrapple.

"What's up, boys?" called out Bruce, wiping his hand on his grease-covered apron before extending it toward us for a fist bump.

One by one, we reached between the regulars — who sat on their usual stools, reading the paper, talking sports scores and local politics — to tap our knuckles against Bruce's.

Even though it was called New Wyman, there was nothing new about it. From the dim glow of the overhead menu display to the faded off-white linoleum countertop and tables, the diner felt like a relic of the past. What it lacked in size and modern amenities, it made up for in heart. The locals who populated this cozy spot were among the nicest we had met in Remington. It had become a classic hangout for us, and the unpretentious wooden booths felt like home.

Donna greeted us with menus, and after giving my dad and me a hug, she walked us back to our usual spot, the fourth booth down along the frosted street-side window. The steaming coffee came shortly after we sat down.

"Thanks again for making the time to visit, especially in these conditions," my dad started. "You know us, and we've talked about the vision for Seawall to empower and unite. We've also talked about our idea to turn the Miller building into the Center for Educational Excellence. We know this is going to work, and the pieces are falling into place, but our biggest obstacle right now is how to pay for it."

My dad paused to take a sip of his coffee.

"You guys are the best in the world at making the impossible happen," he continued. "We love the idea, and we want to help bring it to life."

Then my dad calmly stated the problem.

"There is a sixteen-million-dollar gap in the financing for the project. What do we do from here?"

It may have taken longer in real time, but in my memory, Bart's answer came almost immediately.

"You've got nothing to worry about."

My dad and I shared a brief glance of mutual disbelief. What did he mean?

Then Bart and Joe came in full force. They told us about New Markets Tax Credits, a federal program designed to help spur commercial investment in low-income communities. They schooled us on Historic Tax Credits, another way the government provides financial incentives to encourage the reuse of our country's beautiful old buildings. Their previously stiff and frozen movements became more animated as their excitement rose and the coffee kept coming.

I frantically scribbled notes, my fingers beginning to defrost. It was effort to try to record all the knowledge they were dropping. To be sitting across the table from a legend like Bart Harvey was surreal in and of itself, but to watch his eyes light up about the project's potential was even more powerful.

For almost two hours, as we ate our fluffy hotcakes, crispy bacon, and soft omelets, my dad and I took in all the expertise that Enterprise had in turning a dream like the Center for Educational Excellence into reality.

Our doubts melted away. Even though no agreements were signed that morning, the weight of the $16 million gap began to lift. Of course Bart loved this idea. He had spent his career fighting to provide housing for America's most underprivileged people. The idea of serving and protecting the underdog, in this case teachers and nonprofits, was near and dear to his heart.

By the time Donna slid the bill onto the table, it had become very clear that Enterprise was going to make sure not only that this project succeeded, but also that they were intimately involved in it. The team who would join the educators and the Remington community in seeing this project through to completion was starting to take shape.

■ ■ ■ ■ ■

In less than a week, the miracles began to take place. Bart and Joe immediately began introducing us and the idea to local and national circles that — even with my dad's connections — we hadn't had access to and, in many cases, hadn't even known existed. Having Bart and Enterprise believe in Seawall was like having Nelson Mandela's foundation back PeacePlayers: their vote of confidence was the tipping point that gave the project great credibility and allowed it to move forward.

We already had a spectacular architect and general contractor on board, both of whom specialized in the adaptive reuse of historic buildings. What's more, even though Seawall had no track record and we had yet to build a building, Marks Thomas Architects and Hamel Builders each donated their time during the early exploration phases of the project. They too had become committed to the idea of taking great care of teachers and nonprofits. After Bart's endorsement, the phone began ringing off the hook with others who wanted to join the team. People wanted to be a part of the first ever Center for Educational Excellence.

Banks, tax credit investors, lawyers, and accountants, very few of whom we had had any luck in finding before that meeting with Bart and Joe, came out of the woodwork to help piece together the opportunity and navigate the complex tax credit financing that Enterprise had turned us on to, which ended up contributing $14.5 million toward filling our gap. In the end, even the state of Maryland and the city of Baltimore jumped in by making low-interest loans of $1.5 million to help erase the last of the deficit.

Within a few months' time, the $16 million hole in the capital stack was gone. The team of investors had the same sense of pride and ownership in the idea as the teachers, the nonprofits, the community of Remington, my dad, and I did. It was as much theirs as it was everyone else's. With each day that passed, the project gained more momentum. Hundreds of inspiring individuals joined in and made significant contributions toward moving the idea forward. It got to the point that people felt left out if they weren't a part of it. Even my mom had become a believer, lovingly bragging about how cool the project was around the house with Charlie and at dinner parties. She beamed with so much pride about what my dad and I were working on that he joked that she was now taking credit for the idea.

■ ■ ■ ■ ■

In the summer of 2008, a couple of months before Lehman Brothers collapsed and the world's financial markets spun into free fall, we managed to close financing and started construction on Miller's Court.

Enormous excavators, powerful Bobcats, and lumbering dump trucks swarmed into Remington. Crews of abatement professionals in white hazmat suits spread throughout the building, covered from head to toe so they wouldn't be affected by the lead paint, asbestos, and other contaminants they were systematically cleaning out of the decaying factory. Masons scaffolded the entire building and artistically repointed every square inch of the facade, an exercise that would take close to ten months to complete. The plywood came out of the boarded-up window openings and was slowly but surely replaced with ten-foot-tall windows that poured massive amounts of beautiful sunlight into the building for the first time in decades. News reporters, both local and national, showed up with TV cameras and photographers, and each attempted to tell the amazing and heartwarming story that was unfolding.

As construction got underway, the neighbors watched the building at night like hawks. There were several occasions when a would-be thief entered through an open window late in the evening only to find Randy, several other pissed-off neighbors, and the police waiting for him when he got out. Those neighbors would proudly call us on our cellphones in the middle of the night to let us know they had caught someone messing with *their* building.

Three months after the crews first showed up, and nine months before we finished construction, the building was 100 percent leased. With the exception of the Miller's Court website, which the teachers had helped to design, we never spent a dollar on marketing. We didn't need to. Those ten teachers led the way for the ninety tenants that followed, with the word spreading to hundreds more. It had extended far past any network we had or any advertising reach that money could buy. The word went viral because the end users felt like they owned it.

The same thing happened with the office space. Nearly all of the nonprofits who had helped us think through the idea had signed leases. We quickly found ourselves with no space left.

For me, the excitement about the success of this powerful idea was paired with a huge sense of relief and stability. During the two-year process, Lola and I had gotten married, and we were expecting our first child. All the while, I was still living off savings. Developer fees don't find their way into bank accounts until financing closes. My dad and I were bootstrapping the whole thing, so we weren't taking salaries from money the company didn't have yet. Lola supported and believed in our work, but there was considerable pressure on my shoulders to deliver as someone starting a new family. Once the financing had closed and the funds were in the company's account, I finally was able to catch my breath.

During the summer of 2009, we put the finishing touches on Miller's Court and opened the doors to our residents. The adaptive reuse of that once-forgotten historic 100,000-square-foot factory was spectacular, and the corner of Howard and Twenty-Sixth Streets was glowing for the first time in decades.

The governor of Maryland, the mayor of Baltimore, the CEO of the school system, the president of SunTrust Bank, the president of the city council, and several other distinguished guests came to the opening. I was asked to give a speech on the stage they set up for the occasion.

In front of me was a crowd of more than three hundred people, who had gathered to help cut the ribbon. The crowd was made up of neighbors, teachers, employees of the nonprofits who would be moving in, CEOs, plumbers, electricians, accountants, carpenters, roofers, lawyers, employees from the permit office, our family members, and dozens of others. These were the unsung heroes, many of whom had worked on the site through freezing-cold winters and blazing-hot summers. Though their names would never be associated with the building, together they had carried the project forward as if it was their own. Which it was.

To my right, where there had once been a forest of overgrown weed trees, was a brand-new parking lot surrounded by fresh mulch and lush green landscaping. To my left was the newly rehabbed building, which looked exactly like it must have appeared 119 years earlier, when it was first built. Only this time, instead of a state-of-the-art tin can manufacturing facility, it had become home to so much more. The community had come out in full force to see their idea come to life. Earl Bell, the president of the United Citizens of Remington, stood in awe among them. The impossible had happened, and everyone had played a part.

■ ■ ■ ■ ■

After we ran out of space at Miller's Court, teachers and nonprofits on our waiting list started asking us to build a second Center for

Educational Excellence. Soon after those conversations, we stumbled across another forgotten mill building less than a mile away. We assembled the same team to replicate what had worked so well the first time. The teachers, nonprofits, community associations, web designers, lenders, architects, contractors, and city and state agencies all rolled up their sleeves again and helped us push Union Mill across the finish line. The two projects eventually received many local and national awards, including being recognized by the Obama White House as a Champion for Change.

Two years after the grand opening of Miller's Court and three months after the opening of Union Mill, I was on a train with my dad and Evan Morville, who had joined us shortly after Seawall got started. Evan helped run our development projects and had become one of my closest friends. That day we were heading up to New York City to see the senior leaders at Teach For America. They had invited us up for a meeting, which they said was important.

"Guys," started Matt Gould, the head of their real estate team, as we settled into their Manhattan conference room. "Miller's Court and Union Mill have blown us away. We didn't really believe you when you first pitched the idea. Those two projects have made it so much easier for us to recruit and retain both teachers and staff in Baltimore. You guys were right, and these projects have far exceeded our expectations."

We waited for the "but."

"And," continued Matt, "we want to work with you to replicate this model in all twenty-six cities across the country where Teach For America is working."

We were speechless. It had felt miraculous to pull off the first two teacher-housing projects in our hometown; the thought of doing twenty-six of these all over the country was massive. We were honored, petrified, and excited — all at once. Most of all, we were proud that the end user — the Teach For America community and those they impacted — had developed such a sense of ownership of the idea that they would even think of doing more of these.

As the Amtrak train sped back to Baltimore later that afternoon, Evan, my dad, and I spent the entire ride talking about what had just happened and how enormous the opportunity was. And that was just the beginning; later that week we got a call from our partners at Enterprise who had helped to finance Miller's Court. They too wanted to meet.

Over lunch, Joe Wesolowski began by saying, "The Miller's Court project has become a major story in so many national publications across the country."

It was true; Miller's Court had been featured on national television. In fact, the *NBC Nightly News* segment had reminded me of what Linda and South African Broadcasting Corporation had put together for PeacePlayers.

Joe continued, "And it's one of the most impactful projects we've ever been part of. In fact, it's the poster child for the kind of work we want to be doing. We can't stop here. Would you guys be interested in replicating the model in other cities?"

The following week we were on a plane with Joe out to St. Louis to meet with US Bank, one of the major lenders and financial partners in our two Baltimore deals. They too wanted to see more Centers for Educational Excellence. They also wanted to help start a fund that would make it easier to get more built.

The team had spoken loud and clear. They too owned this concept and were caught up in what had been created. These weren't the traditional real estate projects these banks were used to financing. These were projects with a soul and with a purpose. These were projects they were happy to take risks on and devote extra time to. These projects made them feel like true partners and not third-party lenders.

That's when I first started to understand that we had now become part of a movement. Movements change the way the world works. They unify people and allow us to do things together that we can't do alone. Movements give individuals the encouragement, confidence, and permission to help bring bold and audacious ideas to life because we feel supported by a larger group. Movements remove the boundaries, obstacles, and inhibitions that we may experience along the way and make us feel like we are part of an unstoppable force.

That's how you know a movement — when an idea has been born

and has taken on a life of its own, way past the reach of the initial group that helped it come to life. The potential began with the idea to house Baltimore teachers and education-focused nonprofits all under one roof. From there, everything just needed to be built inside out, not from the top down, with the end users, the community, and the team having the same sense of pride, ownership, and authorship in the finished product.

All the years I'd spent instinctively building companies and projects inside out, driven primarily by love and respect, began to make sense. It had allowed the Center for Educational Excellence idea to become a movement. Looking back, the same thing had occurred with PeacePlayers, even though back then I did not have any idea how much power the word *movement* actually had. When the end user, the community, and the team are simultaneously asking for more and are willing to do anything it takes to get there, you are a part of a movement. At that point, nothing can stop you.

I'm convinced that if we had taken all of the credit for Miller's Court and touted the Center for Educational Excellence as our idea, the concept would have fizzled out. We would have alienated those individuals, organizations, and institutions that were the most crucial components to the idea's conception, success, and longevity. We would have been seen as a bunch of real estate developers who stole the idea from a handful of passionate teachers and nonprofits in an attempt to make a bunch of money. Miller's Court might have worked, but it would have been just another real estate project and not the movement it became.

I realized then that the French poet Victor Hugo was right: the most powerful thing in the world is an idea whose time has come.

■ ■ ■ ■ ■

National replication of the Center for Educational Excellence movement started in Philadelphia. The building at 100 West Oxford Street in the South Kensington neighborhood was once part of one of the largest textile manufacturing complexes in the city. With our partners there,

D3 Development, our team was able to turn it into a 170,000-square-foot urban oasis: 114 apartments marketed mostly to Philly's public school teachers, 38,000 square feet of office space for Teach For America and other nonprofits, and a 1,300-square-foot community café.

We spent time in cities like New Orleans, Denver, and Washington, DC, helping share the lessons we had learned in making our centers in Baltimore. We welcomed visitors from places like Pittsburgh and Detroit into the city to tour Miller's Court and Union Mill. We gave speeches and shared ideas and resources with others trying to accomplish similar goals. Soon incredible projects like Teachers Villages in Newark, New Jersey, and Hartford, Connecticut, came to life, making teachers in other cities feel listened to, taken care of, and part of a greater community. A movement that had sprouted in the improbable Baltimore neighborhood of Remington had, incredibly, gone national.

# 14

## The Dynamism of Love

*"Small things done with great love will change the world."*

— MOTHER TERESA

"Enjoy," said Brenda. The barista slid me a tall glass of chocolate milk, my go-to drink.

I thanked her and found a seat in the small café.

The exposed brick walls, freshly repointed, looked exactly like they must have 124 years ago when the tin can factory was first built. The massive south-facing factory-style windows with their green trim were perfect replicas of what had been there long before the building had been shut down and left to rot. In the old days, factories didn't have much electricity and were designed to take advantage of natural light, which was being beautifully displayed as the cold winter sun filled the tiny space.

The team from Charmington's — the name of the café — had done an amazing job keeping the historical appeal and blending it with the modern amenities they needed to make great coffee and serve delicious food in a welcoming environment. By this time, seven years had passed since Bart Harvey offered his guidance to me and my dad in

Remington's beloved New Wyman Park diner, helping us find the resources needed to bring the first Center for Educational Excellence to life. In the end, thanks to the serious young man at the United Citizens of Remington meeting, Charmington's café took over the southwest corner of the restored building, right at the intersection of Howard and Twenty-Sixth Streets.

As I sipped my chocolate milk, my good friend Amanda Rothschild, one of the owners of Charmington's, approached.

"How's it going, Amanda?" I said, standing up to give her a big hug.

"Hey, Thibault," she said. Then she cupped her hands to whisper into my ear. "So listen, there's this guy here who wants to talk to us."

I peeked past Amanda to see a huge man impeccably dressed in a black suit, white shirt, and black tie. Topping it off was his expressionless face, hidden behind dark sunglasses, and a cord coiling from his collar to an earpiece.

*What's a guy like that doing here?*

He moved quickly to stand between me and Amanda.

"You the owner of this building?"

"I am," I replied, confused.

"Sir, I'm Agent Johnson with the Secret Service. Please step aside with Ms. Rothschild and myself." He motioned for us to follow him.

Agent Johnson ushered us into the back of the shop. Glancing around, I noticed two other similarly dressed men standing at the oversize wooden door that served as the main entrance into the café. They had their arms crossed over their chests and stood motionless, like two well-dressed bouncers. By that point I had ruled out anything that I might have done.

*Maybe there's a shooter around the corner? An armed robbery nearby? A murder?*

Whatever it was, these guys weren't playing around. This wasn't a drill.

Amanda and I followed the agent out of the seating area, past the single bathroom, and into the quieter corridor at the rear of the café. I shot her a nervous look as we walked. Amanda, however, was all smiles.

*What does she know that I don't?*

■ ■ ■ ■ ■

If we'd had it our way, Charmington's might have never existed. We thought that there was too much perceived crime and blight for any kind of retail establishment to ever work there.

Nonetheless, we were clear that it wasn't only our building, so we had agreed to the community's request and started interviewing potential operators. Over the course of a year, only three groups showed any interest at all.

One was a woman who ran a coffee kiosk on the Johns Hopkins University campus. She drove a hot-red Hummer and spent the majority of the time crunching numbers as she tried to figure out how much money she could make if she expanded her operation to the building. She spoke about profit, not purpose.

The second was a young husband and wife who made cupcakes. They were really looking for a bigger kitchen to bake out of, and they had convinced themselves that selling coffee alongside their baked goods would be a good fit for their startup. I really liked their energy, and they spoke as if success was inevitable. At the end of the day, though, it was clear they were primarily focused on how they would get their products into Whole Foods and other national retail chains, not on how their shop would serve the neighborhood.

The third group was Amanda and her team. I'll never forget my first meeting with them, sitting out in the building's courtyard on a warm spring afternoon. Nine of them showed up. Black, white, short, tall, gay, straight, men, women. It was beautiful. They were Baltimore, and they represented our city's amazing diversity. More important, they were Remington.

During the meeting, they explained that they wanted to create a co-op, meaning that the people who worked the business owned the business. They had worked together several years before with the hopes of creating a coffee shop and high-end organic furniture showroom, all under one roof. They had rented space in a part of town that hoped to become one of Baltimore's most prestigious neighborhoods, but their timing couldn't have been worse. The neighborhood was slower to take

off than everyone had hoped, and they were hit hard by the 2008 re-
cession. The furniture wasn't selling and the coffee couldn't support the
massive rent, and they were forced to close their doors.

As I listened to them talk that afternoon — underneath the heavy
steel trusses that we had salvaged to remind us of the rich history
of how buildings used to be built — there was so much love in their
voices. Their first attempt had fallen short, but they didn't give up. They
were now coming together as a more united group, a true cooperative
focused on the people who worked there, with the larger purpose of
serving great coffee and food to help unite Baltimore and create community.

Just like the young man at the UCR meeting who had brought up
the café idea in the first place, Amanda and her team weren't ready to
take no for an answer — even if it came from us. They were willing to
keep pushing until they made their dream a reality. They had spent
months looking all over the city for a new shop, and before they found
us, they had been moments away from signing a lease in a trendy and
well-known part of town.

As I told the story of Miller's Court and of Seawall, I explained
our philosophy that buildings should be used to unite our city, to give
communities a voice, to put like-minded people focused on making
Baltimore better all under one roof, and to help launch powerful ideas.
By the end of our conversation we all agreed that we were the perfect
match for each other.

After that initial meeting, while Amanda and her team spent time
underwriting the opportunity and making sure it made financial sense,
it became clear that they were more focused on how they could serve
the community and their workers than on how much money they
could make. The team wanted to play a small role in helping teachers
by opening at 6:00 a.m. so they could get a fresh cup of coffee on their
way to school. They believed their tiny, 1,000-square-foot shop could
give the community of Remington a powerful place to meet, gather,
and share ideas. They asked themselves how they could create jobs
where their employees didn't just feel like they had ownership of the
business but were actual owners. They couldn't have been a better fit.

Once they were up and running in the space, Amanda bought a house in Remington. Dan Scott — or Action Dan, as I call him — who became another one of Charmington's owners, also moved into the neighborhood. They employed locally and participated in helping grow and strengthen the community by involving themselves outside of Charmington's four walls. They attended Greater Remington Improvement Association (GRIA) meetings, Remington's second community association, and they served on the Land Use and Transportation Committee. They weren't guests; they were neighbors. They became vital parts of Remington, both personally and professionally. Amanda, Action Dan, and the rest of the co-op had done something special — and proved to us how wrong we'd been about a coffee shop not working in the first place.

■ ■ ■ ■ ■

In the back corner of the café, Agent Johnson paused. Then he said, "In exactly seven minutes, the president of the United States of America will be here."

I was unable to speak.

"We are going to secure the premises, and anyone inside will not be allowed to leave for at least an hour, and no one else will be permitted to enter. Anyone wishing to stay will have to go through an extensive search by our team."

He paused at that point, looking for a reaction from us.

*The president? Barack Obama?*

I stood there in silence for a good five seconds, the giant Secret Service agent towering over me. The sounds of clinking ceramic plates filled the space between us.

"Yeah, I want to stay," I said at last, the sharp spray of the milk steamer almost overpowering my voice.

I gulped and glanced over at Amanda.

*Barack Obama is coming to Charmington's.*

Now that I finally understood why she couldn't wipe the smile off her face, it hit me: this was her doing. The community wanted it, and she had delivered. Of course Obama would come visit this spectacular space.

Amanda and I walked back into the main area of the shop. We both followed the Secret Service agent, who moved with robotic rigidity. We must have looked like children behind him, buzzing with energy, eager to meet the president.

While this was a huge moment for Miller's Court and for Remington, it was especially big for Amanda and the team at Charmington's. Part of the reason they had wanted to start a co-op to begin with was to help create a sustainable working environment not just for their employees but also for employees of other small businesses all over the country. That visionary thinking had led Amanda to make trips to Washington, DC, where she had testified in front of Congress in support of the Obama administration's proposed Guaranteed Paid Sick Leave program. Amanda wasn't just fighting for paid sick leave for the employees at Charmington's; she was fighting for paid sick leave for millions of Americans who also worked at small businesses.

Amanda's spirit and drive are enormous. She had caught the attention of the right people in the right places. It turned out that President Obama was coming to Charmington's to announce the Guaranteed Paid Sick Leave program, and he wanted Amanda by his side.

The two men guarding the door moved squarely in front of it, crossed their arms even tighter, and planted their feet. Agent Johnson stood in the middle of the space to address the forty or so people who were quietly enjoying their meals, clearly not knowing what was about to hit them.

"Good morning," he said, his voice and presence instantly commanding attention.

The café became silent as everyone turned to look at the huge man in the dark suit. Even the background traffic seemed to stop.

"In four minutes the president of the United States will be arriving here for lunch."

I could hear muted gasps from people at their tables.

"You can stay or you can go. If you stay, we will be conducting a thorough search of each of you. If you go, please leave now."

As if timed to a T, as soon as the agent had finished his ten-second speech, dozens of Secret Service men descended on the once-abandoned corner of Howard and Twenty-Sixth Streets. Some emerged out of a train tunnel that ran alongside the building. Others came running through doors I had forgotten we had. They wore black jumpsuits with big guns visibly displayed on their hips, and they moved quickly and decisively.

The buzz in Charmington's was electric while a German shepherd sniffed down the place. Not a soul left after learning the news. Instead, the café had filled to the brim with people who had been lucky enough to receive a text from one of the excited diners and close enough to arrive during the narrow window of time before the lockdown. The agents' pat-downs made airport security look cursory. It was a search worthy of a meeting with a president.

A motorcade of police on motorcycles, pitch-black SUVs, and stretch limousines made its way up Howard Street and stopped in front of the building, disrupting traffic for miles. President Obama got out of one of the limos, flanked by some intimidating-looking men who were whispering into microphone cords attached to their earpieces. While the president walked effortlessly toward the building, a massive ring of protection — a human force field — formed around him and the building. Word of the president's visit had quickly spread with the motorcade's arrival. A crowd of hundreds who had missed the cutoff to get inside Charmington's had gathered on the street.

With an enormous smile, the president made his way into the little café that most people, including me, had bet against.

I still couldn't believe it. Nelson Mandela and the Dalai Lama had supported PeacePlayers while I was there, but I had never had a chance to thank either of them in person. Now the leader of the free world was walking around shaking hands with everyone in the same building that Randy had watched drug addicts creep around in for decades. After Obama shook a few dozen hands, I had my moment.

"Welcome to Remington, Mr. President," I said, introducing myself and shaking his hand. "Welcome to Charmington's."

I rushed to explain a little about the soul and history of the building.

"We're reinventing real estate so that it's used as a vehicle for positive change," I said. "This building was one of our first projects, and it was built to take great care of anyone focused on kids and education."

I knew I had only a few seconds to share our story. It felt like I was trying to put a lifetime of work into this one brief moment. I wanted to tell him so much more. I wanted to tell him about Bongani's ability to forgive, about Menzi carrying the hoops, and about Nathi's bravery in the face of his HIV/AIDS diagnosis. I wanted to tell him about the teachers who had designed their own apartments and about the amazing community of Remington, which was helping to bring about thoughtful and inclusive change. I wanted the president to know how it was all driven by an intention to help the children of Baltimore get a better education. I wanted to tell him about all of the hard work that we had put in to help create something we really believed in.

I didn't have time to say most of those things, but with his eyes locked on mine, I felt I had gotten my message across all the same.

"Thibault," the president said to me, "our country needs more companies like Seawall."

I couldn't believe he had remembered my name. He even pronounced it correctly.

"Always lead with purpose and never give up," he continued, shaking my hand once again and moving on to melt the heart of the person standing next to me.

Our entire interaction lasted less than twenty seconds, but it felt like an hour. I knew he got it. I knew he cared.

The little space in this once-abandoned building had become worth a visit by the highest official in the country. While it was an incredibly heavy lift to get to this point for all involved, it had actually happened so naturally, seemingly without trying. Charmington's, like so many other projects, had a life of its own. It was a movement all on its own, evidenced by President Obama coming to visit.

Standing there, soaking up the moment, with all of the things I had wanted to say to one of the busiest men in the world swirling through my head, in this café I hadn't even believed in, I realized the full extent to which real estate could be used as a platform to unite. Had Miller's

Court been a regular real estate project, like the high-end apartments the previous owners had tried to make happen, or had Charmington's been a Starbucks, there was no way that President Obama would have shown up.

Measuring less than 1,000 square feet, Charmington's was very small. If so much influence, inspiration, and impact could arise from such a tiny space, I couldn't help but imagine how much more we could do if we continued to provide other thoughtful and inclusive places for people to live, work, and play.

For the remainder of President Obama's visit, I stood at the back of Charmington's and took it all in. It reminded me of watching the kids from Saphinda and Clifton playing together in Umlazi. Against each and every no, even the ones I had given myself, it was a resounding yes that would resonate around the country and into the future.

# 15

## Deep Listening

*"The essence of community, its very heart and soul, is the
non-monetary exchange of value. The things we do and things
we share because we care for others and for the good of the place."*

— DEE W. HOCK

"**W**hoa now, that's what the old heads say." The music floated through
the balmy afternoon air.

I stood in the courtyard at Miller's Court. Realizing that the
weather was going to be pleasant, we were in the midst of throwing one
of the spontaneous cookouts that our teachers had come to appreciate
during the warmer months. Taking great care of everyone who lived in
our buildings was so important to us that we were always thinking of
creative ways to show our gratitude for the important work our tenants
did on a daily basis. In addition to the cookouts, we started to offer
monthly breakfast spreads at the main building exit so they could grab
a bagel, a bowl of fresh fruit, some juice, or coffee on their way out into
the morning rush hour toward their schools. Exceeding expectations
was something that my dad always talked about.

That day, the residents, who now felt more like family, were mixing
and mingling about. They soaked in the sunny Friday afternoon after a

long week in the classroom, pumping beers out of a nearby keg, grilling burgers and hot dogs over an open charcoal flame, and catching up on the week. The radio station 92Q — Baltimore's legendary hip-hop and R&B station — provided the jams for the occasion, including B Rich's famous hit from the early 2000s, "Whoa Now."

My three-year-old son, Finley, was running around the courtyard kicking a soccer ball. He was born the month we opened Miller's Court. Our second son, Durban, who was just one at the time, was snuggling in my arms as I sampled the food. A few minutes later, one of the teachers, Andrew Gorby, and his wife, Ashley, came over to say hello.

"Listen, Thibault," Andrew said, after we'd exchanged pleasantries and small talk. "Can we speak with you about something?"

The couple had been with us since day one. Andrew was a teacher at Collington Square Elementary/Middle School. He was originally from eastern North Carolina but had moved to Baltimore to teach. Miller's Court was his first home in the city.

"Of course, brother," I said, finishing the last of the delicious burger. "What's up?"

Andrew waved a few other teachers over.

*Uh oh,* I worried silently. *Is this an ambush?*

"So, we've been thinking," continued Andrew. "Miller's Court has exceeded all of our expectations. It's even better than what we ever thought it could be."

His fellow teachers and Miller's Court tenants nodded their agreement between sips of beer.

"We want to stay in the classroom and continue teaching," Andrew said, checking the faces around him. "I think I speak for everyone when I say we're all in. We want to make Baltimore our permanent home."

I could hardly control my excitement. That was the exact reason that Miller's Court was created. It was supposed to be a temporary landing place for teachers like Andrew who were new to Baltimore, a landing place that would allow those teachers to focus 100 percent of their energy and attention on the kids and the classroom. We had all hoped it would make the teachers' lives easier, which, in turn, would help them fall in love with their profession and remain committed to kids and education. We also hoped that after a year or two at Miller's Court, the teachers would have a better understanding of Baltimore and be ready to move out and make room for the next group.

Then Andrew said something that I'd only dreamed of hearing when I really got carried away thinking about what a building like Miller's Court could do.

"We want to buy houses."

I paused. Baltimore was famous for people abandoning it. Its population had perpetually dwindled since the glory days of the manufacturing boom, declining from one million to about 600,000, an almost 40 percent drop. While people across the country were moving back to urban centers, the reality for Baltimore at the time was that the majority of the stories I heard were still about folks leaving. While city planners and developers were busy trying to figure out how to get people to come back, too few people were talking about building for all those people who never left, who helped hold the city together through the storm of such a mass exodus. Now, to add a third dimension to it, standing here in front of me was a solid group of young people who had no prior roots in Baltimore telling me they wanted to make this city their permanent home. They wanted to put their own hard-earned economic investment back into the town they'd grown to love living and working in. They wanted to stay in Baltimore.

Once the gravity of the moment had passed, I said, "I love it, guys. That's amazing."

"Hold on; we're not done just yet," Andrew said. "We want our houses to be in Remington." Then he added one more detail. "And we want you guys to build them for us."

My excitement turned to shock. The first points that Andrew had made were brilliant. I was with him until those last points.

"Wait a second," I started, collecting myself. "First, we have no idea how to build a house. Also, where did you have in mind?"

"Look around us," Andrew said. "There are thirty vacant houses surrounding this building alone. We've all invested so much time, energy, and love here. Those vacant houses have absentee slumlords. I see people selling drugs out of them daily. They are holding the neighborhood back."

I nodded as Andrew continued.

"If we don't reclaim those houses, then we are part of the problem, not the solution."

It sounded as if Simon — my young friend from my flight from South Africa — was whispering into Andrew's ear as the young teacher pleaded his case. Andrew didn't want to wait for someone else to do it. He wanted to seize the moment.

Andrew and his teacher friends had my attention. They weren't talking like tenants. They were talking like owners and partners. Like change agents.

Andrew wrapped up his pitch. "If you buy those houses and fix them up, we'll buy them back from you."

■ ■ ■ ■ ■

After hearing the teachers' request for permanent homes in Remington, I immediately looked back on my experience with PeacePlayers. Initially, we'd been focusing mostly on sports until those wise Zulu mamas had approached us to ask us to include an HIV/AIDS component in our program. It had been tempting then to hear their concerns and brush them aside. We might have argued that the request was out of our scope and too far out of our comfort zone, relying on someone else to come along someday to address them. In the end, however, because of change agents like Nathi, the life skills program became one of the most impactful parts of what we did.

*Buying and remolding homes may be out of our wheelhouse, but that's what they asked for — what if we can make it happen?*

Later that evening I hooked up with the rest of the Seawall team and pitched the idea the teachers had come up with. In the fading daylight, we walked around Miller's Court. Perhaps for the first time, we really noticed the vacant houses. They had been there since we had first arrived in the community years before, but we had always just assumed that someone else would take care of them at some point in time. We had done our part by building Miller's Court, and we had no real intention of ever building anything else in Remington. At that time, as far as we were concerned, those abandoned and boarded-up houses clearly weren't Seawall's responsibility.

*But Andrew is right. There are so many vacant houses.*

The more we walked and discussed it, the more we fell in love with their idea. Our role was evolving and becoming clearer. We began to understand that we existed to listen deeply and help others, especially those with seldom-heard voices, realize their dreams through the built environment. If this was one of those dreams, then we were in.

We met with some residential real estate brokers to get their take on the project. Just as some of our early advisors and the real estate community had told us Miller's Court would never work, the brokers told us we would never sell a house in Remington for more than $100,000 — especially not as many of them as we were looking to do at one time. The biggest problem, though, was that the construction cost alone to fix up each house was at least $150,000, and the idea was to do thirty of them.

We knew that this wasn't just a real estate development or a housing project. It was a project whose purpose was to provide permanent for-sale housing for teachers and other hardworking people in Baltimore. It could help us prove that it was possible to make major investments in a neighborhood in an inclusive way and still keep prices affordable. It was another part of the momentum that had been building in Remington. The end users, the teachers who had started it all, were now asking us to take it to a completely different level. They'd become consumed by that raw and powerful feeling you get when you are part of a deepening and expanding movement.

■ ■ ■ ■ ■

Baltimore's row houses — blocks and blocks of connected dwellings that share a party wall with neighbors on both sides — are fascinating. Built primarily in the early 1900s, there are more of them in Baltimore than in any other city in America. At their worst, they give you no privacy. At their best, they create an amazing sense of community, a tribe, a village.

By then, Seawall had done $100 million worth of impactful development. Our reputation as a group that listened and led with purpose over profit was emerging in Baltimore. Several local families began asking us if it was too late to invest in Miller's Court or Union Mill. They loved the idea that their money could be put to work in a way that made a real, positive impact in their city and provided them with a financial return at the same time. While we were honored by the request, to date we had been lucky. The creative financing we had used had allowed us to complete those complicated projects without needing to put in any of our money or any other investors' money. We had never taken outside investment as a company, but with this new idea that Andrew and his friends had come up with, it was time. And if we were going to do it, there was nobody we wanted to work with more than Eddie and Sylvia Brown.

The Browns are well known in Baltimore as an investment, entrepreneurial, and philanthropic force. Eddie was born in central Florida at a time where African American families like his were kept separate from white families with Jim Crow laws. He went from working for his uncle's moonshine bootlegging operation to graduating from Howard University to having over $18 billion under management through his Baltimore investment firm, Brown Capital Management, which he founded in 1983. Both Eddie and his wife, Sylvia, are often among the first Baltimoreans to support many of the most innovate initiatives around town. They had reached out to us before, but we just hadn't needed the investment. But when we came to them about the new project, they eagerly jumped on board, putting up the money to help us acquire and fix up the homes for the teachers.

With the Browns behind us, over the next sixty days we set out to buy all thirty vacant row homes the teachers had identified. The community supported our proposal to buy ten of the homes, which were owned by the city and had been vacant for more than thirty years. Those ten houses were in such bad shape, the roofs had literally collapsed all the way down into the basements. The city had put out a Request For Proposal for a developer to acquire them, and thanks to the relationship with Remington, Seawall was awarded the chance. The truth is the condition was so awful we probably overpaid by giving the city a dollar for all ten of them.

The other twenty houses of the thirty identified were privately owned, and we purchased them one by one. We bought out slumlords and absentee owners. In many cases we overpaid for the houses just to make sure that they ended up in the right hands. We didn't have a plan yet, but we trusted a process that started with listening deeply to our community.

After we acquired the properties, we called all five of the couples who had challenged us with this idea during the cookout. We playfully told them that they were in trouble because we were in trouble. We explained that we had bought all thirty of the houses they had identified and that they now needed to buy them back from us. Like we had done with Miller's Court, we invited those five couples, along with some of their teacher friends who had heard what was happening, to tour one of the collapsing houses we had just purchased and sit in on a focus group to share their thoughts.

The look of terror on their faces as they walked in was priceless. Rotten wood floorboards splintered under their shoes. Lead paint flaked off the walls. Cockroaches scurried between the cracks, surprised to see humans for the first time in decades.

After a brief tour of the house, we made our way back to our office. Then, armed with some pizza and beers, we got down to business.

"Okay guys," I started. "These are your houses. We want you to dream big. We want you to reinvent the experience you can have from both the inside and the outside."

We had brought our design team, who had sketched out a couple of rough ideas about what could be done with the houses. The teachers essentially ripped up those plans and started from scratch. They told us that Baltimore row houses, with their two small windows on the second floor and their one small window and door on the first floor, were boring. They needed to be reimagined. They wanted a ton of natural light. They wanted to make a statement from the outside.

They pitched an idea to take out almost the entire second-floor facade and replace it with a massive steel I beam and an enormous picture window. They asked for fixed planter boxes on the second floor so that, in the spring and summer, bright-purple vines could flow down. They suggested oversize numbers marking the addresses. At the same time, they wanted to keep the charm of the historical homes intact — asking us to leave the brick and wood floor joists exposed where possible.

We feverishly took notes as they fired off ideas. I could see it in their eyes and hear it in their voices — they were bought in.

We continued meeting with the community to discuss the idea the teachers had come up with. They too loved it. We were going to make a major investment with the goal of keeping the finished product affordable and at a price point picked by the teachers. We were going to replace blight with hardworking young families who, in addition to becoming neighbors, were also going to pitch in and help support the neighborhood.

We then started to assemble the team. We found an architect who could translate the notes we had taken from the focus group. We found a builder who could help turn those notes into a spectacular finished product.

Since affordability was a priority of both the community and the teachers, we had to get creative with the financing in addition to the support from the Browns. The Abell Foundation — a local community-driven institution that had completed their own apartments for teachers in Baltimore and that had been incredibly helpful in sharing their lessons learned as we brought Miller's Court to life — heard about what we were doing. They pledged $25,000 grants to any teacher or police officer who bought one of the houses and committed to staying there for at least five years. The city of Baltimore gave $10,000 to every buyer who purchased one of the newly rehabbed homes. The state of Maryland had a Live Near Your Work program that contributed up to $15,000 to each buyer per home. All in, most of our buyers qualified for close to $50,000 of incentives that greatly helped with the affordability.

Armed with an idea and a design driven by the end users, the support of the community, and a financing team to back the development and sale of the houses, we were ready to start. The project was going to be called 30 by 13. We were going to build and sell thirty fully rehabbed houses in Remington all in 2013. This was an audacious goal; I don't think that thirty fully rehabbed houses had sold in Remington in the past ten years combined, maybe even the past fifty.

We reconvened the teacher focus group and developed a simple website with a quote from one of our teachers. It read:

> I first moved to Baltimore in 2009 as part of the Baltimore City Teaching Residency. Miller's Court has provided me with a beautiful and convenient home base from which to explore the city and has allowed me to get to know other teachers with similar interests. I am buying a Miller's Square (30 by 13) house and I couldn't be more excited! Not only am I making a great investment in my new home, but I'm making an investment in this community. And that's a great feeling.

We also started construction on a model unit to figure out how we were going to actually build those thirty houses. As it began to take shape, we scheduled an open house. Armed with nothing more than a Facebook page and a website, we asked the teachers, the community, and the team to help spread the word.

■ ■ ■ ■ ■

I'll never forget the day of the 30 by 13 open house. It was a beautiful fall Sunday morning in early October. Not having ever sold a house, we had no idea what we were doing, or what to expect. I remember talking excitedly with our team as we tied balloons to the railing, wondering if we would get ten or fifteen people to show up that day, which would have been a really successful first open house by anyone's standards.

By 10:00 a.m., the posted start time of the event, there was a line out the door waiting to get in. By the time the thirtieth person came inside to tour the house, we had run out of the flyers and promotional materials we had printed. The case of water we had bought was gone.

We hadn't run any ads in local magazines, bought any airtime on local radio stations, or even hired a broker to help promote the project.

We had relied primarily on word of mouth, and we once again proved how powerful an idea can be when its time has come.

By 5:00 p.m., as the last visitor left for the day, we were exhausted, inspired, confused, and ecstatic. In the end, three hundred people had showed up, and all thirty homes had been claimed within the first hour. We couldn't believe it.

■ ■ ■ ■ ■

The next morning, we regrouped to try to figure out what the open house meant for the future of Remington, a neighborhood that so many had unfairly written off. That day taught us that Remington was about to have a lot more eyes on it. We began to realize that there were three main factors at play.

The first was that Remington's physical location is perfect. Baltimore has a major Interstate — I-83 — that acts like a conveyor belt. It shuttles hundreds of thousands of people in and out of the city on a daily basis from Baltimore County and even as far north as Pennsylvania. Most of the exits off Interstate 83 dump drivers out onto windy streets that eventually lead into the various neighborhoods. In contrast, the Twenty-Eighth Street exit in Remington drops people right smack in the heart of the once highly industrial and now largely residential community. Furthermore, the Remington exit is perfectly sandwiched between Baltimore's Inner Harbor and Baltimore County.

Second, the neighborhood is actually connected to the Johns Hopkins University's campus, one of the most prestigious universities on the planet. Urban legend has it that for years, because of Remington's reputation for crime, poverty, and drug problems, the administration at Johns Hopkins warned all of its students, faculty, and staff never to go below Twenty-Ninth Street, which is where the campus ends and Remington begins. However, in 2011, armed with a dynamic and visionary new president, Ron Daniels, who believed that strengthening the neighborhoods surrounding its campus would also strengthen the university, Johns Hopkins committed to become a true partner and anchor institution. They worked collaboratively with the ten neighborhoods that surround the campus's borders and rolled out the Homewood Community Partners Initiative (HCPI), pledging tens of millions of dollars to help strengthen those communities. None of those other HCPI neighborhoods was closer to or better positioned than Remington to start benefiting from that partnership and investment.

Third, because Remington had been written off by many and largely ignored, it was one of the few remaining neighborhoods that still had an amazing stock of old historic warehouses that were prime for redevelopment. These gorgeous buildings featured massive factory windows, fourteen-foot-high ceilings, and beautiful old bricks — the kind of building that would be too expensive to recreate today. Had any of those buildings been in one of the more established neighborhoods in Baltimore, they would have been turned into high-end restaurants, condos, apartments, and shops a long time ago. The fact that they were sitting underutilized — and in many cases abandoned — made no sense. It was only a matter of time before the word got out.

While all the attention was exciting, it also made us nervous.

*What if the properties end up in the wrong hands? What if they are bought by people who don't share the neighborhood's vision? What if the new owners are more focused on profit than purpose?*

With those questions swirling, our team decided we weren't done in Remington after all.

# Part III

# GROW

**Years before the birth of Seawall,** while I am still dribbling basketballs around the world, a rusty yellow bulldozer idles in front of a construction gate that runs across the entrance to 2901 Smith Street, unable to move forward. Its massive mud-caked tires grip the pavement. Exhaust billows out in angry plumes and drifts away in the chilly fall wind, but the thirty-ton machine remains still. The bulldozer has met its match.

Just a few feet away, chained to the gate — the machine rumbling forebodingly in front of him — is Earl Bell. The president of the United Citizens of Remington is hell-bent on blocking the bulldozer's access to the construction site. There is no way he is going to stand by and let this apartment building get built.

The contractor and developer are beside themselves. They thought this was going to be a fairly straightforward project. The developer assumed the community would welcome him and his new building with open arms. He's going to bring fresh development to Remington, after all, and perhaps these apartments will be the tipping point for more exciting projects to come. Most of Remington welcomes him, but not Earl.

The United Citizens of Remington president has already delayed the project for more than a year, fighting tooth and nail at every juncture with various appeals and lawsuits. Now, just when the developer has finally obtained all the necessary approvals to proceed with the building, this happens. The physically unassuming middle-aged man with short brown hair and round glasses is chained to the gate. He has taken his tremendous resolve to the streets and put his life on the line to halt this project.

No one knows what to do with him. The construction superintendent paces back and forth about ten yards down the road, watching the whole thing unfold, stopping to pull off his helmet and scratch his head. He's never seen anything like this. If he can't get the bulldozer onto the land, he can't level the previous building, and he can't start the project.

He radios his boss, frantically asking for guidance. There are some short exchanges, then his boss goes quiet. The line fizzles with static in the early morning air. He's not getting any guidance. There isn't any to give. This is a first for everyone.

The bulldozer operator inches forward, turning the scene into a game of chicken. Another puff of black smoke shoots out of the machine's exhaust pipe, and a deafening sound roars out of its diesel engine. Earl, tennis shoes laced tight, fall jacket half zipped, doesn't budge.

Every community in the world has that person who is such a conservative thinker that he or she will challenge new projects no matter how valuable they seem to be on the surface. In fact, the world needs these conservative forces because they actually help keep developers honest; their challenges can spark important, healthy conversations. They exist on the margins of almost every project in almost every community, thwarting thoughtless development, questioning assumptions, and driving the community to be clear about what it needs and what change should look like.

Every neighborhood has folks like this, but few neighborhoods can boast a figure quite like Earl Bell — a person with such determination that he has become a Baltimore legend.

The air hangs thick with uncertainty as chaos surrounds the jobsite. No one can believe what they're seeing. The giant machine remains frozen dead in its tracks, the driver unsure what his next move should be.

In Earl's eyes, this is his neighborhood. He's been here since the late 1990s. Nothing goes up without the UCR's approval. He is committed to stopping the construction and keeping Remington just as it is despite its surplus of dilapidated buildings, forgotten homes, and empty lots.

The neighborhood has never fully recovered from the loss of jobs and the depopulation brought on by deindustrialization. Too many abandoned row houses from the 1920s surround unused old factories and warehouses. Even during the economic boom of the early 2000s, when construction cranes dotted the city's skyline and investors were pouring money into neighborhoods throughout Baltimore, Remington sat quietly unchanged.

On the other hand, the city, the country — the world at large — has countless developers who take advantage of situations like these, charging in and changing a neighborhood to suit their own ideas and increase their own profit.

The tense standoff lasts for well over an hour, everything brought to a halt by one small, determined person.

When all seems lost, Earl unchains himself and walks away without saying a word. He doesn't need to; he's proven his point. He intends to continue fighting the project every step of the way — and that's exactly what he does.

The twelve months the developer had scheduled for construction take three and a half years. Just as Earl caused an obstruction that day with the bulldozer, he continues to place countless appeals and lawsuits in the developer's path at every turn. Local newspapers write numerous articles covering the battle, further propelling Earl onto a citywide stage as the protector against development. It looks like it may never end.

Finally, despite Earl's efforts, the building goes up. Yet even after the twenty-unit apartment building finally has its lights on for new residents, Earl refuses to quit and continues to appeal the project, hoping to tear it down. Even though the developer eventually made it past Earl and completed the building, the conflict-fueled delays crippled them financially. The developer is forced to sell the building shortly after finishing it. The saga sends a clear message: Earl, the UCR, and Remington won't stand for just any development.

# 16

## Purpose Driven

*"Reimagine a way communities can be rebuilt."*
— CANDY CHANG

"I don't know, Thibault," said Evan. "I know it's not your idea. It's not our idea. It came from the community, but I just don't know."

A blown-up map — printed on several massive sheets of paper — was stretched out along the front wall of our office. It featured the Baltimore neighborhood of Remington, the place that over the past five years had begun to feel like home to the small yet determined Seawall family.

Circled on the map were several parcels of land and structures spread throughout the neighborhood. I stood next to it, my eyes darting between the map and the rest of the team: Evan Morville, Jon Constable, Matt Pinto, Kirsten Lessner, and my dad.

I began to address Evan's concerns. "Look, we thought we were going to do teacher housing in Remington with Miller's Court. Then there was 30 by 13. Well, now there's this."

"This" was an early draft of the community's master plan. It was being dreamt up by the Greater Remington Improvement Association

(GRIA), the second community organization in the neighborhood. We knew they were working on it, and they had asked us questions over the years, sharing material as they made progress. When we had our hands full with Miller's Court, we hadn't been very involved, but as GRIA picked up steam and we became clearer in our purpose, we began to pay closer attention to the details in their emerging master plan. The meeting that day centered on how we could help bring a part of their vision to life. There were numerous projects outlined in the plan, but the one that excited us the most was the idea of turning Remington Avenue, which ran through the heart of the community, into what they described as a commercial corridor.

GRIA had imagined a future Remington Avenue that they hoped would include things like outdoor seating, adequate parking, ground-floor retail stores that would benefit the neighborhood, office space, and new housing. In their master plan, GRIA had zeroed in on several abandoned or underutilized properties that they envisioned being re-developed.

"Think about it, guys," I said. "While GRIA's plan is amazing, what if we could help them dream even bigger. What if we were able to add a few more properties along Remington Avenue? Perhaps an even greater vision for that commercial corridor could be brought to life? An actual Main Street." Our contribution in this dreaming phase of the process was to imagine what it would be like to be able to combine three contiguous city blocks into one project, rather than a patchwork of commercial businesses here and there. The properties that GRIA had identified and that we had added were circled on the map that now hung on the wall in front of us.

"Let's be honest," said Jon, a passionate guy who had helped us launch Seawall's property management company and evolved to over-seeing many of our development projects. "We know the direction Remington is trending. Someone is going to buy these properties. The word is out."

The speed with which we had sold the row houses we were refur-bishing for teachers confirmed that Remington was suddenly in high demand. And the three factors that made it so attractive — the number of really cool, underutilized industrial buildings and warehouses that were prime for redevelopment; the proximity to the interstate and to downtown; and its physical connection to to Johns Hopkins University — weren't going to change anytime soon.

Kirsten — our accountant, office manager, and the glue holding all of us together — added, "And though it's not impossible, it's at least unlikely that any other developer or real estate investor would move forward with the neighborhood's best interest at heart."

I loved watching our team at Seawall think through ideas together. Wading into uncertain waters, poking and prodding at the seen and unseen challenges inherent in new projects: this was how we worked as a company. I listened as we talked about what a commercial corridor might mean, how it could be expanded upon with intentionality, and whether we could be involved in a helpful way.

"Okay, I get it," said Evan. His uncertainty about the idea had dissolved. "This is a way to protect the community and work with them to play some small role in helping them implement a piece of their master plan."

"And to serve them," added my dad.

As those words sank in, we all stared at the map again. More than fifteen acres of properties were circled in red. At its core, assembling large parcels for development is tricky and challenging, but it's what real estate developers do. The difference between us and traditional developers stemmed from our reasons for wanting to assemble the properties and what we planned to do once we had them.

Real estate, for the most part, seemed like it needed to be reimagined to us at Seawall. We saw it as our responsibility, and opportunity, to reinvent what it meant to be a developer. We were by nature a company of socially conscious self-starters, ambassadors for those who didn't have as loud of a voice in their communities, and entrepreneurs who just happened to use the built environment as our tool to serve. We saw buildings as a way to help unite and empower communities, provide kids with better education, take care of teachers and others doing important work in our cities, and allow like-minded people to live and work collaboratively. While my dad and I had started out with a vague idea of what we wanted to be part of, that vision was expanding with every new person we encountered. It was evolving in real time.

It was possible to argue that getting involved with the master plan didn't make any sense. That wasn't how real estate development normally happened, and I hadn't heard many stories about neighborhoods including developers in their visioning process. More often than not, I heard stories of developers' fighting the community and using their muscle and influence to steamroll anyone standing in their way. Normally, developers know exactly what they want to build and are relentless in getting it done because they are primarily focused on maximizing the financial returns for themselves and their investors.

In an example that hit close to home, a developer from out of town had tried to bring a Walmart to Remington a little after Seawall became involved in the neighborhood. The developer wasn't able to get the right team in place and wasn't well versed enough about the conditions in the community. A public fight that dragged on for five years erupted over the project. In the end, the developer lost millions of dollars, and the whole thing fizzled out completely. That out-of-town developer had not been a good partner to Remington, and we did not want a similar situation to unfold now. To ensure that those important properties did not end up in the wrong hands again, we decided we wanted to purchase them ourselves.

I said, "These are some of the same properties involved with the failed Walmart. And remember, a big chunk of the community had wanted that project to happen, yet it still failed."

Plenty of folks around Baltimore and around the world have concerns about Walmart, especially its potential effects on local business. The reality was that the poorest and most vulnerable citizens of Remington didn't share those concerns. These were usually legacy residents who didn't have cars and relied on buses to get around. Many of them were tired of having to travel so far — often all the way to the county — on public transportation just to get their basic shopping needs met. They were thrilled by the idea that they could shop somewhere convenient and affordable so close to home.

As our meeting wrapped up that day, I glanced at the properties highlighted for redevelopment in GRIA's master plan alongside the ones we at Seawall had circled on the map hanging at the front of the room, and I felt that sense of growing momentum I'd become familiar with over the years. A new sense of purpose was beginning to propel us forward.

■ ■ ■ ■ ■

If streets could talk and tell stories, Remington Avenue — which runs right smack through the heart of the neighborhood — would be able to describe the community's rise and fall perfectly. In the early 1900s, when industry was booming, it had been home to lush green trees, a fancy car dealership, successful businesses, beautiful three-story houses, and nice wide sidewalks. Gorgeous new cars navigated the impeccably clean street, and a trolley line ran only a few blocks away, shuttling people to and from work. At that time, Remington Avenue had a Main Street feel to it and was clearly the epicenter, both in geography and soul, of the neighborhood.

The Remington Avenue I experienced when we first came to the neighborhood in 2007 could not have been more different. That quaint and safe Main Street feel had vanished long before. The three blocks that had once been the pride of this little community had traded life and vibrancy for vacant cinder-block garages, derelict old warehouses, shuttered pizza restaurants, and contaminated construction yards filled with junk. Trash from a tired old 7-Eleven convenience store blew unchecked and collected along both sides of the street. The once-thriving car dealership had closed long before and boarded up all its windows with cinder blocks, only to be replaced by a body shop that neighbors complained about, saying that it pumped toxic paint fumes into the community. More than half of the houses on the 2800 block had sat vacant for close to thirty years, visibly deteriorating and providing a daily reminder of disinvestment and unfilled potential.

GRIA, along with many of the Remington neighbors, had faith that the master plan would unite the community and bring the neighborhood up to date with the progress of the twenty-first century. Most of those who lived in Remington were tired of being held back. Residents were excited about the possibility of development, and they wanted it to happen in a responsible and thoughtful way — and hopefully on their terms.

The overarching goal of Remington's master plan was to ensure that its physical, social, and environmental development were consistent with the vision of those living and working in the community. The plan focused on mixed-income housing, multifaceted businesses, open space, transportation, and public safety. It was incredibly well thought out and thoroughly inclusive. The diversity of the many people who had contributed to it was staggering. Thousands of volunteer hours had been poured into the effort, and a solid strategy had emerged.

Turning Remington Avenue into a kind of Main Street for the neighborhood would be an ambitious, incredibly heavy lift and would require us to work in a more calculated fashion. For one, the three blocks contained fifteen different parcels of land with about fifteen different owners. Some of the title holders were absentee owners without a real stake in the neighborhood, trying to squeeze out all the money they could without regard for the well-being of the community. Others were long-term, responsible owners who deserved to make a fair profit from their property. Assembling that many properties into one parcel at the heart of a tightly knit and very protective community would be incredibly hard to do. If people knew a developer was eyeing their property for a large assemblage, everyone would start talking and prices would skyrocket. If it was economically impossible to acquire the properties, then the project had no chance.

Even so, we believed that GRIA's idea to create a commercial corridor here not only was possible but also was needed to fuel the growing momentum in Remington. Luckily for us and for the community's plan, development opportunities were still clouded by the word of how tricky development there had been. Conversations between Seawall and the owners were able to happen discreetly without spurring speculation or word getting out that a single company was buying so many buildings.

For the next twelve months, with very few people knowing it, Seawall bought fourteen of the fifteen properties along Remington Avenue that were needed for the project to move forward. Covertly buying up land in Remington reeked of the kind of thing many real estate developers did when carving up neighborhoods to suit their bottom lines. It wasn't a tactic that came naturally to us. We liked having constant dialogue with the community and working together from the beginning. But in this case, because we knew we were paying all owners a fair price for their properties, and because the stakes were so high and the margin for error so small, we focused on doing whatever it took to serve the greater purpose.

Eventually we reached the point where we had only one more property to get. Unfortunately, we knew it would also be the trickiest, since it had been there for generations and was a part of the fabric of the community. We knew that to buy that last property, we would need to help the owners see the purpose too. This project wasn't about one building or a specific type of resident in Remington — it was about the entire neighborhood.

■ ■ ■ ■ ■

As I walked into the Baltimore Glass Company, the old bell that hung off the door handle clinked awkwardly, announcing my arrival. Their building stood proudly, perhaps defiantly, surrounded by abandoned and underutilized structures in the last block on Remington Avenue.

The bell bounced off the door, and a young woman sitting at the receptionist desk looked up from a stack of invoices.

"How can I help you, dear?" she asked enthusiastically. Her thick Baltimore accent drawled off her tongue and instantly helped me relax, even though I knew this wasn't going to be an easy conversation.

I paused as I took in my surroundings. Fake wood paneling from the 1970s lined the interior, and fifty years' worth of old invoices, boxes, and scraps were taped to the walls or stacked in piles on the floor. A modest glass wall separated the waiting area from a single semi-private office and from the glass-cutting operations in the back. It felt like I was inside of not just a neighborhood institution but a living museum.

From the outside the Baltimore Glass Company's building was spectacular. I had been staring at it since we had first arrived in Remington six years earlier. The tiny, 2,000-square-foot building had originally been constructed in 1910 as a two-pump gas station and tire shop that was an integral part of the tight-knit, Main Street experience along Remington Avenue. Looking at the beautiful old brick exterior walls and the massive window openings, worn only slightly by a hundred years of weather, I could close my eyes and imagine how the little service center had once functioned at the end of the perfectly manicured Main Street — a place where the attendant knew everyone's name, a place that was an anchor of the community.

When Remington began to lose population and businesses closed down, so did the gas station. Luckily, in 1960 the Baltimore Glass Company purchased the abandoned building and proudly made it their home, refusing to let it be swept up in the community's decline. Now, a little over fifty years later, the family-run business was still stable — a fixture not only in Remington but for the entire city of Baltimore.

The receptionist smiled and introduced herself as Carlene. I smiled back, returned her greeting, and said, "May I please speak with the owner?"

"Maybe," answered Carlene. She tilted her head sideways and gave me an inquisitive look. "What can I tell him this is about?"

"I'd like to talk to him about this building," I said, trying to remain vague.

Carlene clearly didn't like that answer and read right through me. I could see that she had quickly figured out why I was there. Her friendly tone and demeanor changed instantly.

"It's not for sale," she said, turning back to her stack of invoices.

I took a few more steps into the jumbled shop and walked closer toward Carlene's desk. She had taken my request personally, and her role as the charming greeter had turned into that of loyal protector. Past her, I could see a man on the phone in the small office off to the right, less than ten feet from where I was.

"I understand, but please, could I have a couple of minutes with him?" I asked. I motioned with my head toward the guy on the other side of the glass wall, who I assumed was the owner.

Carlene was visibly angry, but I sensed that she was professional enough to pass along my request. Sure enough, she got up from her chair, pushing it hard against the cluttered wall behind her for effect, and walked loudly toward the back room.

I understood why Carlene was angry. Nobody likes to be displaced, and Carlene saw in my eyes that I was there to buy the building that provided not only her livelihood but also the livelihoods of more than a dozen other employees who had counted on a paycheck from the Baltimore Glass Company for perhaps longer than I had been alive.

Their building was the most important piece of the assemblage, and not just because it was the only one we hadn't yet been able to buy. It bookended the southern and most significant block that the community had flagged for development. I wanted to tell Carlene that without it, the Remington Avenue project was impossible. Without their property, the community's commercial corridor idea, expanded upon by us to turn it back into an actual Main Street, would remain nothing more than a great idea on a piece of paper.

# 17

## *Can't/No* as the Catalyst

*"Don't give up. Don't ever give up."*

— JIM VALVANO

Carlene didn't even look at me as she stormed back into the room, followed closely by Caleb Kelly, the owner of the business, who was wearing a light-blue Baltimore Glass T-shirt. He walked up to me and wearily shook my hand, introducing himself and inviting me to his small office in the back.

Caleb picked up a stack of automotive and hunting magazines from the top of an old brown folding chair and threw them onto the floor, motioning for me to have a seat. I scanned the small room, noticing the exceptional photographs that hung on Caleb's wall. A few featured the old service center that existed in the building before Baltimore Glass took it over. Others showed what the neighborhood had looked like in its prime.

What caught my attention most, though, was a grainy picture of a strapping young guy surfing a massive wave in clear blue water.

"Is that you?" I asked.

Caleb's eyes lit up as he swiveled his chair around to admire the picture. It turned out that Caleb was once an avid surfer.

We spent the first two hours of our conversation talking about the various waves we had ridden around the world. He told me all about his adventures during the 1960s in a VW van surfing the coastline of Southern California and his time chasing big waves in Hawaii. I told him stories of surfing the shark-infested waters of South Africa and the freezing-cold emerald waves of Northern Ireland. Caleb even took me up to the rickety old attic where he kept his surfboard, coated in decades of dust. He picked it up proudly, as if a thousand memories of waves were flashing before his eyes, and dusted it off as if inspired to give it another go.

Our surfing conversation turned to a history lesson about the neighborhood and the business. Caleb, who was married to the founder's daughter, Maureen, told me all about Baltimore Glass Company, which was established in 1928. In his early twenties, Caleb had gone to work for Maureen's dad. When his father-in-law died unexpectedly, Caleb stepped up to run the business. There was great pride in his voice. It was clear why the company had remained so relevant for all these years.

Unlike the fourteen other properties we had bought along Remington Avenue, Caleb's Baltimore Glass Company was still full of life and buzzing with employees, many of whom lived in Remington. Unlike our other purchases, I wasn't there that day to buy out a slumlord or an absentee owner who had let his property deteriorate at the expense and safety of the community. I was there to start a relationship and work in concert with Caleb to find a mutually beneficial solution that would work for him while allowing the Main Street project to move forward.

Eventually, the conversation shifted to me, and I shared with Caleb the inspiring work that I had been part of, both around the world with PeacePlayers and now back home in Baltimore. I told him that our purpose at Seawall had become crystal clear, and that we saw ourselves as the neighborhood's ally, simply there to help them realize their dreams. I told him all about the community's master plan and about how neighbors wanted inclusive progress.

Then I did what not many other developers would ever have done. I told Caleb that we had acquired all the other properties needed for the Main Street project to move forward. All that was left was his. Finally, I asked him if he would be open to discussing selling the Baltimore Glass Company building.

Silence filled the small office as Caleb's gaze shifted down toward his feet. Not knowing where else to look, my eyes scanned the messy office as I waited for Caleb to process the magnitude of the question I had just dropped. An article from *The Baltimore Sun* newspaper praising Baltimore Glass Company's work hung proudly framed above the cluttered desk. This had long been his company, a place he put his heart and soul into, and a staple of the community for years. He knew those rooms and walls so well. He knew his employees. Clearly he cared and was taken aback by the implications of selling the physical space he'd worked so hard in for decades.

While I had just met Caleb a couple of hours earlier, I trusted him. I knew that if I was genuine, loving, and open with him, he might be able to trust me too, and that he might be drawn into the vision that was coming to life. By approaching Caleb this way, I could create an atmosphere of mutual trust, which in my experience had always resulted in the critical open dialogue needed to make impossible things possible.

After what seemed like an eternity, Caleb looked back up at me and repeated exactly what Carlene had told me earlier: "It's not for sale."

■ ■ ■ ■ ■

By then, I had heard answers like this many times. I had heard it in South Africa when principals of white schools wouldn't let their students go into a Black township. I had heard it when we first presented the idea of Miller's Court to our most trusted financial advisors, who had all told us that the project would never work and that investing time, energy, and resources in Remington was a bad idea.

I wanted to tell Carlene and Caleb that the words *can't* and *no* inspired us at Seawall. What mattered was that we had read the community's master plan and loved the idea of playing a larger role in Remington and empowering the neighborhood. We were beginning to understand that the more impossible something seemed, the more a shift in perception was needed to bring that idea to life.

Baltimore Glass Company's building was key to Remington's grow-ing momentum. We weren't just buying it for ourselves, we were buying it to combine GRIA's and Seawall's visions and begin to implement a piece of the master plan. We were buying it so the neighborhood could move forward in a responsible way. We were buying it to demonstrate that real estate could actually empower and unite a community rather than tear it apart.

Caleb just wasn't on board yet. I knew that relationships and trust take time. I was fully committed to helping him realize that he was going to be a part of something big. Selling his building was not only going to benefit him, it was also going to benefit his community and his city.

Before my meeting with Caleb that day, Seawall had spent close to $4 million on assembling the first fourteen properties, but there was a catch. None of the other properties were worth that investment if we couldn't get all fifteen, because each property was part of the puzzle that made up the vision. When pieced together, the sum of the parts allowed for a dream to become a reality. It was an all-or-nothing prop-osition.

We had taken an enormous risk getting to that point without any guarantee that we would be successful in purchasing the Baltimore Glass Company building. Compounding the mounting pressure of the situation was the fact that we were financing this project differently than we had funded others in the past. Whereas our earlier projects cobbled together tax credits, loans from banks, and a lot of creativity, this one was on a completely different scale, and we needed signifi-cant additional help. After the Browns had been the first outside inves-tors for our 30 by 13 project, we had welcomed eight more Baltimore families into our tight-knit group of investors — along with my father, who put in $250,000 of his own money. Our group believed deeply in what we were doing. These weren't just investment funds. They were real human beings with real families who had worked incredibly hard for their money. While there was great risk and pressure in borrowing money from a bank, it paled in comparison to ever disappointing one of these generous families who had just placed so much trust in our hands. While we knew they were more focused on the positive social impact than on the financial returns we could offer, we also knew we never wanted to let them down.

They had trusted us and were swept up in Remington's movement too. While those families wanted to make money, they were more focused on making Baltimore better. Each wished to play a role in helping the neighborhood's plan become reality. They wanted to be able to walk their grandchildren proudly through future construction projects, explaining that they had been a part of helping the community's vision come to life.

Even though Caleb wasn't there yet, an unwavering faith in the process had kept me calm and laser-focused on the purpose of the work we were doing and on the larger picture. While he had just said no — as I had anticipated — we had also clearly connected. I trusted that with enough time, he would come to understand the value of the master plan to the community and to his company. I had total confidence that we'd eventually see eye to eye on the powerful reasons why this project had to happen.

Over the next few weeks, I came back again and again to the Baltimore Glass Company.

"You again," Carlene always said when I walked in, giving me the stink eye before Caleb came out to meet me.

"I'm not getting rid of you, am I?" he usually asked.

I always shook my head and pressed on.

Through the course of several more visits over the next month, I learned that Caleb wasn't the only one I had to convince.

"Why don't you come by the house to meet my wife, Maureen," Caleb told me one day with a smile. "She's the one who makes all the decisions anyway."

Of course I accepted the invitation. I was beyond committed to helping carry forward the vision of the community, and I had to do something; I couldn't let the conversation end here, especially since Caleb and I had begun developing such a strong friendship in the small amount of time we had spent together.

■ ■ ■ ■ ■

For the next three months, I visited Caleb and Maureen at their home almost every Sunday, building the relationship and discussing the opportunity. They too loved Remington and wanted to see it flourish. They appreciated GRIA's master plan and the potential for the Main Street project to unite the community behind a single shared vision. As our friendship strengthened, Caleb and Maureen came to appreciate that Seawall wasn't just a developer and that we, like them, cared deeply about the well-being of their neighborhood, their company, and their employees.

On one particular Sunday, as we sat watching the Ravens football game on TV and drinking Coors Lights in their living room, Caleb turned to me with an unusually serious expression on his face and asked me a question out of nowhere. He spoke with a kind of directness I hadn't heard him use before.

"Thibault, even if I sold you my building, how are you going to get around the Earl Bell factor?" he asked, taking a sip of his beer. "No one else seems to be able to get past him, and he seems to fight every single project ever proposed in Remington."

Earl's reputation had spread throughout the entire community — in fact, throughout the entire city. Caleb had heard the story of him battling the bulldozer. I paused to think about how to answer his question. In a way, it was the same question everyone had asked us before we started the Miller's Court project. It reflected what people had asked PeacePlayers as we had gone to war-torn countries where peace and reconciliation had seemed impossible. It was the "There is no way, so why are you so fixated on this?" question. I had heard it before and recognized the thinking behind it.

*If all the evidence is to the contrary here, why do this? Why burn out fighting to make the impossible happen?*

"Look, Caleb, while Earl has upset a lot of people, he has worked with us in the past," I explained. "We plan to include him every step of the way and make sure that he too feels a sense of pride, ownership, and authorship in the finished project. This is larger than Earl, and I believe he will understand that and be supportive of the community's vision."

There was an awkward silence. I could tell that Caleb didn't want to spoil my optimism, but he was also clearly unconvinced. His eyes told me that with Earl in the picture, the road would not be as easy as I was making it out to be. He was questioning why he would even spend time considering selling to us if at the end of the day we could never get the project past Earl.

Still, I kept spending time with Caleb and Maureen. I told my stories. Over time, they began to come around to the notion of selling their property for the greater good. Their only request, if they were to sell, was that they wanted to find another building in Remington out of loyalty to their employees, many of whom still walked to work. We loved their commitment to staying in the neighborhood, and we never wanted one of our projects to displace anyone who didn't want to leave. We began to work with Caleb and Maureen to find the perfect replacement property for the Baltimore Glass Company.

Of course, the word *no* reappeared again as we brought them around to different buildings. Sometimes Caleb loved a place but Maureen shut it down. Other times it was the other way around. Again and again our team thought we had found the perfect building, only for them to pass. Ultimately, they were determined to find the right place. We were too. To Seawall, it was worth it to get a company like theirs the best building possible. In the end, all of their objections were right.

After a few months of exploring various opportunities, we showed Caleb and Maureen an 8,000-square-foot warehouse, three times bigger than their current facility. They fell in love with it. The building was two blocks away from their existing shop and provided them the opportunity to grow and streamline their business.

A month later we had signed all the paperwork, and Caleb and Maureen were the proud owners of a beautiful new building. Finally, the three contiguous blocks of property along Remington Avenue were ready for reimagining. The next step was to share the expanded Main Street vision of GRIA's commercial corridor plan with the whole community, including Earl.

# 18

# Co-ownership

*"Growth is never by mere chance;*
*it is the result of forces working together."*

— JAMES CASH PENNEY

On a warm early-summer morning in June of 2013, a hundred Remington residents vied for space inside one of the conference rooms at Miller's Court. Whispers of anticipation and excitement bubbled against the brick walls. More people filed in and began to take their seats, unsure of what they were about to hear. There had been rumors of a large Seawall project in the works, but there were very few facts to substantiate the gossip that passed through the narrow streets of Remington.

I recognized many of the diverse faces who poured into the room. I hugged the people I knew the best. The Gorbys and several other young teachers who had just bought houses were present. Randy and our fearless neighbors who had guarded the building at night during construction were there. Some local business owners and many of the neighbors who had lived in the community their whole lives came too.

Anyone who was curious to hear what all the buzz was about joined us that day.

Even though we'd acquired the land needed to bring the Main Street project to life, the first significant phase of the community's master plan still faced an uphill battle. The properties weren't zoned correctly to allow for the mix of apartments, offices, and retail that the community envisioned being built there, and simply rezoning them, for a number of technical and legal reasons, was not an option. The only way forward was to get the green light for a planned unit development (PUD) — in essence, a binding contract between a community, a developer, and the city that allowed the uses in large projects to be shifted as long as the community supports them.

For traditional developers, a PUD is often the least desirable option, because it opens the developer up to unlimited financial and programmatic demands from the community. They can ask for large donations, special favors, or even unrelated, extra projects. Essentially, it takes the control out of the developer's hands and puts it into the hands of the community. At Seawall, however, we loved PUDs. In fact, our Union Mill project was one of the fastest PUDs that had ever been approved in Baltimore. Since we liked the idea of a contract with the community, we didn't mind pursuing a PUD, and, because of the bond we'd formed with the people in the neighborhood, we were confident that we could work together. The only thing nagging at us was the fact that the previous PUD attempted in Remington, the $70 million Walmart project, had been fought by a small number of people in the community.

Another reason a PUD is so challenging to pull off is because of the massive layers of government and neighborhood approvals that developers need in order to proceed. Dozens of public meetings are required, and many city agencies need to meticulously sign off at every step of the way. With luck, a developer may be able to obtain a fully approved PUD in about a year, but most PUDs take far longer. Many never even make it to the end.

As the last of the neighbors settled into their chairs in the conference room that morning, Evan welcomed everyone and began the conversation.

"Thank you all for coming," he said warmly. He looked surprised by the number of people who had shown up. "We've been following your plan to redevelop several properties along Remington Avenue with the hopes of one day turning it into a commercial corridor, and we love it. We've given it a lot of thought, and we believe that the idea can be made even stronger. By adding a few more properties into the equation, we believe that the vision can be expanded upon and we can actually turn Remington Avenue back into the Main Street it once was."

Evan paused for a moment. Even though we had quietly checked in with several Remington neighbors throughout the process, he knew this expansion might come across to the rest of the community as abrupt. He also knew that, because Seawall had acquired the properties under the radar, the next news he was going to share might be a shock — hopefully a good shock, but a shock nonetheless. But since he heard no objections and sensed the same excitement we all had for the project, he continued. "Over the past twelve months, we've purchased all the properties needed to allow our combined idea to move forward. We fully acknowledge that this is a major project for Remington and that we are at the very early stages of its ideation. As always, we'd like to work with you to make sure that this is everything you had hoped it would be, and more. We want to hear directly from you about what you think is missing here in Remington and how these three blocks, fully reimagined, can really help fulfill your commercial corridor vision."

Evan walked everyone through a series of early presentation boards we had put together to help start the conversation. He detailed the impressive size and scope of what the three blocks could look like with a bit of creative thinking. When he finally paused, the room was instantly filled with surprised and giddy chatter. Many people raised their hands as both long-term residents and newcomers starting calling things out.

"We need a bank," shouted one person.

"What about a dry cleaner?"

"We don't have a pharmacy," added another.

Soon a bike shop, a doctor's office, a barbershop, a beauty salon, and a day care were among the other businesses added to the list.

One by one, Evan meticulously addressed every question and

suggestion thrown his way. With each answer, he continued to build trust and confidence among the neighbors.

Just as the PeacePlayers team hadn't shown up in South Africa and told the people there that we had figured out how to solve centuries of racism and conflict, the Seawall team hadn't shown up to the Remington meeting telling the residents that we had come up with the perfect project that was going to improve their community. Instead, we explained to the neighbors gathered there in the room that we had listened and that we intended to continue to listen. We wanted to help.

By this point, the energy in the room was contagious. Finally, Remington was going to get the goods and services it had been asking for, in a project that it could be proud of and rally behind. All the hard work and planning that had gone into the master plan was going to start coming to fruition. The countless volunteer hours that the members of GRIA had spent getting input and buy-in for the plan were going to result in better street lighting, more safety, better walkability, opportunities for jobs, and, perhaps most important, something to believe in and a way to begin to unite Remington. What had started as just a dream and a vision on paper — a seemingly impossible one at that — was now being expanded upon and looked ready to come to life.

But no big project is ever that simple. As I scanned the crowded room and I gauged people's reactions to what Evan had just said, I became fixated on one person: Earl Bell. He sat all by himself, feverishly taking notes while the community discussed what would become the largest project that Remington had ever seen.

While we had remained vague about the reason we had invited the neighborhood to the meeting, it felt like everyone had shown up out of love and support for the unusual relationship that had been forming between a developer and a community. Most people were there because they had been positively impacted by what we had created together so far, and they wanted to have a voice in what was going to come about as we moved forward. There was a sense of camaraderie and optimism in everybody — except for Earl.

■ ■ ■ ■ ■

Five minutes before the meeting was set to begin, I had watched Earl Bell march into the room without saying hello to anyone. He had avoided eye contact and rushed to an empty chair as far away from everyone else as possible. As helpful to us as Earl had been in the past, he was hard to read. It always felt like we were skating on thin ice with him and with one wrong word he might instantly turn against us.

Earl didn't appear to appreciate the element of surprise that came with this meeting — or GRIA's master plan itself. As the president of UCR, Remington's other community organization, he had received several open invitations from GRIA to engage in the planning process but had refused to participate, claiming that GRIA wasn't a real community association. During Evan's presentation, I watched out of the corner of my eye as Earl stared down at his legal pad, flipping through his notes as he fidgeted in his chair.

This was an important meeting for the community, and we wanted everyone, including Earl, to feel welcome and involved. By this point, after more than ten years as head of the UCR, Earl had frustrated most of the neighbors. Many people believed his conservative approach had held Remington back, and they had grown displeased with his leadership. Lines of communication between Earl and much of the rest of the community had evaporated. His once-thriving neighborhood association, at one point the only group in town, had dwindled to a shadow of its former self as his members had stopped coming to meetings or left to join the more inclusive GRIA. The people of Remington wanted progress, and they wanted to see development past the small handful of projects that Seawall had helped them complete.

As the meeting progressed, Evan explained that the fifteen properties we had just purchased weren't zoned properly for what the community was proposing. He explained to the neighbors about the challenge at hand — namely the PUD process. The PUD was something we wanted to be optimistic about, despite how hard it might be to pull off.

We had begun the meeting that day with a contagious amount of energy and excitement at announcing this impactful project for the community. While we knew it wouldn't be easy, we were confident we could work with GRIA, UCR, and Earl to get buy-in from all parties. We had proven we could do that in our previous projects, and until the moment that Evan mentioned the PUD, we had no reason to think that we couldn't do it again.

I watched as Earl put down his pen; his shoulders and chest appeared to rise and fall as he gave an enormous sigh. He adjusted the glasses on his nose and grazed his fingers against the stubble on his chin as he looked up from his notepad, maybe for the first time since sitting down an hour earlier. He smiled as if he'd finally found our weak spot.

My heart sank.

It wasn't just anyone who had derailed the Walmart PUD. Earl had played a significant role in leading that charge. The appeals and lawsuits were just too much, and the developer had no choice but to walk away from the project and from Remington altogether, defeated, embarrassed, and $6 million poorer. All it takes is one person opposing a PUD to ensure that the developer is stuck in court for years, unlikely to ever get the project going. And Remington had that one person.

Earl was the guy who had chained himself to a gate to stop a bulldozer. Along the same lines, he was the only person to impede a tiny French restaurant's pursuit of outdoor seating for more than four years, even though others in the neighborhood supported the request. He had thrust himself onto a citywide stage in the fight that defeated the Walmart-anchored shopping center that the majority of his constituents wanted. And now, sitting in the meeting that day, with every squiggle of the pen he appeared to be gearing up for another fight.

As the meeting wrapped up and people started to leave, Earl bolted out of the room. Watching him, I had a gut-wrenching sense that we no longer saw eye to eye. So much of the spirit of Earl's opposition to development came from an important place, one we respected greatly. Every neighborhood needed a diligent and bold watchdog. Still optimistic, we weren't about to give up working to keep him as an ally and partner. This was the biggest and riskiest project we had ever taken on, and we needed Earl's guidance more than ever before.

# 19

## Beyond Comfort

*"To bring about change, you must not be afraid to take the first step.*
*We will fail when we fail to try."*

— ROSA PARKS

Dodging a few patches of snow on the sidewalk, I tapped the envelope gently against my palm. Winter was giving way to spring, but Baltimore's biting chill breezed down Huntingdon Avenue as I stopped in front of a regular Remington row house that sat just a few blocks away from Miller's Court. I sighed and pulled my jacket closer. It was dusk, and a trickle of rush hour traffic sped by behind me.

I scooted along the sidewalk and briskly climbed the stairs. Taking one last deep breath, I exhaled, then knocked on the single glass pane at the top of the old wooden door.

*I hope he's home.*

It had been months since we announced the Main Street project, which was now being called Remington Row. But as I had feared, the majority of the community's enthusiasm for change was being countered by Earl's preference to keep the neighborhood as it was. Since the presentation, our days at Seawall had been filled with countless meetings, emails, and conversations with the myriad of committees that are needed to inch a PUD forward. Earl began to fight the project by filing one negative letter after another with the various governing agencies, trying to undermine, delay, and derail the process and the project the way he had so effectively done for past developments he didn't want.

Despite all the pushback, we still desperately wanted to connect with him. We didn't believe that Earl needed to be our adversary. Convinced that we could still collaborate, we worked tirelessly to include him in the process. We weren't going to give up on him, and we certainly weren't going to exclude anyone in the community from these important conversations. We were simply asking for a chance to sit down and talk with Earl so we could begin to understand why he was so adamantly opposed to the community's plan.

Showing up on someone's doorstep unannounced for a complicated conversation is never easy. In times of electronic communication and social media, we often hide behind our screens because it is easier, less personal, and more comfortable. In this case, I had failed to get in touch with Earl in all other ways, so I was left with no other choice but to just show up.

Standing there on Earl's porch, waiting for him to open his door, I looked up at the awning and the partial view of sky at its edge. It was getting darker outside, making it easier to see that the lights were clearly on inside his house. To be treated like this, to be left on the doorstep, didn't feel right.

*Why isn't he willing even to have a conversation?*

■ ■ ■ ■ ■

From what I came to understand, when Earl first arrived in Remington in the late 1990s, his watchdog mentality was new and even needed. The neighborhood, which had been overlooked for so long, now had an individual who was extremely tenacious in his fight against development. However, as the years rolled along, the community began to realize that Earl wasn't fighting these projects because of a horrible political issue that was being overlooked or to stop some violation of the human rights that the people of Remington were entitled to. He was standing in front of the bulldozer because *he* didn't want this kind of change in *his* neighborhood.

Earl was so driven in these goals, he appeared to pay little attention to what others wanted. It didn't seem to be in his nature to seek out or try to understand the many dimensions of a project or what the people who lived in Remington were asking for. Once he had his mind made up, it seemed hard for him to change it again.

Rather than listening to the desires of the community that were rising quickly all around him, Earl opted to fly solo. His style began alienating the people who had once counted on him to protect their interests. As time passed and nearby neighborhoods began to flourish again, too many buildings in Remington stayed vacant, street corners remained dark, and job opportunities lagged behind. Worst of all, too many people in Remington felt they were being left behind.

Some neighbors had started to push back against Earl and what he represented. His ideas of preserving Remington felt to others like a desire to keep it frozen in time. Many of the people who lived in the neighborhood — including those who'd been there decades longer than Earl — wanted Remington to return to its glory days when businesses, jobs, and a unified community spirit existed. They remembered when kids played freely and safely in the streets. There was a time when almost every corner had a thriving business on it, and during those days, people took pride in where they lived and why they lived there. Now the folks of Remington wanted change for themselves, for future generations, and for the community at large.

Sensing that Earl and the UCR were holding back progress, members of the community had gotten together and formed GRIA in 2007, around the same time that we had first visited the Miller's Court building. This association, which was full of change agents like our coaches in South Africa, was infused with the passion, purpose, and drive of a group yearning for something they felt entitled to.

GRIA represented the growing number of people living in Remington who were tired of their neighborhood being overlooked by opportunity, only to see it taking root in the next community over.

They too wanted to see positive progress and thoughtful and inclusive development. They weren't a group of millennial transplants descending on Remington in search of the next hot neighborhood. The GRIA members were incredibly diverse in age, gender, and socioeconomic background, and they represented a healthy cross section of the people living there.

GRIA wasn't interested in just being a backup organization for those who simply didn't agree with the UCR. The members of GRIA reimagined what it meant to represent a community, and they put their social purpose — preserving Remington as a diverse and vibrant neighborhood where opportunity was accessible to all — at the forefront of everything they did. Their determination to lead with that purpose is exactly what drew many of the people of Remington to them.

Even the location of the monthly GRIA meetings, which took place in the basement of an old weathered church, spoke to the fighting spirit of this amazing group. There was nothing fancy about the building or its fading yellow paint, but its huge stone foundation and thick hundred-year-old walls were rock-solid and built to last. GRIA wasn't messing around. They were committed to moving steadily and inclusively.

The group had started small, with tree-planting projects, community gardens, neighborhood cleanup days, and ongoing beautification initiatives that showed both long-term legacy residents and new residents that there was a renewed sense of pride and ownership in the community. They brought forth an infusion of energy, unity, and care that Remington hadn't had in more than fifty years, since the factories supporting the blue-collar families had left the city. This stood in stark relief to Earl's commitment to keeping Remington as he had found it in the late 1990s.

The movement that GRIA started picked up energy with every new flower that was planted. Remington's time had clearly arrived, and a culmination and convergence of powerful forces, both positive and negative, were beginning to unite this little community, which was becoming crystal clear in its resolve.

In order to rise above any one individual's influence, Remington needed a project and a plan to unite behind. It had waited long enough. The Remington Row PUD was that project.

■ ■ ■ ■ ■

As I continued to wait on Earl's porch after knocking for the second time, my feelings were deeply and profoundly hurt. Earl had emphatically supported our Miller's Court project. We had worked well together on many other ideas. In fact, Earl and I used to talk all the time. At one point, he had been our first call anytime we thought about doing anything. When we had wanted to redevelop an old tire shop into nonprofit office space, a community black-box theater, and a restaurant, he had advised us about the rezoning process. He had held our hand and supported us every step of the way, all the way down to the liquor license for the restaurant. The same back and forth would take place whenever new projects were on the horizon. We talked about the smaller things too, like how much I admired the gusto with which Earl organized a water table every year for a local charity 5k run.

*Now this?*

It felt as if one of the PeacePlayers coaches had turned on the program and accused it of making the divides in South Africa worse. It felt as if one of the Baltimore teachers had accused Miller's Court of exploiting the education problem in the city for commercial gain.

Evan and I had emailed and called Earl more than two dozen times during a six-month period requesting the opportunity to meet and talk. Each time he had brushed us aside with one excuse after another about why he was too busy.

*Too busy to have meaningful, face-to-face conversations about the largest project in the history of Remington?*

My third knock lightly rattled the door again.

Seawall had met numerous times with GRIA and all of the city agencies by that point. Everyone was on board. Not only were they incredibly supportive of the plan, but they were actually helpful in molding it to better meet the neighborhood's needs. But we couldn't get through to Earl, and that scared us.

There seemed to be only one way to get Earl to see that Remington Row was larger than any of us, and that was to talk to him in person. I wanted to see the man I had once grown to call a thought partner. I knew what tumultuous working partnerships were like. Sean and I had butted heads, but it never stopped our ability to talk through important decisions. Surfing had brought Caleb and me together the way I'd seen basketball do for myself and so many others. Even Charlie and I disagreed a lot about what was possible in the world based on the different circumstances and times under which we had been raised. Yet in all these instances, despite all the differences, it was always possible to find common ground.

I tapped the letter, my contingency plan for connecting with him in case he didn't come to the door, against my palm during the incredibly uncomfortable stretches between knocks.

*His lights are on. His car is out front. He must be home.*

I knocked again, less out of hope than disbelief.

*I'm being totally iced out.*

After what felt like the longest two minutes of my life, I finally dropped the handwritten letter in his mailbox and turned away from the door. The streetlights were on. It was late. It was time to call it a day.

*This feels wrong, but he's left me with no other option.*

The letter to Earl was deeply personal. I had written from my heart to make sure he knew how hard we were trying to connect with him, how much we valued his guidance on the past projects we had worked on together, and how important it was that he play an active role in shaping the direction of this big, new opportunity that the community was dreaming up. It ended with an open invitation to meet together. It was all I could do.

With the letter out of my hands, I felt relieved. Once again, getting knocked out of my comfort zone made way for a new realization. With or without Earl, this project had to happen. Failure was not an option.

As I walked away from Earl's house, I realized that Seawall's role in this project was to be the silent leader. It was less about actually building the buildings than it was about bringing the community together and empowering them to get what they wanted: forward progress so that Remington could get back to its once-thriving self.

A convergence of smaller and larger forces — teachers and nonprofits through Miller's Court, Charmington's, community members, and Seawall — had miraculously aligned their missions and purposes with Remington's success at the same moment in time. Even our neighbors at Johns Hopkins University had joined the conversations to see how they as an anchor institution could help Remington achieve its dreams. That perfect alignment had created a groundswell that, if guided humbly in the right direction, could help expand that energy. Our job was to amplify that groundswell and make it so large that no single person could stop it.

My experience on Earl's doorstep was sad, but it was also sobering. It inspired me to do something unexpected, something above and beyond any action I'd taken with any of Seawall's previous projects. It would forever change the way that I would go about helping to bring ideas to life.

# 20

## Inside Out

*"When you talk you are only repeating something you already know.
But if you listen, you may learn something new."*

— HIS HOLINESS THE DALAI LAMA

A few days later, clipboard in one hand, backpack slung over my shoulder, I trudged down the sidewalk past a line of red-brick row houses on Twenty-Seventh Street between Remington Avenue and Howard Street. I stopped in front of a house with the porch light on. The streetlights had already been illuminated for the evening. I looked down at the ink-squiggled papers snapped to my clipboard.

*Maybe it's too late for one more?*

In the week since my final attempt to speak with Earl at his house, I'd already collected fifty signatures. The plan was to knock on as many doors in Remington as possible. Even though Earl wouldn't open his, I wanted to see if the rest of the neighborhood would.

*Might they not just open their doors but also deeply connect with me and engage in a conversation about the well-being and future of their community?*

I had to know. I also wanted to see if every neighbor I connected with would sign a petition in support of the project. The final land use

216

hearing, where the fate of the PUD would be determined by members of the Baltimore City Council, was still six months away. While I wasn't sure how many signatures of support I could get, I hoped whatever number I could gather would help demonstrate that the Remington Row PUD truly was by and for the community. Going door-to-door was the only way to be sure about the one doubt that clawed at the back of my mind.

*After all the listening, what if I discover that there actually isn't the support in the community I think there is?*

I climbed the stairs to my third house visit of the evening. If the objective was merely to collect signatures, we could have divided up the task among the Seawall team or even hired outside help. Instead, I was determined to show people that Seawall wasn't some monster hedge fund from New York City with a billion dollars in capital as rumored. I wanted people to know that we were a company of local folks, like my dad and myself. I wanted them to know that we cared deeply about Baltimore and neighborhoods like Remington. Mostly, I just wanted them to know that we were human beings and would be honored to hear their thoughts.

Every door knock began uncomfortably — showing up unannounced is always awkward — but I hesitated in front of this third door even longer than usual. The early spring sun had already set, and the sky was losing its blueness by the minute. I didn't like to bother people after dark, but my earlier conversations at the two previous houses had been so fascinating and inspiring, I couldn't help but keep going. Remington was pretty diverse as far as Baltimore neighborhoods go. Its population was about half white, a quarter Black, and a quarter Asian, Latinx, and mixed-race residents. There were older residents and millennials. Some people were new to the area; others had been here for generations. Remington had residents who had never graduated high school and residents who had earned post-graduate degrees from Johns Hopkins University up the street. No matter who they were, I wanted to know more about each and every one of them.

I raised my hand, braced myself, and knocked, thinking that I'd give it one quick try. Almost as soon as I took my hand from the hardwood of the door, an older white gentleman clicked the lock and greeted me with a half smile. He had a bandanna covering his hair and looked like he might have been busy with something in the house.

"I'm sorry, sir," I managed to blurt out. "I lost track of time, and I didn't mean to bother you. I can come back another day." I started to turn to walk away.

"No bother at all, man. How can I help you?" he responded.

"Thank you," I said, shifting myself to face him again. "I'm Thibault. I work with a company called Seawall, which built the teachers' housing project around the corner from here on Howard Street."

I pointed in the direction of Miller's Court, a silhouette in the fading light.

"I'd like to tell you about another project that we are helping the community pull together and hear your thoughts on what is happening here in Remington."

"I know who you are, man. I love you guys. I'm John Bales," he said, shaking my hand warmly.

John invited me to sit on one of the two white plastic chairs on his porch, which overlooked the abandoned block we had just purchased on Remington Avenue down the street from his house.

"Thank you," I said as we both took our seats.

I leaned forward in my chair, drawing myself closer to John. I wanted him to know that nothing was more important to me than the conversation we were about to have.

"John, I'm here to listen. I've been going door-to-door throughout Remington hoping to understand people's stories as well as to share ours."

As if he'd been waiting for this moment for years, John didn't need any more guidance to start. I listened to him talk for an hour as dusk turned to night. He told me that he had grown up in Remington, in this very house, where he had been living for more than fifty years. He told me stories of how great and safe this neighborhood had been and what it was like growing up around here. He described riding bikes with friends to the old ice house building and playing stickball on the street after dinner. He recalled when there were thriving businesses throughout the entire neighborhood and no one ever really needed to leave because everything they could possibly want was right here in Remington. John's tone and demeanor shifted, though, as he explained how drugs and crime had taken over as jobs had been lost.

Every now and then I'd interject with a question to get John to tell me more about a detail that fascinated me, but for the most part I sat quietly with my eyes locked onto his as I created the space for him to open up about what was on his mind and in his heart. More important, John's life and stories, along with the hundreds of other stories I would hear, helped shape my understanding of the area's rich history and the fragility of the opportunity that lay in front of it.

Gradually the conversation shifted from the past to the present, and John explained to me why he was excited about the progress and improvements he was seeing.

"It's not until you guys from Seawall showed up and started making things happen that we saw a glimmer of hope," he said.

"John, have you heard about the Remington Row PUD that we are working on with the community?" I asked him.

"Yeah, I love it. Everyone is talking about it. We are all sick and tired of staring at vacant lots and boarded-up houses," he said, motioning toward the site of the proposed development, which was now barely visible in the darkness. "We are all pissed off that the Walmart project didn't happen."

He looked into my eyes as if checking to see whether he had permission to vent.

"I want to be able to walk out of my house and down the street to buy things I need, not to have to go all the way out to the county just to shop. I want more happening around here. I want people out and about. I want it safe again."

I pulled out some renderings of the Remington Row project to share with John so he could get a feel for the design, size, and scale of what was being proposed.

"It's beautiful," he said, examining the drawing I had placed on the small plastic table between us. "Looks like an old warehouse that could have been sitting there for the last hundred years."

"Thanks! We worked hard to design something that would fit in nicely. We've also been asking people what kind of shops they'd like to see when the project gets going. Do you have any suggestions?" I asked.

"I'm easy, man. Although a pharmacy would be really helpful."

"I think that's fair, John, and we're going to work on making that happen for you."

John and I shot the breeze for a few more minutes. He told me more about his memories in the neighborhood. We both laughed as I told him how I used to pick up the wonderfully greasy cheesesteak sandwiches for lunch from Corky's, one of Remington's classic dive bars of yesteryear, when I worked for the painting company here in high school.

"We'll have to get a beer sometime," he offered.

"I'd like that, John," I said, realizing I should probably get going. "Thank you so much for all of your time and stories tonight. The rest of the community has been signing this petition in favor of the project. Would you be interested in signing it as well?"

I presented the clipboard, our breath now visible in the cooling air.

"Lynn," called out John, without even pausing. He turned his head back toward the house. "Get out here and sign this for these guys. The more support they have, the more likely the project is to happen."

With that, John and his wife added their names to the growing list of people who believed deeply in Remington's potential.

My conversation with John was just one of many that I would have over the next six months. Almost every evening I went door-to-door in Remington, focusing mostly on the blocks closest to the proposed Main Street project. I listened to hundreds of residents sitting on stoops and porches, relaxing in living rooms, or just passing on the street.

In the occupied houses that surrounded the proposed development, I collected 250 signatures — a total of 99 percent of respondents — for a petition in support of the Remington Row PUD project. I spoke with pastors, heroin addicts, teachers, drug dealers, college students, legacy residents who had lived in Remington their entire lives, young professionals who had just moved in, nurses, firefighters, and veterans. The people I spoke with were Black, white, South Asian, and Latinx, and they beautifully represented Remington's diversity.

It became a running joke throughout the neighborhood as I inevitably bumped into people I knew every single evening: "There goes Thibault, with his backpack and petitions."

This humor aside, Earl's steadily intensifying fight against the PUD was not to be laughed at. It was frightening. However, I knew that every signature we received in favor of the project would go a long way toward convincing the various city agencies that the community's support was enormous, and that it dwarfed Earl's opposition to the project.

All of the conversations I had were fascinating not only because they allowed me to hear the stories of the people who lived here, but also because they allowed the people who lived in the neighborhood to hear Seawall's story. It allowed us to connect. The residents came to realize that despite the rumors, we were from here. We'd been to Preakness. We remembered when the Baltimore Colts left in the middle of the night. We watched the Ravens win two Super Bowls. We witnessed Cal Ripken Jr. break the record for consecutive games played. We went to the giant farmers market under the freeway together every Sunday. We craved the famous crab cakes from Faidley's in Lexington Market. We were multigenerational and as much a part of Baltimore as anyone. Unlike the group involved in the failed Walmart project, our capital came from passionate, local families.

Whether folks had been living in the neighborhood for generations, like John, or they had just moved in, the responses were all the same. They loved the project. They appreciated being able to get to know us and give feedback.

I was on a mission to connect deeply with as many people as possible in Remington and make sure this massive project was indeed something the community wanted. It spanned several city blocks and was going to cost more than $60 million to build. I wanted everyone to know that while we at Seawall were going to play an enormous role in helping the project come to life, it wasn't our idea. A project of this size and magnitude would work only if it was truly driven — not just supported — by the community. It needed to be sought after, contributed to, and advocated for in order to improve the quality of life for those who called Remington home.

I now realized that the Miller's Court and 30 by 13 projects were easy for people to get behind. After all, we hadn't been building anything new. We had just been taking abandoned buildings and boarded-up houses, fixing them, and filling them with teachers and nonprofits. It is really hard to argue against that. Seawall's purpose of providing great space for all those focused on kids and education had been obvious, and our work had been on a small enough scale that it hadn't really bothered anyone.

In this case, however, that original purpose was evolving and growing. It was beginning to encompass communities beyond the teachers and nonprofits that we were originally focused on. We weren't just impacting the children, the schools, and those who lived or worked within our four walls. With the proposed Main Street project, we were about to impact an entire neighborhood, every resident on every corner. The gravity of that wasn't lost on us, and we didn't take the responsibility lightly.

I wanted to know what all of Remington thought about our company, about our soul and our purpose, and about this project. I had heard countless times from the people I knew well who were active in the community. Many of them went to the GRIA meetings each month, but that wasn't enough. I wanted to know what the other 2,458 people living in Remington were hearing and saying. I wanted to listen to those who had the quieter voices, who might not have known they had a platform from which they could be heard. I wanted them to trust us to carry out the community's vision and dream. I wanted them to know about the work we had done and about the work we were proposing to do, all of which was for them, and all of which was being done with their best interests at heart.

After all of those conversations, over the course of all of those months, I began to notice that an incredibly powerful shift was taking place — a shift that only happens when we are swept up into the spirit of a movement. This time, the community of Remington began to understand that it actually did control its own destiny.

Remington was going to unite and start its next chapter. However, if the PUD was going to succeed in the face of Earl's opposition, we needed to make sure the project was as fully fleshed out as possible. That meant building the project inside out. That meant not just hearing from people like John Bales, but listening to them deeply.

■ ■ ■ ■ ■

One day, as I was pulled off to the side of Remington Avenue to check my phone for emails, I suddenly noticed someone moving between the houses on Remington Avenue. As I began to watch, I saw that the man was walking up to each house, reaching into a folder, pulling out a piece of paper, and sliding it into each mailbox. As he walked toward my car, I realized it was Earl.

Two months earlier, it had taken me an entire week to cover that same amount of ground on that very same block. Each night I had sat for long periods of time and just listened to people's ideas, stories, and dreams. Earl's approach looked different. He was covering an entire block of twenty homes in less than ten minutes.

By this point, with only four months left until the final land use hearing that would either approve or deny the Remington Row PUD, Earl's letters to the various city agencies hadn't slowed down the project. Now he was going door-to-door in his own way. While I disagreed with many of the points Earl raised, he was still a member of the community. If he felt strongly enough to print and distribute flyers to each of these houses, maybe it was best I take a look at one myself. Since he had never responded to my letter or countless additional attempts to communicate, it was really the only way I could begin to understand his concerns.

After he'd moved on to the next block, I left my car, walked up to one of the houses, and knocked on the door. By that point, I was friendly with every single person who lived on the block. My buddy Kenny Rogers, an amazing teacher and author who had purchased a house in Remington after living at Miller's Court for four years, opened the door with his newborn daughter in his arms.

"Kenny, how are you, my man?" I asked as we shook hands.

"Great, Thibault. How are you, bud?"

"I'm great too, Kenny," I said. I reached out to tickle his daughter's dangling foot. "Man, Earl just dropped something into your mailbox. I'm curious to see what it says. Would you mind if I have a look?"

"No problem," said Kenny. He shifted his daughter to the other hip so he could pull the flyer out of the mailbox.

"Good luck," he said, after taking a quick glance and handing it over with a grin.

I thanked him and walked back to my car, opening up the flyer to see what it said. On it was a rendering of the Remington Row project with one bold phrase on top:

**STOP The Remington Row PUD!**

The flyer, designed in a way I found misleading, invited anyone who read it to come to "Straight Talk" about the Remington Row project with the UCR later that night. By now, and with time working against him, Earl's campaign opposing the PUD was in full swing. He was clearly hoping to enlist others and, like he had done before, stop the project in its tracks.

I went to the impromptu UCR meeting that night, disappointed but not surprised that we hadn't been invited since Earl was going to be discussing the project. I walked up to the community center where the UCR held their monthly meetings, wondering if Earl's flyers had created a sudden wave of opposition and packed the house with angry neighbors, all there to voice their hatred for Remington Row, the PUD, and Seawall.

I breathed a sigh of relief as I walked in through the metal side door. Only about a dozen people had shown up. Earl's canvasing of the neighborhood hadn't been as powerful as our talking to folks door-to-door. The three dozen or so mostly empty chairs that had been set up facing the front of the room actually made the room look cavernous in the harsh fluorescent light.

As I watched, Earl stood up in the front of the room to call the meeting to order. I could almost see a wall between him and the attendees, a kind of invisible barrier that kept the people in their seats separated from him.

Earl paced as he spoke in front of the tiny gathering, never making eye contact and constantly staring down at his notepad as he critiqued the Remington Row project. As Earl argued that no one should support the PUD, he pointed to the set of plans that he had printed.

That night I began to realize how different our two approaches to leadership were. My idea of an effective leader, one who can galvanize people and create movements, was someone who works quietly behind the scenes, letting everyone else shine and only stepping up when absolutely necessary. Earl was proving to be the complete opposite of that. He sought to lead in the direction he believed was best, rather than letting the community and those he represented set the course.

I felt angry that Earl wasn't giving me, or anyone else, an opportunity to say anything about the project. As he spoke about how threatening Remington Row was to what he saw as the well-being of the neighborhood, I took my focus off him and let my eyes scan the room, looking at his small handful of board members. Their blank stares and slumped-over body language made me feel that they were disconnected from Earl too. Perhaps they were also tired of Earl's leadership style, which involved shutting down opportunity at every possible chance.

What bothered me the most in that moment was that almost all of Earl's board members were some of the beautiful elders who had lived in the community their entire lives and who had seen a lot in their many years in Remington. Their parents had probably ridden the trolley cars to work when the neighborhood was thriving. I knew that Earl thought he could always count on them to support his opposition of any given project, but I wasn't convinced that they too didn't want to see their neighborhood improve.

After Earl had uneventfully wrapped up that meeting, I stayed late and helped put away the chairs. While we worked, I began to get to know his board of directors, many of whom I hadn't connected with yet.

I sensed that the people who regularly attended these meetings had a palpable fear of going against Earl as well as a desire to connect in a

positive way with others in their community. I realized that this was
an important part of Remington that I needed to immerse myself in
more fully. From that day forward, I attended every single one of the
monthly UCR meetings. I usually got there early to sit with Miss Sue
or Miss Roxanne, who had both spent every one of their combined
150 years right here in Remington, and I carefully listened to their stories of the past or their complaints about the present.

After each meeting I drove Randy, our early friend from Miller's
Court, back to his house, which he had lived in for more than five
decades. During those short rides home from the community center, I
could tell Randy was gritting his teeth, trying to control the frustration
he felt about Earl's constant fight against progress.

One night he said to me, "Thibault, you guys are amazing. The
neighborhood hasn't been this nice since I was a kid. Things are so
much better now that you guys are in town. Please don't let Earl stop
you."

Covered in paint from his day job, he lumbered out of the car after
I parked in front of his twelve-foot-wide row home. After slamming
the car door, he looked back at me and added, "I'm serious."

My connections also went way beyond the monthly UCR meetings. I visited the board members individually at their homes between
meetings and simply listened for hours. Based on their response, it felt
to me like this was the first time they were being given the opportunity
to open up freely about what they wanted. Their honesty and candor
were inspiring, and they didn't hold back.

As I suspected from that initial meeting, it turned out that Earl's
board members were also unsatisfied with his inability to collaborate
and compromise. They too loved the Remington Row PUD project,
and they wanted to see their neighborhood become safe and walkable,
the way that John Bales had described it to be in its heyday. What was
even more powerful, because of their long history in Remington and
memory of how wonderful the neighborhood had been, they were
the ones who wanted to see change the most. They wanted to see the
neighborhood return to its safe and thriving self. What upset them
even more was that Earl wasn't even originally from Remington.

As my relationship with Earl's board members grew stronger, some of them began to call me after their private board meetings. After voicing concerns about what Earl would say if he ever found out they had called me, they told me everything that Earl was planning to do to stop the project. They became allies because they felt the sense of pride, ownership, and authorship that compels us as human beings to love, protect, and take care of the things that are important to us, and nothing was more important to Earl's board members than their neighborhood. They were no longer going to sit on the sidelines and let other people control their destiny.

It wasn't just Earl's board members who wanted to see progress and who were quietly helping the movement grow. The two city council members representing the community wanted to see the project happen as well. Every time Earl emailed them a complaint, they would forward the email on to us so that we could prepare ourselves to address the issues he was raising.

What I realized as a result of my hundreds of conversations in the community was incredibly powerful. Earl had become the very person he was trying to fight. He had become the disconnected developer — the person who comes into a neighborhood, tells the community what he thinks it needs, and pushes everyone else in the process aside. Earl, like too many developers, had his own vision for what he wanted to see happen, and no one else's opinion seemed to count, not even the opinions of the very people who attended his monthly meetings. Because of that, it became increasingly clear to me that Earl's campaign against the PUD and the project was dead on arrival for one main reason: he struggled to connect with people. Earl led by instilling fear in those around him and making them think that he was the only one who could protect them. History has proved that this kind of leadership isn't sustainable. It only lasts until something more positive and inclusive comes along.

# 21

## Trusting Leadership

*"To lead people, walk behind them."*

— LAO TZU

Groggy-eyed from a night spent tossing and turning, too nervous to find any real sleep, I gazed up at Baltimore City Hall. The leaves on the trees in War Memorial Plaza behind me were changing into beautiful oranges, reds, and yellows. I made my way up the massive steps of the historic downtown building.

*This is it.*

It was October 23, 2014, and after a fascinating eighteen-month process of setting the Remington Row project up for approval, the final hearing was scheduled to take place. I arrived an hour before the proceedings were scheduled to start so I could thoroughly absorb the energy of the day. I replayed over a year and a half of engaging in conversations, planning, and learning. My mind raced back and forth between the hundreds of inspiring connections I had made sitting on people's porches, the Sunday afternoons spent with Caleb and Maureen at their house, the $4 million our investors had trusted us with to allow the project to move forward, the never-ending tension

228

of Earl's sudden turn against us, and the powerful life lessons that had come to us every step of the way.

There was no downplaying the significance of this one day; it marked the culmination of thousands of hours of work. It had started before Seawall even existed. It all came down to one meeting and one last committee.

Remington's fate — Seawall's fate for that matter — rested in the hands of the seven-person panel of the Land Use and Transportation Committee, made of members of the Baltimore City Council. We needed four votes in favor of the project in order for the PUD to be approved. Anything less than that would topple the Remington Row PUD and all of the goodwill behind it. There was so much riding on this one hearing.

After going through security, I walked up the stairs to the fourth floor and passed through the open doors to the Curran Room. The soaring thirty-foot-high ceilings, spectacularly decorated in ornamental plasterwork, were supported by massive columns that wrapped the exterior walls. An elevated, judge-style bench sat perched importantly on the far side of the room, surrounded by heavy wooden tables. Empty rows of chairs were lined up facing the front of the room, waiting to be filled. The courtroom-style setting was appropriate for the magnitude of the event.

Usually these hearings included the developer, the developer's team of attorneys, and anyone opposing a given project. But not this one. There was too much at stake. While no one from Remington was there yet, we expected a big turnout given how much this project meant to the community. It was clear that Earl would be there arguing against the project, and the neighbors were not going to let him have the last word.

By 1:00 p.m. the Curran Room had filled up, and it was standing room only for anyone who trickled in late. The vibe in the usually stale chamber was buzzing with a mixture of excitement, uneasiness, and optimism as the growing crowd whispered and joked nervously, waiting for the meeting to begin. More than thirty neighbors had taken the afternoon off work to come support the project, something which was unheard of.

The chatter died down for a few seconds as Earl walked into the massive room. He walked in without greeting a single person, arms full of notes, plans, and folders, and moved to the seating area on the opposite side of the aisle from where the rest of the neighbors had gathered.

Shortly after 1:00 p.m., Councilman Edward Reisinger, the chair of the Land Use and Transportation Committee, called the meeting to order. Even he appeared to be shocked by the enormous turnout. His voice was stern as he laid out the ground rules for the day. This wasn't his first time dealing with Earl, and because of how litigious he was, he and his committee had altered the format of this hearing. Chairman Reisinger had stringent time restrictions on how long any one person could speak so as to keep things moving forward. Earl had a habit of talking far longer than was usually allowed. The chairman was clear that he was not going to allow that today.

As the proceedings got started, each city agency that had contributed to the Remington Row PUD stood up and gave its staff report, explaining why it recommended approval: planning, traffic, zoning, legal, stormwater, fire, public safety. Each of them was also more than familiar with Earl, so hundreds of pages of reports and briefings had been meticulously prepared.

I noticed that the staff members who testified that day had an air of pride and defiance in their voices as they spoke, as if to indicate that they too felt Remington's pain. It was clear by the sheer volume of each report, and by the resolve in their voices as they presented their findings, that the staff had taken this task very seriously. It felt like they too owned the Remington Row PUD and that they wanted to see it succeed just as much as the actual residents of the community.

As the staff members read their reports detailing months of preparation, I couldn't help but flash back to the dozens and dozens of meetings that had taken place with each of them and their departments to get to this point. The city of Baltimore had been extraordinary throughout the entire process. They too understood what this project meant to Remington and to the city as a whole.

After the last staff report was delivered, the chairman thanked everyone for their incredibly thorough work and turned the floor over to us to present our case. We had given this presentation an enormous amount of thought. We had spent the past year and a half working with some of Baltimore's best land use attorneys, who had guided us every step of the way; any of them would have loved the opportunity to get up and present the case as to why this project not only was legal but also was vital to the city. We had a better plan.

This wasn't about highly paid attorneys and their egos and how long and eloquently they could recite the case law and zoning codes of the city of Baltimore. This was about the people of Remington — who were being represented that day by the thirty citizens who had taken the day off work to attend the hearing — getting the chance to passionately defend their neighborhood. One by one, each member of the community who had shown up in support of the project stood and took most of the five minutes allotted by Chairman Reisinger to tell their stories.

Randy got up and made his way to the microphone at the front of the room. He walked past Earl, who seemed surprised to learn that one of his own board members was speaking against him. Once at the lectern, Randy repeated what he'd told me in our many conversations over the years. He explained to the committee that he had lived in Remington his entire life and that for the first time in a long time he felt that the community was improving. He explained that Remington had declined for decades but now it was taking a turn for the better. He finished by saying that the project had his full support.

Amanda and Action Dan from Charmington's each explained that they supported the project wholeheartedly because it would bring more local businesses to the community.

Maureen from Baltimore Glass Company thanked us for working with her and Caleb and for helping them find a new building in the neighborhood. She explained how important it was that they could stay in Remington so their employees could continue walking to work.

An older gentleman named Michael Burke, who had just purchased a house on Remington Avenue the month before, proudly stood up as well. Michael was probably the newest member of the community, yet he had quickly become known as the "mayor of Remington" because of his engaging personality and his deep desire to help everyone with whom he came into contact.

"This is my first home," he said. "I'm a young sixty years old, and I plan on living to be a hundred, but I would like to own my house and would like to see my house go up in value so that I can have a legacy to leave behind."

Michael had become a fast friend, and I knew that his road through life had not been an easy one, which made his testimony that much stronger. He concluded by voicing his full support for the project. Others also spoke about how they had just bought a house in Remington, moving to the community because of the proposed Remington Row project and because of the beautiful spirit that existed there, explaining that they wanted to contribute to it.

People thanked Seawall for our dedication to serving the community, for our transparency and willingness to collaborate, and for helping them realize their dreams, saying that we had developed with the community and not in spite of the community. Almost every single person mentioned how bad crime had been in Remington and how for the first time in a long time they were starting to feel safe again on their streets. People pointed out that over the past few years, vacant houses were getting fixed up and blight was being erased.

These were the same stories I had heard while I collected the 250 signatures of support across the community. While most of those individuals hadn't made it to the hearing that day, it felt as if they were with us. No one from Seawall said a single word: not Evan, not my dad, not even myself. We didn't need to. We had led from behind the scenes, helping others shine, making way for the entire neighborhood to march in front. As a result, Remington was on the verge of getting what it had wanted for so long, which was what it deserved.

# 22

## The Oxygen of Love

*"Those who are the hardest to love need it the most."*

— SOCRATES

As the land use meeting gained momentum, I repeated the move I had made on that spectacular day when Clifton visited Saphinda in the township of Umlazi, the day that changed the complexion of Peace-Players and the day that many said would never happen: I got up and stood in the very back of the room, taking it all in. Once again, I was moved to tears, this time as I listened to the sound of the movement picking up steam as it roared through City Hall.

The moment was particularly emotional for me because just seven years earlier, before I had even heard of Remington, I had been walking down Pennsylvania Avenue, realizing that the United States, including my own city of Baltimore, was more divided than any of the other so-called war-torn countries where I had just spent so much time and energy. I had arrived back in Baltimore with no experience in real estate and only basic knowledge about it from light conversation with my father growing up. I simply had a sense that the industry, reimagined, could become one of the great forces for empowering people and communities, and that it would allow me to continue doing the work I was so passionate about.

As I stood in the back of the Curran Room that day, the voices of the people of Remington confirmed in my heart that I had found something powerful and meaningful. I could help lead effectively from behind the scenes. Real estate, done right, could unite our neighborhoods and our cities.

As the last of the Remington Row supporters finished their testimony, Chairman Reisinger asked if there was anyone there that day who opposed the project. Earl raised his hand and walked up to the microphone.

■ ■ ■ ■ ■

Some of the people who had been negatively affected by Earl had called him out in their testimony. Many of their voices had trembled as their emotions got the better of them. I realized with each heartwarming testimony that Earl, as powerful as he had been in the past, was dwarfed by the size of the movement the community had created. It turns out that they weren't fighting him, they were fighting to reinstate the peaceful way of living that had once existed in Remington before drugs, vacancy, disinvestment, and crime had taken over. By standing in the way for as long as he had, Earl had actually galvanized the community behind a shared vision for restoring the neighborhood that Randy and hundreds of other legacy residents remembered.

Earl's opposition to the PUD hadn't stopped at the streets of Remington. He had shown up for more than a year and a half at every one of the countless public hearings held downtown in Baltimore's municipal buildings, using his iPad to record every word that was said. During those meetings, he had voiced one concern after another to the various committees who oversaw the PUD process. Even though he had refused to meet face to face with us, Earl had threatened us every step of the way by email, saying that what we were proposing was illegal and that he didn't think it would be fair, under any circumstance, to compel the neighborhood to participate in supporting the Remington Row PUD — even though so much of the project was their idea.

Earl was relentless and he was brilliant, perhaps smarter than any land use attorney in the city. In the past, Earl had helped find every single loophole that could stall and delay the Walmart project, until the developer couldn't take it any longer. Today, sitting all by himself on the other side of the aisle, he was doing the same thing with the Remington Row PUD, asking questions that no one had ever thought of and bringing up case law that expensive attorneys never imagined an ordinary citizen would know.

But as hard as he had tried, Earl had been unable to find a single neighbor to stand by him in opposition to the project. Not one. His voice was shaky and his thoughts seemed to be a bit scattered as he spoke into the microphone that day.

Watching from my place in the back of the hearing room, my feelings for Earl suddenly changed. For the better part of a year, Earl had disrespected me on a personal level, and he had done everything in his power to question Seawall's true intentions. I had seen a relationship with someone I respected turn sour. There had been moments, like when I stood on his porch in the cold, when I struggled to cope with Earl's behavior toward me and the project. Friends and family helped me talk through those experiences over the months, but it wasn't until this instant, as he began delivering his testimony at the land use hearing, that an overwhelming sense of gratitude appeared.

As he spoke, his words seemed weightless in the shadow of the community's outpouring. I realized it wasn't just gratitude that I felt. It was an unexpected sense of love. Not just love for all the people working toward getting the project approved but absolute, deep love for Earl. He had made us stronger.

As Earl's testimony became more frantic, Chairman Reisinger announced that his time was up. Although he protested that there hadn't been enough time to examine the materials, Chairman Reisinger interrupted and politely asked him to sit down.

As Earl slowly took his seat, he was even more alone. The old way of being had no roots in Remington anymore. What he represented was separate from what the rest of the community wanted. Still, through all that, he had made us better — he had made me better.

As the committee prepared to vote on the PUD, the love I felt for Earl deepened because I could now empathize with his struggle. Even if I wasn't sure whether we could ever connect as I had always hoped, I loved his contribution to the movement, even his opposition to it. I had reached a deeper appreciation that day about just how healthy, even vital, opposition can be. It helps to strengthen movements. It actually brings people together with more clarity.

Earl had taught me so many lessons over the years. Sure, sometimes it was about how not to be a leader, but it was also about how passion and diligence can make all the difference when it comes to neighborhood development. If he hadn't existed or opposed the movement, I'm not sure if we at Seawall would have paid as much attention to all the details. I don't know that we would have even thought of going door-to-door to connect deeply with everyone the project affected. Indeed, it's possible that Earl's very opposition was actually the reason the community's support of the PUD was so strong.

The hearing was reaching its end. The committee had heard more than two hours of emotional testimony. The vote had been taken, and it was time to hear the result.

"It seems the committee has come to a unanimous decision," said Chairman Reisinger, pausing, "to approve the planned unit development for the Remington Row project."

The room erupted in applause, cheers, and laughter. People got up and hugged one another, overcome with joy and relief.

I gave Michael Burke a big bear hug. I embraced Maureen. Then, my dad and I had a moment of our own. Just like the hug we had shared before I hopped on the plane to South Africa, there were no words exchanged. Back then, I had felt his love as a father but I hadn't fully appreciated him as a man, as a leader. Now, after all we'd been through, I could feel more than pride in the strength of his hug. He was edging again toward retirement, starting to transition out of Seawall. It was possible that this was the last thing we'd work on together. The way he hugged me then made me feel like I was capable of leading myself, like we were almost equals. It was all I could do not to cry again.

This wasn't a real estate project. This was an idea whose time had come. We were all driven by purpose. We all felt like we owned it because it was built with love, in all its forms.

■ ■ ■ ■ ■

Early the next morning after the land use hearing, I wrote an email to all of those who had shown up. It read:

> When you all started testifying yesterday, I went to the back of the room because I was moved to tears. It is clearer to me than ever that this is your project. It's Remington's Row.
>
> We are honored to be able to play a small role in helping you all continue to shape the fabric of your wonderful neighborhood. Your words yesterday were powerful, decisive, direct, emotional, and from the heart. Please know how thankful we are for the time and energy you have put into this.
>
> We at Seawall have always been huge believers in the concept that the most powerful thing in the world is an idea whose time has come. It's Remington's time.
>
> This is just the beginning...
>
> Love —
>
> Thibault

After the approval of a PUD, there is a thirty-day window when anyone can appeal the project. If he wanted to, Earl could appeal the committee's decision. We expected him to continue to fight. Of course, we were nervous that all our hard work could still be undone. We got word to our lenders that an appeal would likely be on the way. We wanted them to be prepared for the worst. Their answer — that they had our back, were confident that we had done everything right, and were ready to move forward — felt like a milestone given all the pressure we'd put on ourselves about taking on multiple outside investors for the first time. In the end, even Earl seemed to realize that the community had spoken. There was no appeal by him or anyone else. Remington Row's time had come.

■ ■ ■ ■ ■

On a particularly mild weekday in January of 2017, I sat having breakfast in one of the warm and cozy booths inside the new food hall we had just built on Remington Avenue. Baltimore's winter sun shone timidly through the massive floor-to-ceiling windows. It was 9 a.m., and the tables around me were bustling — couples and friends, commuters and locals, students and colleagues.

After two short years of construction, the Main Street vision had come to life. On the ground where Baltimore Glass once stood, Remington Row had come to fruition, completed in the summer of 2016 and now fully leased. The impressive replica of an old factory included 108 mixed-income apartments; a 30,000-square-foot community medical center run by Johns Hopkins; 15,000 square feet of neighborhood retail that checked off boxes including the pharmacy John Bales had asked for, a bank, a community acupuncturist, and a dry cleaner; and close to 300 underground parking spaces.

I was enjoying my breakfast on the next block, the former site of a boarded-up body shop filled with beat-up cars. It had been replaced by R. House, a 50,000-square-foot space focused on creating community and launching new ideas. On the first floor was a modern-day food hall, the result of our listening deeply to chefs who asked us to do for them what we had done for teachers: to give them a collaborative plug-and-play space that would make it easier for them to successfully run their businesses. Breakfast, lunch, and dinner hours buzzed with some of the most innovative and diverse food in the city. The upstairs held a fitness studio called Movement Lab, where my wife, Lola, introduced alternative forms of movement from all over the world, as well as the Seawall office. There was also plenty of room left over for cutting-edge space for startup companies. On the next block, Seawall converted another abandoned warehouse into 20,000 square feet of storefronts for local retail businesses and an incubator space called Fast Forward for Johns Hopkins undergraduates working to launch companies.

As my eyes scanned the crowded room again, a new sensation arose in the pit of my stomach. I was proud to have played a role in bringing this to life — alongside my colleagues at Seawall and all the people in the community — but now seeing it complete, it was a lot. The dream had been big, but the result felt bigger somehow — and I wasn't sure that was a good thing. On one hand, the explosive growth the neighborhood was experiencing felt inevitable based on geography and trends in cities all over the country — all over the world, even. It had been a match that someone was going to light at some point. On the other hand, although we'd tried to be careful and deliberate about how we went about contributing, we'd poured gas on the fire all the same. As the people around me were enjoying their own breakfasts and conversations, new questions bubbled up inside me.

*Has the growth been too much and too fast for this little community? Is it Seawall's fault? My fault? People seem to love R. House, but at what cost? What are the downsides and unintended consequences of the project's success? What have we missed in all this?*

As these questions swirled in my mind, it dawned on me that when it came to Seawall's quest of using real estate as a tool to empower communities, the most difficult challenges of all might have only just begun.

# Part IV

# EVOLVE

"Where my hustlers at?" Joe Jones asks the group. Joe is the CEO of the Center for Urban Families (CFUF), a powerful Baltimore nonprofit committed to dismantling poverty.

Joe is dressed in an impeccable black designer suit, crisp shirt, and pristine blue power tie. His dark-brown eyes reflect his stern expression as he scans the conference room and the faces of the several dozen people crammed into it. It's mostly young men here, with a handful of women and older guys scattered among them. There's one white person; the rest are various shades of black and brown.

There is no response to Joe's question. Perhaps the group is unsure whether it's acceptable to volunteer self-incriminating information; no one raises a hand. Instead, they glance around nervously, as if seeing whether anyone else is foolish enough to admit to being a drug dealer.

"Come on y'all, I ain't playin'," Joe continues. "Where my dope boys?"

Half of those present, who are there to participate in the monthly STRIVE kickoff program, slowly raise their hands. A couple of people are in suits, others rock a sports jacket or poorly tied necktie, and some are in jeans and a hoodie. There are a few fitted baseball caps on top of bald heads or dreadlocks, tattoos of every size and design, and an assortment of Timberland boots and sneakers.

"How 'bout my stickup boys?"

Now nearly three-quarters of the men in the room have their arms up. As Joe talks, a few newcomers sneak into the room and try to take a seat. Instead, they are ushered over to the side to stand in a line against the wall with their fellow latecomers.

"That's more like it." Joe grins as he looks out at the hands raised in the air.

At six foot three, with broad shoulders and a shiny, cleanly shaved head, Joe is intimidating. Not in a scared-to-meet-up-in-a-dark-alley way, but because everything about him exudes confidence. He's got a no-nonsense attitude.

"I've been out of the game awhile, but let me break down a little story for y'all and you tell me how it ends."

These words don't seem right coming out of the mouth of such a prestigious-looking gentleman, but there is something in the way Joe says them. Everyone in the room knows he's not playing. No matter how dressed up this guy is, he is no stranger to the drug game.

Joe grew up in East Baltimore. His father left when Joe was nine. Joe started dealing and shooting up heroin not even four years later, around his thirteenth birthday. He was in jail before he was legally able to drive. After going in and out of prison several times, he decided it wasn't the life for him. He caught a break at a recovery center and got on a work release program. There he began to realize that no one was paying serious attention to the role of fathers in urban families. There was a lot of time, money, and attention focused on mothers, but not on dads. So with no real experience to speak of, but driven by his own personal story and understanding about how hard life could be, he launched the Center for Urban Families to tackle that very problem.

Joe will never forget where he came from, and that's precisely how he helps those who want to get on a better path to find their way. The group Joe was addressing that day had gathered for the kickoff of the newest class in his STRIVE program, which was offering them a chance to gain both skills and employment.

"I'm on the corner of Wylie and Park Heights Avenue. Deep in that hole. You guys know the hole I'm talking about?"

They each nod their head. There's some pride in the acknowledgment, but their eyes betray their general attitude about being here. It's torture for most. For others, it's just a hassle, something their parole officer made them do. Some look down at the floor. Others peer cautiously at the front of the room. Joe has to really search for the flickers of hope in their gazes, but it's something he knows is there.

"So I've got a kilo with me, and I'm waitin' to off-load it to a couple of chumps I don't know. My two lieutenants are supposed to meet me down there early before the other guys show up, but they are at the Burger King around the way, and guess what?"

There's a pause across the room. Those looking down raise their eyes and stare ahead at Joe. They're into the story now. They know the exact hole that Joe's talking about. They've been in it.

"They start to holler at a shorty behind the register, asking for her digits, forgetting all about lil' old me waiting in the hole."

One fellow closes his eyes and scoffs. Another laughs uncomfortably. A couple shake their heads. One of the few women shrugs. Joe's commanding their attention.

"So these two chumps come to pick up the kilo and they see me by myself. What do y'all think is about to happen?"

The answers come quick: "You dead." "Bang." "Game over." There are also a few expletives.

Now it's Joe's turn to nod his head.

"That's right. Being late out there can be the difference between life and death. Well, guess what?"

He pauses to glance over at the line of folks who arrived late.

"It's the same in here," Joe says, switching deftly between street talk and business talk. "We're here to prepare you for consistent employment and you can't afford to be late."

Now most of the room's attention is half on Joe and half on those in the we-came-late lineup, most of whom are either scratching their arm or nervously clearing their throat, feeling the eyeballs on them.

"All right," says Joe, now fully turning his attention to those who arrived late. "How come all these people were on time but y'all were late?"

Those in line rattle off excuses: "The snow." "Bus was late." "Cops pulled me over." "Childcare was late."

Joe takes it all in. He's heard it all over the past two decades.

"Life is ten percent what happens, ninety percent how you react," he says eventually. "And look, there's all these other people sitting in chairs. They knew that this is a really important first day, and they made sure to do whatever they needed to get here on time."

Then he turns to everyone seated in the chairs in front of him and asks, "What should I do with these guys? What should their punishment be for being late?"

Half of the people say, "Kick them out. Send them home."

"Give them a second chance," shout the others.

Joe identifies one guy, someone who doesn't exactly appear to have his full act together but who is also among the second-chance advocates.

"You, come on up here."

The guy leans out of his chair, gets onto his feet, and sluggishly approaches the front of the room.

Joe shakes the guy's hand. "What's your name?"

"It's Trevon."

"Congratulations, Trevon," Joe says sarcastically, offering a hypothetical situation. "You've just been promoted. I've started a company that's doing well, so I need to expand it by hiring a supervisor. Trevon, you are now my supervisor. And you know what your first assignment is? You've got to pick three people in the room you want as employees to report to you."

Trevon looks out at all the people in chairs. He never, even for a second, looks over at the eight late people standing against the wall behind him. He instead points to two guys and a girl — Malik, Paris, and Andrea — who've been more vocal, look decently dressed, sit in or near the front row, and generally appear responsible.

It's exactly what Joe expects. No one ever choses someone from the late group. He gestures to the lineup.

"Why didn't you pick any of these guys behind you? These are the guys you said deserve a second chance."

"Well..." Trevon pauses, knowing he's been had. "They were late."

The whole room erupts in laughter.

"You know what?" says Joe, corralling Malik, Paris, and Andrea. "I'm not going to give you those three. I'm going to take them myself." Joe pauses for effect, then says, "You're getting these eight guys behind you."

The group of latecomers roll their eyes or simply look at the ground, clearly pissed off they made it down here only to get treated this way.

"Now," he says to Trevon. "You still sure you want to give these guys a second chance?"

Trevon shrugs but then nods his head yes.

"Shoot, it's on you to decide their fate," Joe says, switching back to street talk for just an instant before he's back to business. "So why don't you go out in the hallway with these latecomers and decide?"

And with that, he sends the lot of them out into the hall to talk over what to do with this hypothetical company they've been tasked with starting.

"Just don't come soft, Trevon," he says with a serious look on his face as the door closes.

After a few minutes of waiting as Trevon and the group discuss their fate, the nine of them return to the main room.

"What's the verdict?" asks Joe.

Trevon explains that the group of latecomers will be forgiven and allowed to continue the program but that they have one check against their record.

"That's it?" Joe is almost chuckling. "I thought I told you not to come soft, Trevon."

After giving the others in the room enough time to laugh at the moment, Joe gives a real punishment.

"Your first assignment is that at 8:30 a.m. on Monday, all nine of you owe me a five-hundred-word essay about the importance of showing up on time. Otherwise, you're all kicked out of the program."

Trevon will have to write an essay himself, and he'll also be kicked out if anyone else in the group fails to submit an essay or shows up late again.

"It's on you now, bruh," says Joe. "What do you say?"

The group talks in quick whispers among themselves.

"We accept the punishment," announces Terrance, one of the latecomers, a guy who'd robbed banks at home and abroad and was hoping to find employment as a midnight-shift mortician. "But if this doesn't work out, I'm going back to the continent of Africa to join one of the militias and rob banks again."

Some of the people in the room look at one another awkwardly.

Others chuckle out of discomfort. No one questions whether Terrance is serious. These are the kinds of options folks who come to Joe consider seriously, and he knows they deserve every chance to do something greater.

■ ■ ■ ■ ■

It's January of 2017, and I'm sitting in a chair in the back of the room watching Joe work his magic. It must be the thirtieth time I've done this. The first time I saw him run one of these STRIVE kickoffs was back in 2006, right when I first got back to Baltimore. At that time, CFUF was in a run-down class C office building donated by the city. It wasn't good enough to accommodate the program's growth and aspirations. It wasn't good enough to help local residents like Paris, Malik, Trevon, and Andrea get the best shot at their second chance.

Joe and my dad were friends, brothers if you were to ask either of them, and Joe had heard that we had launched Seawall together. He immediately reached out to ask us if we could help him find, design, finance, and construct a state-of-the-art building that would give CFUF the base they needed to better dismantle poverty. Their new headquarters was among Seawall's very first projects, one that started construction just after Miller's Court, and it has helped Joe and his team impact at least thirty thousand men and women in Baltimore.

The beautiful new $8 million building sits on the corner of Monroe Street and Windsor Avenue, the former site of the Baltimore Coliseum, which was the first home of the Baltimore Bullets (now the Washington Wizards NBA franchise). Every day CFUF plays its part in a much more important kind of teamwork — one that President Obama came to see for himself when he was in office — that is improving the quality of life for individuals and their families in Baltimore's most underserved communities.

This was where it also all started for me, a few blocks from here on the corner of Pennsylvania and North Avenues, when I realized I was in an American township. That's where the idea to use the built environment to empower and unite instead of oppress and divide began to take shape. In Seawall's ten short years, that idea had grown into more than $250 million of projects that are transforming Baltimore and a couple of other cities.

Since that plane ride with Simon and that first walk down Pennsylvania Avenue, I had worked with the Seawall team to do so much more outside of Remington. We had built Centers for Educational Excellence, state-of-the-art charter schools, workforce housing, neighborhood retail that provided launchpads for passionate local entrepreneurs, breweries, community doctors' offices, restaurants, affordable for-sale housing, and so much more. And we took great pride in the fact that not a single one of the projects we'd worked on had been our idea. They'd all come as a result of us deeply listening to the end users and the communities where we work. Since the very beginning, projects like the Center for Urban Families were the result of leading with purpose over profit and Seawall's burning desire to reimagine an entire industry.

# 23

# Principles in Motion

*"You've got to always go back in time if you want to move forward."*

— SNOOP DOGG

Twenty of us were nestled in my parents' living room on a cold February day in 2017. Flames snapped and popped as a fire began to roar to life. This was the same house where about ten years before, when I'd just returned from my last trip to South Africa, I had tossed and turned in my bed because I was so worried that I would never find anything as meaningful as the work I had been a part of with PeacePlayers. Instead of pushing that uncomfortable feeling aside, I had embraced it — and dived even deeper into it — by going to Pennsylvania Avenue, which led to the creation of Seawall, which was why all twenty of us were gathered there that morning. It was Seawall's tenth anniversary, an amazing occasion to celebrate at our annual strategic planning retreat.

I couldn't believe there were twenty of us there that day. I never thought Seawall would be much more than just my dad and me. Then it was my dad, Evan, and me. Then after five years, there were five of us. Here, after ten years, an amazing family had been born, twenty of the most inspiring people I've ever met. Except for my dad, Evan, and Jon, none of the twenty had any real estate experience before joining the company. We intentionally didn't hire anyone from the industry out of fear that they would come with preconceived notions of how real estate was supposed to work, which would get in the way of reinventing the industry. There was very little hierarchy or infrastructure. If you worked with Seawall, you were your own boss, and you worked passionately on the things you loved the most. You were a self-starter. You had autonomy to explore and create — even to mess up.

A ten-year anniversary is a big deal for anything. I had no idea where the conversation would go during our strategic planning meeting. While we always measured our success based on impact instead of on finances, I wondered whether we would talk about doing another $250 million of projects over the next ten years, or perhaps doubling that to shoot for $500 million. I wasn't sure, but to help set the framework for the day, I had sent out this email before the meeting:

What up, Seawall Family —

2015 and 2016 were heavy, yet amazing years. So much was accomplished through sheer willpower and determination. In thinking through the theme for this year earlier this week, the one that kept coming to the surface was not becoming complacent and constantly reinventing ourselves. With so much development completed, it would be easy to go into property management mode and execute on the great systems that have been implemented over the last two years. However, just like we did 10 years ago when we launched Seawall and Seawall Property Management, we have to continue to strive to reinvent the experience people expect out of their landlords and development partners.

With that as a backdrop, and before laying out the agenda, I would like for each of us to come up with a personal goal for Seawall that we will share with the group during the planning retreat. Not something that is already expected of us in our roles here. Please spend some time thinking of an audacious goal for the organization, maybe one that seems unattainable, but that if realized could change the trajectory of Seawall forever.

Can't wait,

Thibault

As the meeting came to life and the conversation started, I settled onto my beanbag in the circle, staring at the people I loved the most in this world outside of my family. I was ready for whatever direction the meeting would take.

Shawn Brown went first. She had been an amazing event planner at a large nonprofit organization before we hired her to lease our apartments, even though she had zero leasing experience. Of course, she excelled at her job because she deeply loved people and wanted to help them.

"We've become such an integral part of the fabric of the Remington community, and it's a huge honor to have been accepted this way," Shawn started. "We are also a victim of our own success, and we can't hide from that. While we've been so focused on creating apartments for teachers, workforce housing, collaborative office space for nonprofits, and launchpads for small businesses, the reality is that Remington has changed drastically over the last ten years, and if we are not careful, major displacement will begin to happen. Gentrification has already become a very real problem because of the work we're doing."

I was immediately struck by Shawn's candidness and her insistence that we have the conversation about a topic anyone wanting to work in real estate — even those setting out to reinvent it — struggled to face. My whole working life, the cause that pulled at my heartstrings more than anything else, was the chance to bridge divides. The catchall concept *gentrification* was the exact opposite of that. Projects that put up barriers, whether cultural, economic, or otherwise, ran contrary not just to everything Seawall stood for as a business, but also to what I stood for as a human being.

"I know that gentrification was never our intent, but it's real. We can't ignore it or sit on the sidelines and hope that someone else addresses it, because they won't," Shawn continued. "My audacious idea is that we dive even deeper into Remington and the other communities we work in, where we become even more outward facing and transparent."

I couldn't wipe the smile from my face or heart. Shawn had articulated succinctly why our role had to be so much more than just that of a developer. No movement is perfect. There were downsides, mistakes, and unintended consequences in every project I had been involved in, but part of reinventing industries and being a leader meant owning those imperfections and not hiding from them. The fear of making mistakes could jeopardize, stall, or cause us to abandon good projects entirely. While it was never our intention, Seawall's projects had displaced some people. The more vibrant the neighborhood became, the more the living cost increased. There was a whole tool kit of things Seawall did and could start doing to minimize the downside of even the most forward-thinking development, but our projects could never be perfect, and although I may not have been okay with that when I was younger, I had now discovered it was an inevitable part of making movements. There will always be more divides to bridge.

Almost before I could catch up, others started chiming in.

"Let's organize trash pickup days," said one team member.

"Or serve on committees in the neighborhood to protect legacy residents," said another.

"What about organizing a neighborhood festival to help outwardly celebrate how special the place is to the community?" said a third.

"Exactly," Shawn replied, nodding her head. "And maybe most of all, we must actively engage in the gentrification and displacement conversation instead of running from it and pretending that it doesn't exist or that we weren't responsible for the fact that it has arrived."

The conversation reminded me so much of the way my dad and I had riffed on the idea of what the company could be a whole decade earlier at our seemingly ordinary Outback Steakhouse dinner.

*Who would have known it would have turned into this?*

This was total ownership by Shawn and the others. If they didn't feel that profound sense of ownership, these audacious ideas would have never crossed their minds. As I reflected back in that moment, Shawn was right, and we had been so focused on the projects at hand that we never stopped to think through the downside of this kind of success. I wholeheartedly agreed that we had to actively fight for the community to protect it from outside forces that weren't aligned with its inclusive vision.

A log collapsed; the fire ate it up and continued to burn before us. I thought about Charlie, who had lived with my family for twenty years before passing away peacefully in his sleep in 2011. I thought about how grateful I was that he had had the chance to meet both of my sons. I thought about the way he used to hang around the fire when my mom's uncle from France visited and the two of them would pass boxed wine back and forth, smoking cigarettes and communicating even though neither spoke the other one's language. Connecting deeply was all about a sense of knowing that conveyed more than any specific words could explain. It was a feeling.

I listened as we went around the room, sharing our audacious ideas, many of which piggybacked off Shawn's idea that the next ten years of Seawall weren't about how many hundreds of millions of dollars of work we would do. As a matter of fact, no one ever even mentioned a single dollar amount; instead we talked about how we would further engage with and protect the neighborhoods we worked in.

By the end of the meeting, the beginning of a blueprint for helping Remington create the world's first ever Inclusionary District was beginning to come into focus. The idea was to prove that a neighborhood, an anchor institution, and a developer could actually work together to create a set of guiding principles to govern how community decisions are made, which projects are supported, how jobs remain local, how to protect legacy residents, and how new ideas are both welcomed and included in Remington. It could become a platform to continue to unite and empower the community so that the people who live and work there continue to feel a sense of pride, ownership, and authorship in helping to shape an inclusive and diverse neighborhood. With that platform, they could continue to feel like they were a part of something larger than themselves. While it's impossible to say as I write this book whether the Inclusionary District will come to life, the thinking behind it is what sets us apart.

In many ways, that ten-year anniversary gave me clarity. With our Seawall projects, like with leveraging my privilege itself, there will always be judgment and criticism — and rightfully so — but that doesn't need to lead to fear or avoidance of difficult truths. No matter who you were, where you came from, or what kind of work you do, you still have to be brave enough to lead with love.

The meeting was inspiring for so many reasons. Most of all, it gave us a true sense that we were just getting started and that there was so much more important work to do. We knew that Remington was only the beginning and that a whole city, in fact a whole world, was waiting — all guided by our founding principles and our bold dedication to putting others first.

# EPILOGUE

# Full Circle

I park my truck on North Bentalou Street in West Baltimore. To my right is Senator Troy Brailey Easterwood Park, and to my left is Carver Vocational-Technical High — the same school where Michael Tobass teaches and Freddie Gray was once a student. I'm half a mile from the Center for Urban Families and less than a mile from the corner of Pennsylvania and West North Avenues, the intersection where it all started for me.

I'm with my two sons, Finley (age nine) and Durban (age seven), who can't wait to get out of the truck. Before I have time to turn off the ignition, they've grabbed a basketball from the back and are sprinting across the grass toward the court. It's early in the morning, so we're the first ones here. We begin warming up with a game of HORSE. After about ten minutes, two kids who look about thirteen come out of no-where and run onto the court, asking if they can play. That's my cue to step aside and disappear. I've seen how this works all over the world. I make my way over to the sideline to watch.

"Sure," says my younger son. "I'm Durban." I watch as they struggle awkwardly to find a cadence between Durban's go-to hand greeting and the kind his new friend prefers.

"I'm Finley," says his older brother. "Let's split up the teams."

Each of the neighborhood boys joins one of my sons, and they begin a game of two on two. One Black kid and one white kid per team.

Neither one of the older kids is a great athlete. One's actually wearing soccer cleats, so he keeps sliding all over the place, but all four of the boys are enjoying themselves.

Finley scores the first three baskets of the game. Of course, I'm beaming with pride. When Durban's team finally gets the ball, he dribbles it and proceeds to line up a fifteen-foot fadeaway jump shot.

It's sort of a ridiculous shot, but I'm used to seeing him take it. Durban has never met a shot he doesn't like, and he isn't ever afraid to let one fly. Complicating the shot is the fact that he is being guarded tightly by a kid who is almost twice his height. As Durban is taking it, his teammate adds another layer of difficulty. "Noooooo," he screams. "Don't shoot that!"

It's probably a fair request — given Durban's size and the situation — but the ball leaves Durban's hands all the same. It sails through the air, like my soccer ball soared in rural South Africa that unforgettable day, then swishes through the net.

Immediately, Durban walks up to the kid on his team to get the high five he clearly feels he deserves. Then he asks, with a perfectly straight face, "Why didn't you want me to shoot that?" I can't help but crack up on the sideline.

In that moment, things really begin to open up, and all four boys laugh hysterically. The game rolls on. One team is up, then the other rallies back. The scoring is spread around pretty evenly among all four players in the end, each of them learning to trust their teammate when they've got a shot they like.

A while later, once they've played enough basketball, the older boys invite Finley and Durban to come meet their other friends, who have arrived at the park. A bigger group of them arrange a quick game of flag football on the adjacent field. I find a seat at a picnic table and take it all in. Even after all these years, I still marvel at the power of sports to unite disparate groups of people, anywhere in the world.

Twelve years after first coming home, sitting less than a mile from where I realized that parts of my hometown were essentially American townships, I have just watched my kids build a relationship with two kids they'd never met, kids whom society might otherwise have kept them from meeting. A familiar series of questions comes to me.

*What is daily life like in Baltimore's inner city, beyond the one-dimensional news stories about the violence and destitution? What are the experiences of those who actually live here? What causes these divides between races and communities, and how can we channel the diversity and vibrancy of our city to bridge them? How can we counteract the years of neglect and lack of access by leaning into all the things that are already Baltimore's greatest strengths?*

I know that these questions are challenging to examine and answer. While I can appreciate how far I have come as a leader, as a husband, and as a dad since I first asked them, I also know how far I have to go. I know that the work I have been part of, while inspiring, has barely begun to scratch the surface. There are so many more questions to ask, people to listen to, ideas to help bring to life, and movements to help launch. I am proud simply to be in the mix.

To a certain extent, I never felt I had the right to write this book. Though I was taught from a very early age to work hard, I have never had to struggle for basic needs; I have never been poor, hungry, or homeless. I was never discriminated against or racially profiled. I have never lost friends or family to violence. My story isn't one of rags to riches that brings tears to the reader's eyes because of the incredible obstacles that the author had to overcome to get to the top of the mountain. The only mountains I attempted to climb were ones I got to choose.

I understand that I have the privilege of choosing to bring my boys into this community and of going back to the comfort of our apartment in a safer neighborhood later on. I understand that, because of inequity, so many people have no choice of where they can live or go. The boys from the basketball game may not be able to simply leave and go to another part of town after the game.

*So does my story matter? Is it even worth telling?*

Moments like these, watching my sons connect with kids in West Baltimore, help me realize a bigger truth. The story of movements isn't about me. It's not really even my story. It belongs to all the people I've been lucky enough to meet and work alongside. It belongs to all those who have come before me and devoted their lives to bridging divides. It belongs to everyone here in the United States and abroad who works to make the world a more united place, no matter what barriers they face. It belongs to anyone interested in a life that is *larger than yourself*.

"Dad," the kids say later, when we finally climb back into the truck, "that was so much fun."

# APPENDIX

# Larger Than Yourself Principles

## How to Grow Ideas into Movements

## PART I: DREAM

### Chapter 1: Comfort Zone

What would my life look like if I hadn't moved beyond my comfort zone in Baltimore? What if I hadn't hopped on that plane to South Africa? What if I hadn't gotten out of my car in that rural village? If I hadn't run down that hill?

When we launch something as audacious as a new nonprofit, we face terrifying decisions every day. Oddly enough, this can bring out the best in us. We often learn better after being scared, when our senses are heightened, after we've experienced survival mode. How we react defines our ability to get diverse perspectives, to walk in the shoes of others, and to put ourselves in positions to learn different ways of seeing things.

What have you been afraid of in the past? How did you move beyond that fear? Were you able to see the world differently because you expanded out of your comfort zone? Which fears are holding you back right now from trying to make the world a more just, equitable, and inclusive place? What opportunity for growth awaits on the other side of that fear?

## Chapter 2: Purpose First

Sean's comment that I'd never be more than the number-two guy shook me really hard, and it could have broken me. As I regained my composure, the reason it didn't break me was because every day for years, I had been asking myself two questions:

1. Why are we so divided as human beings?
2. What creative ways can we use to bridge those divides?

That's why I was so excited to have the opportunity to help reimagine the basketball industry to answer those questions, no matter what bumps or degrading comments were thrown my way. I always knew my *why* and my *purpose* were the quest to answer those two questions; I just needed to figure out *what* I was going to do and *how* I was going to do it. At that moment in time, for me, the answers centered around sports, which is what I loved the most.

1. Have you found your purpose, your *why*? If not, ask yourself these three things: What burning questions are keeping you up at night?
2. What is the one thing you could do for work every day for the rest of your life?
3. How can you reimagine what you love the most around the purpose that drives you?

## Chapter 3: Shared Ownership

What if, when I engaged with people in South Africa, I had claimed that the idea of using sports for good belonged to me and that if they wanted to be involved, they'd have to do things my way? If I'd talked about the idea like it was mine alone, would Menzi still have developed the sense of ownership of PeacePlayers in a way that empowered him to feel like it was his own? If I had claimed exclusive ownership, would there have been room for anyone else?

How many Menzis are in your corner? Do you have people on your team who believe so deeply in the vision and the idea that they make it their own? If you have Menzis, are you following their lead? If you don't have people like Menzi, why not? Are you being open enough with sharing ownership?

Think about the language you are using. Are you describing the idea you are working on as yours, in the first-person singular? Or are you describing it as an idea that you are helping to bring to life, leaving the door open for others to also have equal pride of ownership and authorship of what is being created? What are you doing to share ownership?

## Chapter 4: Outside Listening In

In helping to bring the PeacePlayers idea to life, we asked ourselves three questions and identified three answers.

1.  *Who are our end users?* For us, that was the kids and the coaches.
2.  *Who makes up our community?* That was the parents and teachers.
3.  *Who is on our team of guardian angels?* That was the board members and funders.

Next we asked ourselves what we needed to do to ensure that those three groups drove the design and ideation of the program so we were following their lead.

As white Americans with no real understanding of the divides in South Africa, we always knew that we had no right to come in and try to shape the program on our own. We understood early on that we were there to listen and help bring the pieces together. That's why when the parents came to us with the concerns about HIV/AIDS and the life skills component, we could be receptive, even if it wasn't something we had planned on.

Are you so focused on your vision for your project that you are not listening to your end users, community, and team? What are you doing to make sure that everyone is actively engaged in designing the idea for themselves because it is by them and for them? Are you being careful to listen to all iterations of the idea, even if it wasn't part of the original vision?

## Chapter 5: *Can't/No* as the Motivator

Had it not been for Bongani, would I have just accepted Brian's *no*? Without Bongani's courage and willingness to reject *no*, where would PeacePlayers be now? Would the idea have even gotten all the way off the ground? If you deeply believe in something, is there room for accepting a *no*? Or is the real value in a *no* the power of it to motivate you to be better?

Not only did Bongani turn Brian's *no* into a *yes*, but also he did this by transferring ownership of the idea to Brian. Brian was no longer a passive observer. He became an active participant because Bongani helped Brian see how he could change the world and South Africa by allowing this game to take place. That's the power of not taking *no* for an answer.

Think back to every big *no* and *can't* you've received throughout your life. How did you react to them? Did they serve as motivators that inspired you to dive deeper? If not, how could they have served as fuel to your fire if you had approached them differently? What if you reframed rejection to where every *no* and *can't* became an opportunity? What's a recent *no* you received, and how might a different approach to it have turned it into a *yes*?

## Chapter 6: Finding Leadership

I ask myself every day whether I am an effective leader. What if I had been so afraid to trust in my leadership skills that I had tried to adopt someone else's? What if I had given up on who I knew I was and tried to force a style of leadership that felt disingenuous to me? Would PeacePlayers ever have received the support from so many other incredible leaders around the world if it didn't have solid leadership to begin with?

All of us have leadership within us. For me, it took much longer to get comfortable that my style could work, especially since it was so different from Sean's. Building inside out and sharing ownership of an idea requires significantly more leadership than working on something alone. Because you are giving up so much control, you have to carefully ensure that the idea is growing in harmony with the different forces that are helping to guide it forward. While I am always open to suggestions and turns along the way (and welcome them), I make sure that in my head and heart I always have the road map of where we are working to get to. If no one is the gatekeeper of that map, you'll get lost along the way.

If the book's other principles suggest that Larger Than Yourself projects are always free-flowing, organic utopias, then this should be the reminder that true and consistent leadership is required in order for the previous principles to work at all. If anything, the other principles are there to guide you about how to approach and implement leadership differently. Are you clear about what's on your road map? Are you shooting out of bed every day ready to lead people down the path? Have you found a leadership style that works for you?

## Chapter 7: The Power of Love

Would Nathi, Thabang, Bongani, and all our other change agents have trusted me as much if I hadn't shown up and told them how much I loved them? Or if I hadn't been clear at every opportunity to remind everyone that I loved the work we were doing together? Would they have been as committed to growing the program if I had treated them as disposable employees and not as my brothers and sisters? Would they have believed me when I told them that this was their program to grow and mold if they didn't believe that I loved them first? Would Menzi have invited me to perform the sacred Zulu rite of passage to slaughter the goat had he and the rest of the team not known that our hearts beat together, no matter the color of our skin or what country we came from?

The tremendous love for the program shared by the end users, the community, and the team of guardian angels prompted it to grow through South Africa and beyond. This love was the reason why leaders like Nelson Mandela and organizations like the NBA hopped on board to support it.

What does love mean to you? How has love provided strength and support when you've needed it most? Have you allowed yourself to pass that love on to others? Do your change agents know how much you love them and the work you're doing together?

# PART II: BUILD
## Chapter 8: Uncomfortable

What would my life look like if I hadn't gotten out of bed that morning? What if I had dozed off eventually and then had breakfast with my parents, just talking about the things that bothered me in the comfort of my bubble? What if I hadn't driven down to West Baltimore? If I hadn't gotten out of my car when I hesitated?

It was no coincidence that I ended up in West Baltimore that day. Before my PeacePlayers experience, my instinct, like most people's, would have been to stay in my comfort zone. But now I understood that only by getting out of that comfort zone would I have a shot at answering the questions that were bothering me. While I didn't necessarily know what I was looking for that day, I knew that the first step out of that comfort zone was the first step into the place I needed to be.

Let's revisit a question I posed in the discussion about chapter 1: Which fears are holding you back right now from trying to make the world a more just, equitable, and inclusive place? Write that fear down on a piece of paper so you can see it clearly. Next to it, write down a place or situation that could force you to confront that fear in some way. Come up with as many suggestions as you like but put at least three on paper. For example, if your fear was related to rejection, write down one or more situations where you might have to confront rejection, such as applying for a grant for your project or pitching an idea to an investor. Then envision the worst-case scenario of having to face that fear in each situation. Picture all the ways it would make you feel uncomfortable. Finally, envision what would come afterward. Write down a guess about what you think might happen after you've confronted your fear.

## Chapter 9: Purpose Refined

My return to the US left me curious about what I would work on next. I thought deeply about what other industry could be reimagined that would allow me to explore my two burning questions: Why are we so divided as human beings? And what creative ways can we use to bridge those divides?

I'd grown familiar with how it felt to wake up every day with a purpose during my time with PeacePlayers. When I sat down for dinner with my dad, another purpose-first idea was taking shape inside me. I felt it, but it wasn't until he put the right words together that I was able to see it clearly. Just by posing the question *what if* — what if real estate could be rethought to help empower those who are doing the most important work in the city? — my dad injected the idea with new life.

In the discussion about chapter 2, I prompted you to think about what burning questions have been keeping you up at night and what you could imagine yourself working on for the rest of your life. Now it's time to link those two together. Write them down next to each other and reverse the order. For example, let's say technology is the work you love and your burning question is about how you can combat climate change. Now ask yourself the kinds of *what if* questions my dad and I asked each other in chapter 9, making substitutions like this: "What if real estate TECHNOLOGY could play a role in helping inner-city kids get a better education COMBATING CLIMATE CHANGE? What if we could reinvent what it means to be a real estate developer by CREATING TECHNOLOGY to help those doing important work in COMBATING CLIMATE CHANGE?" See if a pattern begins to emerge and if any ideas begin to form. Oftentimes it's as easy as reversing the reason you do what you do to highlight purpose over profit.

## Chapter 10: *Can't/No* as the Teacher

What if the challenged conditions of the old factory building had scared us off? What if we had listened to the banker about how dangerous he thought the neighborhood was? What if we had listened to our closest advisors, who told us that what we were proposing made no sense? What if we'd believed those people who said, "you can't do it"?

Because of my past experience with the words *no* and *can't* where we faced so much resistance during my time with PeacePlayers, when I was confronted with more of that negativity in Baltimore, I was able to sit with it without reacting outright. As we toured the building, I began to understand that another power of *no* is that it could be a teacher, that it might have lessons behind it that could help me through all the uncertainty associated with a new project. In a sense, the blanket *no* taught me how to listen more closely to the positive guiding forces, like the teachers', and how to process the negative reactions, like the banker's, in a realistic way that would inform but not derail the project.

To continue our discussion about chapter 5 and every big *no* you have received, I now want you to write down a project that seems impossible. It could be personal or professional, one you are actively working on or one that's just hypothetical. Then I want you to write down every reason that you or people you know will say that it can't be done. Write down why it won't work or why it won't make money or why it won't gain support. Once you've exhausted each potential *no* and *can't*, read through them and see what they can teach you. Maybe some will offer a way to refine the idea; maybe others will show you why you're on the right track. Be sure to sit with them and be comfortable with them as teachers, rather than taking them too seriously as the end-all-be-all word on a project's viability.

## Chapter 11: Group Ownership

Why is it so hard for us to invite others in to help shape an idea? Why do we always feel like it will be better if we create something alone? What is it about ownership, even of something as nebulous as an idea, that is so appealing it makes us steer clear of working together or makes us suspicious of others' involvement?

Watching my dad avoid claiming that the idea was his was so powerful. By not claiming ownership of the idea, he was giving the teachers the credit for it, and he was inviting the end users to take ownership of the idea themselves. Watching the teachers take full ownership because of the way that we invited them to cocreate was magical.

In the discussion about chapter 3, I asked you to think about the language you are using. Now it's time to write it down. For the next few days or weeks, write down the language you are using to talk about the idea for a project you are working on. Are you using too many words like *I*, *me*, and *my*? When you use *we*, are you including more than just your company or organization? Once you've recorded your list of words, see how that language could be shifted to better share in the ownership and authorship of what you want to create.

## Chapter 12: Inside Looking Out

How would the community have looked at my dad and me if we had rejected their idea about the coffee shop? If we had shot down their contribution the way that so many people had tried to shoot down the idea of us redeveloping the building, how would they have felt about working together? Why was my first reaction to the coffee shop idea to think that I knew what was best for the community and that their idea couldn't work?

Since our original vision for the project didn't include a coffee shop, the initial rejection came from a place of believing that I knew best for the community rather than the other way around. Building trust with your community — just like your end users and your guardian angels — is critical to growing an idea inside out. We tend to focus only on those who are buying what we are selling, but there are always groups of people who are affected by our actions. The community is a group we can't ignore. The more they are invited to cocreate, the more we grow the idea inside out, the more the project can reach the best version of itself — even when it shifts what our vision might have been in the first place.

In the discussion about chapter 4, I challenged you to find your end user, your community, and your guardian angels. Now grab a piece of paper and write down a list of five questions that you could ask each of them that would better inform the idea you are bringing to life. See how far outside of your comfort zone and your initial vision you can push your questions. The more you can show you are genuinely ready to give up control and lovingly share in cocreation, the better.

## Chapter 13: Effective Leadership

What if we'd let the gap in funding derail the project because we weren't ready, as leaders, to look for other leaders to help us?

After the experience with taking PeacePlayers from a program in South Africa and Northern Ireland to one that could flourish overseas around the world, I'd come to appreciate the crucial role that leaders must play in bringing an idea to life. It was all reiterated with our work in real estate as we began to tap into the power of seeing the finished product before a project had even started. I began to further understand the importance of seeing that road map to get there. Even as early as that first day touring the building, I could literally imagine that moment of celebration and the building glowing full of teachers.

As we reflected on during the discussion about chapter 6, no movement can be built on principles alone, without effective leaders guiding the evolving vision to life. Right now, with whatever you're working on, it's time to map out that vision. I want you to write down the story of your project being completed. Literally picture it completed. Focus on every single detail. Envision the people who will help you get there, the people who will stand in your way, the feeling each of them brings, the potential challenges, and what the final celebration looks like when it exists in the real world. Draw pictures if it helps bring it to life. Once you have written the story and mapped out your vision, read it over again and imagine it happening. Grow more confident in it by rereading it every single day, tweaking and adjusting as more details come into focus as it comes alive.

## Chapter 14: The Dynamism of Love

Even though we weren't initially excited about the idea of a coffee shop, what if we had agreed to bring one in only on the condition that they had a proven track record of profitability, like a Starbucks? In other words, what if we had just thought about the same thing many others do — the bottom line — and looked for a café tenant who wanted the same thing?

Amanda never looked at Charmington's as just a café. She looked at the café as an opportunity to unite the community of Remington, to provide meaningful employment, to promote real ownership, and to take care of teachers. In other words, she was coming from a place of love. She wanted to create a space that other people loved — a place to meet, eat, and grind out whatever labor of love was burning in someone's heart. The fact that they served amazing food and coffee was secondary. They were taking an industry we know well, flipping it upside down, leading with their purpose, but following through with their heart. That's why Obama showed up. Out of love.

In the discussion about chapter 7, I asked what the word *love* means to you. I asked whether you've had a chance to pass on that love to others. Now it's time to make that happen. It's time to write a love note. It doesn't have to be written for a specific person or group of people — although that works as well. It could also be written to the project itself, or it could be written to you. At this stage, you should not be concerned with whether you will actually send it to someone or not. Simply begin with just expressing your heart truly, the way Amanda and her team expressed their love and passion for their work when we met. Love is dynamic, so this note can include any kind of expression of love that you want, whatever feels right for you. The only rule is that it includes the word *love* at some point in the note. If it feels right to share it, go for it. If you keep it to yourself, that's fine too. See if you can make expressing your love a bigger part of every day.

## Chapter 15: Deep Listening

What if we had never built that trust with the teachers in the early days of Miller's Court? What if we hadn't helped them understand that this was as much their project as it was ours? What if we had managed the property as landlords and not as partners? Would Andrew and the other teachers have trusted us with the request to help them build their first homes? Would the idea have even come up for any of us? Would those vacant houses still be standing there, empty and abandoned, today? Or would those properties have landed in the hands of house flippers who were solely focused on squeezing profit and who gave no thought to affordable housing?

When you build inside out, the groundswell that is created because the end users, the community, and the team feel ownership in the project is contagious, and it will propel the idea you are working on further than you imagined. Just as improvements to the original idea for the HIV/AIDS life skills class popped up from involved parents, and just as the left-field idea for the café popped up from the community in Remington, our original idea for real estate development evolved the day the teachers came forward and asked us to help them find permanent homes. It was never part of the vision, but by building inside out, the one simple *what if* question propelled all of us forward toward an even truer realization of the idea.

To take the discussions about chapters 4 and 12 one step further, consider the ideas and questions you've generated about building your own projects inside out, and look at an industry or project that's completely different than yours but one where you are an end user. As an experiment, imagine that you get a chance to approach the CEO or board of directors that's behind the project, and come up with three requests you would make to them if you had the chance. Write these down and picture yourself sharing with the CEO or board of directions your contribution to their idea. See what you can gather from the experience of this exercise, and let it inform how you give and receive feedback for projects that you are involved in going forward.

# PART III: GROW
## Chapter 16: Purpose Driven

What if we had seen ourselves as just developers? What if we hadn't actively tried to reimagine the industry with every decision we made? What if we hadn't started out by thinking in purpose over profit?

Would we have been as aware of our desire to protect and serve the community of Remington? Would we have wanted to help the community's master plan begin to come to life? Would they even have trusted us with that responsibility?

Being more driven by our purpose — empowering communities — than by our profit allowed us to pave the way for this kind of opportunity to even be on our radar. Because we looked at ourselves more as social entrepreneurs than as actual real estate developers, the community trusted us. We were on the same team. Seawall's purpose is to use buildings to empower communities, unite our cities, and help to launch impactful new ideas. How much more powerful is that statement than if we'd decided our purpose was to "use buildings to maximize shareholder profit"?

I want to be clear: Making money is important, especially in the for-profit sector. If your business doesn't make money, it will fail and you'll lose your tool to be in service of your purpose. I am, however, suggesting that you'll be more fulfilled, and likely more financially successful, if you lead with your purpose. I believe that future generations have the responsibility to find ways to replace the nonprofit model with for-profit, purpose-driven work. There is no reason that we can't have massive social impact and still make money.

Now it's time to take your work from the discussions about chapters 2 and 9 a step further. Write out a sentence or two that clearly and concisely summarize how you plan to reimagine the industry — the line of work you love the most — by leading with your purpose. If it helps again, here's Seawall's: "Seawall believes in reimagining the real estate development industry so that the built environment empowers communities, unites our cities, and helps launch powerful ideas."

Once your statement is written, it's time to get busy living it. Tell it to people. Write it on a chalkboard in your house or on the mirror in your bathroom. Put it into every conversation when people ask what you do — and use it as a springboard to shoot out of bed every morning, ready to bring it to life.

## Chapter 17: *Can't/No* as the Catalyst

What if I had given up at Caleb's first *no*? Or his second or third?

By this point I had become so used to this word, it began to have the opposite effect on me, motivating me even more to turn it into a *yes*. It also taught me that changing a *no* to a *yes* requires deep listening. When channeled correctly, it actually leads us to ask better questions and dig in deeper to understand why someone believes we can't do something that we know in our heart is important.

Over the next week, write down every time that someone says *no* to you. Choose the hardest three, and dive deeper into each one by writing down three reasons why you think that person said *no*. See if you can understand the *no* from the other person's point of view and then think about what could be done to align your perspectives to turn the *no* into a *yes*. Then go through and actually make it happen by resuming the conversation or being ready the next time you're told *no*.

## Chapter 18: Co-ownership

What would have happened if during that community presentation, we would have said something like, "We at Seawall have come up with the perfect project to solve all of Remington's problems. We are going to build you apartments, a pharmacy, a bank, a dry cleaner, and restaurants, and here is what it's going to look like"? How do you think that would have been received?

Your first connection with your end users, community, and team is critical. It's so important that you understand that the idea you are bringing to life isn't just yours. The more you can explain it in a way that acknowledges all of the people who came before you, and all those who will come after you, the more you invite everyone whom the idea touches to also claim the idea as their own. This is how you set up the opportunity for co-ownership.

The next time you present an idea, whether it's to your kids about plans for the weekend or to a group of employees who report to you, present it in a way that honors the collective learning that it took to get the idea to this point. Don't start out by explaining the idea; start by explaining all of the factors that went into the idea coming to life, and show them how they have a role to play in this idea too. Share the ownership of the idea and make decisions from that place.

## Chapter 19: Beyond Comfort

Why is it so much more uncomfortable to confront someone face to face? Why do we hide behind emails, social media, and phone calls when we have really complicated things to discuss?

Like many people, I'd prefer to be liked by others than disliked by them. When I knocked on Earl Bell's door that day, I was doing it for Seawall and for the community's master plan vision, but I was also doing it for myself. That kind of confrontation had always terrified me, so even walking up to the door was an action that was taking me further out of my comfort zone. The easier thing would have been to continue to leave messages. It wasn't until that day that I finally gave myself permission to move on and grow past Earl because I knew that I had done everything in my power to connect. I had just done one of the most uncomfortable things I've ever had to do: accept that I couldn't please everyone and that someone didn't like me.

You've thought about your comfort zone in the discussions about chapters 1 and 8. You've written down what you are afraid of and at least three things you could do that would make you uncomfortable. Now it's time to take action. Pick one thing from the list you made and commit to doing it. It could be signing up and giving a public speech about something you care about. It could be reaching out to the CEO of the company that you've always admired and wanted to work with and inviting that person to coffee. It could be bringing the homeless man you see every day on your walk to work a warm coffee and actually sitting with him and asking him questions. Whatever it is, take note of how getting out of your comfort zone makes you feel and how you see the world differently as a result of it. See if it sends a pulse of creativity through your system that might not have been there before.

## Chapter 20: Inside Out

What if I hadn't gone door-to-door to deeply connect with those who would be most affected by the project? What if I hadn't spent countless hours listening to the end users and the community about what it was that they wanted? What if we hadn't connected with Earl's board members to really hear their stories and visions for their neighborhood?

It's time to take action on the process you started in the other discussion sections in this appendix by listening deeply to those in and around your project. Talk to your supporters, talk to your detractors, talk to everyone from the end users to the community and see how much you can learn by listening deeply. Avoid falling into cookie-cutter speeches that you've given a hundred times about the idea you are working on. Instead, focus more on asking questions than on sharing your opinion. Be open to letting the idea or project change and grow with each new bit of information you learn.

## Chapter 21: Trusting Leadership

What if I had not remained true to my leadership style? What if I had not been open to observing and analyzing how other people lead? What if, when backed into a corner by someone with a more aggressive style of leading, I'd let go of what had worked in the past in order to "compete"?

While it is critical for leaders to be able to step up and make complicated decisions from time to time, my experience is that when you can visualize the finished product, the road map to get there comes together effortlessly. When your end users, your community, and your team all feel a sense of pride of ownership and authorship in that map and in you as the guide, you'll be able to sit back and watch things unfold with very little need to intervene.

Oftentimes, when you observe someone else's leadership style that doesn't resonate with yours, it helps you become clearer about the style by which you want to lead. Pick one person whose leadership style rubs you the wrong way. The next time you're around that person — or check out that person's speech or interview — identify what, exactly, isn't working for you. Even if you just find three things to pick up on, you can use them to help sharpen your own leadership style and double down on what works for you. Leaders can grow and thrive in any style or approach if they can only learn to trust themselves.

## Chapter 22: The Oxygen of Love

What if I hadn't made room for love?

Love is the most powerful thing in the world; it is the oxygen that ideas need to have in order to grow. No movement has ever sustained itself without love. Anything less than love can only slow us down by consuming us with negativity and pain. My realization that I had nothing but love for Earl was such a pivotal moment for me. To understand that even those who oppose us play critical roles in our growth and deserve the same love and respect as those who join us completely changed who I am today.

Look deep inside yourself. There are people in your life who have wronged you or who are advocating against something you stand for. Some of them are public figures; others are people you work with or know in your personal life. Pick one of these individuals — ideally the one whom you have the toughest time mustering love for — and the next time you come across that person — or that person's words or work — see if you can't imagine that person differently. See if you can identify what the individual is showing you about the world. See if beneath the pain and suffering on the surface, there aren't bigger and deeper truths to behold. Consider, even if you can only manage to do it for an instant, that this is a person worthy of your love — worthy of your gratitude. What does that feel like? What does that openness offer that being closed doesn't?

If you can look at that person as a human being with a unique, individual history, trauma, and agenda, then ask yourself if you can love that person and be grateful to be able to learn from each other. After all, love is the oxygen all great ideas need to grow and keep growing.

# PART IV: EVOLVE
## Chapter 23: Principles in Motion

How else could our ten-year strategic planning meeting have gone? What are all the other directions we could have headed in? There may be thousands of iterations of Seawall, but if an organization is based on shared principles, driven by our purpose, then we end up arriving exactly where we're supposed to be.

What if I hadn't noticed the patterns in PeacePlayers and Seawall enough to begin to identify a set of guiding principles on how ideas grow? What if I'd tried to relay these stories to readers on their own, without boiling down the takeaways I'd experienced? Would the book have resonated more? Less? Would readers feel more empowered or inspired one way or another?

The truth is that I had a hard time deciding whether to include these discussion sections. I generally don't like the idea of being preachy or telling people what to do. I don't like presenting these principles as if they are the "answer" any more than I feel that they fully encompass everything I've learned over these past twenty-plus years working to reimagine what work itself could be. I still feel it's presumptuous to say that these principles are somehow better or truer than principles that others could create based on their own experiences.

■ ■ ■ ■ ■

In the end, it's important to point out that these principles of a movement are just a few of the many important principles others have identified in the past. Principles aren't always linear but are always moving and evolving. By getting out of your comfort zone, reimagining industries, leading with purpose, never claiming ownership of an idea, building inside out, banishing *can't/no* from your vocabulary, and remembering that great movements need leaders, so much is possible. But I know there is more. So much more.

Now, I'll ask you to take time to consider what you've learned on your journey. What principles or ideas have you seen work again and again? What are the patterns that you've noticed? How might you share them so that others can learn, feel empowered, and draw inspiration from your experience? If you aren't ready to share what you've learned, no worries at all, but if you are, please stop by ThibaultManekin.com or reach out to us on social media, and tell us all about it. I'd love to hear all about your experience.

# Acknowledgments

This book itself is a movement. It's the product of hundreds, even thousands, of people who have come into my life and helped show me the way. It would be impossible to properly thank every one of you, so please know that if we are connected, you are a part of this journey, and I am deeply grateful for the lessons I've learned from you along the way.

First, to my amazing wife, Lola: You have been nothing short of heroic, giving me the space for years to wake up and write at four in the morning and late into the evening as I slowly brought the dream to life. Also, I want to thank you for patiently listening to me read every chapter to you dozens of times and for offering the rawest, most loving feedback I ever could have hoped for.

As in all movements, leaders are needed, and oftentimes that leadership is silent. There are no sufficient words to thank Al Dwyer, my brother. You took a giant leap of faith with me and helped to craft these ideas into a coherent and powerful narrative. This book is what it is because of you, and I am eternally grateful that you pushed me out of my comfort zone, provided me with your friendship, and guided me every step of the way.

I am also thankful for my other brother, Ben Allen: You helped to get this project off the ground when it was nothing more than words on the back of a napkin. Even though we had some bumps along the way, your initial belief in me and this project was more important than you'll ever realize.

I want to thank my agent, Leticia Gomez, who was the only one of more than thirty agents I reached out to who showed any interest in the power of this story. And to my editor, Georgia Hughes, and the amazing team at New World Library: Thank you for bringing me into your family. Your mission of publishing "books that change lives" makes you the ideal home for *Larger Than Yourself.*

To my parents: Thank you for giving me unconditional love and the longest leash imaginable growing up so that I could learn to stumble, fall, and pick myself up on my own along the way.

To my three amazing sisters: You have always been pillars of support and stability even when I wasn't able to be the best big brother.

To all four of my grandparents: I'm so grateful to you for humbly paving the way forward for future generations.

To the entire PeacePlayers family: I think of you all every day and am in awe of what continues to be created.

To the Seawall family: You have grounded me and always allowed me the space to dream big and find my highest purpose.

To my author brothers, sisters, and heroes — Wes Moore, Chris Wilson, Alec Ross, Tracy Gold, and Joe Mechlinski: Thank you for the countless conversations and priceless advice you've given me every step of the way.

To Michael Tobass, Amanda Rothschild, and Joe Jones for spending so much time with me to make sure their stories were told correctly.

To Pickett Slater Harrington for thoughtful and invaluable feedback about the implications of the stories I have the privilege of interpreting and sharing.

To Brian Lemek, Andrew Gordon, Tim Guinan, Evan Morville, Jon Constable, Nyha Vanderpool, Erin Mitchell, Peter Diprinzio, Katie Marshall, Peter Burkhill, John Cammack, Richie Frieman, Jinji Fraser, Julie Oxenhandler, Michael Swirnow, Masi Brown, and Lauren Manekin: Thank you for taking the time to read so many versions of the manuscript and making sure I never lost my purpose along the way.

To Bob Embry and Beth Harber of the Abell Foundation: Thank you for pioneering teacher housing and for helping us expand upon the idea.

To the amazing team of donors, lenders, and investors who have believed so deeply in this work: You have given us the support to dream big.

And deepest gratitude to the end users, communities, and guardian angels who have done the heavy lifting alongside us every step of the way.

# About the Author

Thibault Manekin is a speaker, podcast host, author, community organizer, and entrepreneur. He is passionate about reimagining industries by leading with purpose and has made it his lifework to understand what keeps us as human beings apart and what brings us together.

In 2002, soon after graduating from college, Manekin traveled to South Africa, where he combined his passion for bringing people together with a love of sports to help create PeacePlayers, a nonprofit with the mission of bringing together children from war-torn countries around the world through basketball and dialogue. PeacePlayers has since worked with more than 75,000 youths from over 20 countries around the world and has trained more than 2,000 coaches / change agents.

In 2006, Thibault moved back to his hometown of Baltimore, where he helped start Seawall, an impact-driven company made up of passionate social entrepreneurs who believe in reimagining the real estate industry as we know it. The company focuses its energy and resources on providing discounted apartments for teachers, collaborative office space for nonprofit organizations, workforce housing, community-driven retail, public markets, launchpads for chefs, and creative space for inner-city schools.

In 2011, Thibault was honored by President Obama's White House as a Champion for Change, and Seawall's projects have received numerous national awards. Proud husband of Lola Manekin and the father of Durban and Finley Manekin, he lives in Baltimore, Maryland. Learn more at ThibaultManekin.com and Seawall.com.